FRAN ADAMS

Cycling into the Unexpected

Adventures on two wheels at home and abroad

To Al + Amy
With Best Wishes
& Love from Fran xx

FRAN ADAMS

Cycling
into the
Unexpected

Adventures on two wheels at home and abroad

MEREO

Mereo Books

1A The Wool Market Dyer Street Cirencester Gloucestershire GL7 2PR
An imprint of Memoirs Publishing www.mereobooks.com

Cycling into the Unexpected: 978-1-86151-536-0

First published in Great Britain in 2018
by Mereo Books, an imprint of Memoirs Publishing

The address for Memoirs Publishing Group Limited can be found at www.memoirspublishing.com

The Memoirs Publishing Group Ltd Reg. No. 7834348

The Memoirs Publishing Group supports both The Forest Stewardship Council® (FSC®) and the PEFC® leading international forest-certification organisations. Our books carrying both the FSC label and the PEFC® and are printed on FSC®-certified paper. FSC® is the only forest-certification scheme supported by the leading environmental organisations including Greenpeace. Our paper procurement policy can be found at www.memoirspublishing.com/environment

Typeset in 12/18pt Century Schoolbook
by Wiltshire Associates Publisher Services Ltd. Printed and bound in Great Britain by Printondemand-Worldwide, Peterborough PE2 6XD

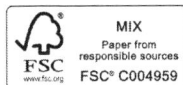

MIX
Paper from
responsible sources
FSC
www.fsc.org   FSC® C004959

PEFC
PEFC/16-33-415

Contents

CHAPTER ONE

Majorcan Retreat

September 1997

Pieces of polystyrene are strewn around the lawn. Frank is cutting up pipe lagging into different lengths to fit onto his bike frame. Then he's giving each piece a unique code with his black marking pen. When we get to the airport, he will know exactly where these pieces are supposed to go. This is how we protect the bikes when we take them on a plane. My pieces are already cut and packed in a nylon bag. They're not perfect, but they're

Frank about to set off for the monastery in the mountains.

coded in biro and I think I know where they all fit.

We've booked a fortnight off work but still don't know where to go. Admittedly, this September weather is beautiful today but we want guaranteed sunshine. Nothing 'iffy.' Maybe the Mediterranean would be our best choice. A friend of Frank's has suggested we should try a retreat; somewhere completely calm and quiet, for a week of pure relaxation. He's aware that Frank has been under a lot of stress lately. It's not the sort of holiday we are used to, but we value his advice.

I'm fed up with hanging around like this. Not knowing where to go is giving us even more stress. So I suggest that I visit the travel agent's up the road. They might have some offers.

I return quite soon. I've taken the bull by the horns and booked two flights to Majorca at £99 each. We must leave home tomorrow evening for an early flight the next day. I'm relieved that Frank's happy with my decision. We've been to Majorca before with our cycling club. On that occasion, we were based on the eastern side of the island. We loved it. But we've heard of a monastery in the mountains to the north. It's called Lluc and is a sanctuary. Just what the doctor ordered!

Tomorrow arrives and we catch an evening train to Gatwick. We have all the time in the world to prepare the bikes. The first thing we do before covering the frame with pipe lagging is to remove the pedals. Then we loosen the handlebars, turn them at right angles and tape them to the crossbar. Finally, we let the air out of the tyres – in case they explode in the cargo hold. In my nylon bag, I've exchanged my pipe lagging for a pair of pedals, a pump, my tool kit and a bell, and I've even squeezed in my handlebar bag. Frank has done the same with his bike parts. This is now our hand luggage. I'm always amazed that these bags get through the scanner without suspicion – but they do.

* * *

Early on Wednesday morning, we arrive at Palma airport feeling absolutely washed out, not having had a wink of sleep in Gatwick. After reassembling the bikes, we hang about in a cool, quiet part of the building, away from the milling crowds, and decide on our next move. We haven't got a map yet, only a phrase book. But the first thing to do is find our way into Palma. Then we can sort ourselves out.

When we feel robust enough, we set off, following the traffic out of the airport. The sky is blue and the air warming up nicely. It looks promising. This road is very busy. We're hooted at several times. Is this a greeting? Cyclists are well thought of on the Continent.

Blimey – it's a motorway! We immediately pull over onto the grass verge, leaning away from the traffic for self-preservation. Through a high chicken wire fence on the outer edge of the grass, there's a small road running parallel to this motorway. We must get onto it somehow. We'll see if there's a gap in the fence. But this strip of grass is so narrow we can't even turn the bikes round, so we have to push them backwards. It's so scary. Drivers are almost skinning our backsides, while our pannier buckles keep snagging on the fence. Sweating profusely, we finally arrive back at the airport. There were no gaps in the wire fence and we've walked back almost a mile. We find the little road we are looking for and spin along it nicely, on smooth tarmac, thanking our lucky stars.

But good things never last and soon our road curves northwards, away from the motorway. Now we're in the middle of nowhere without a map. When we reach a junction with no signposts, we don't know which way to go. We set off down one of the lanes, which soon becomes a stony farm track. So we trundle back and take the second choice. A few miles later we hear that familiar hum of traffic and our little road comes alongside the motorway once more, with just the wire fence separating us from all that hurly burly. Then, sod's law, the road veers off again, and again we lose all sight and sound of the motorway.

We must have got it right this time however, because there are tall buildings ahead of us and we can hear that traffic once more. What a relief. Not that we relish cycling in cities, but at least we have reached Palma. Ahead is a junction on to a busy main road. Here we turn southwards, presuming this will take us towards the coast.

Palma looks much like any other city – rushing traffic and high-rise buildings. At the first big roundabout we turn right into a wide street lined with shops, hoping to buy a map. But we scour the whole street in vain. There's no way we can set off until we've bought a map.

We reach the far end of the street, feeling fed up. Like two lost souls, we plod onwards towards the centre, where soon our spirits are lifted, because now we're in a completely different environment. There are old narrow streets opening unexpectedly onto pretty little plazas. Under the shade of trees, people are relaxing around café tables. It's charming.

Along one long street we spot a sign swinging high on a wall. 'Hostal Apuntadores' it reads. Perhaps we should try our luck and see if they have vacancies. It looks rather run-down, but we'll only be staying for one night.

The contrast from brightness to darkness befuddles us as we walk inside, because we can't see to read our phrase book. Therefore most of our transaction is done awkwardly, through nods, facial expressions and hand gestures. We lock the bikes in a back yard and are shown to our room on the third floor. It's as dark up here as it was downstairs, even though there's a window at each end. Dumping the panniers inside the door, we follow Señora back down to reception; omelettes are being prepared for us in the little café on the ground floor.

After eating, we return to our room, which resembles a featureless cube. I stick my head out of the open back window. It's like we're halfway up a square tube with a deep, dirty inner courtyard down below. Drainpipes emerge from every wall, all the way up. When I look across the nearest corner into an open window, I see the head and bare shoulders of a man sitting on the toilet. I assume this because of the sewer pipe protruding from the wall beneath him. While I'm wondering if he's completely naked or not, a piercing wolf-whistle startles me. I look up to the opposite wall and there's a man ogling me from a top window. Now *I* feel naked. I slam the window shut. There seems to be no privacy here. "Let's get out," I suggest.

Outside, the light is dazzlingly bright for tired eyes, even through sunglasses. Keeping in the shade as much as possible, we explore the sights of Palma but inevitably end up at the harbour, where there is no escape from the sun. The harbour is choc-a-bloc with white yachts. Such opulence. The reflections are painful to look at, but look at them we do. It's a stunning sight. When we can bear the brightness no more, we turn to look inland, and there's the cathedral standing proudly on the edge of the city. We have no energy or inclination to look inside it right now and we realise we've completely forgotten about a map. But enough is enough. Hot and dusty, we arrive back at our room, where we sit on the end of the bed and wash our feet in the bidet – it's that close. Then, flopping back on the duvet, we are soon sound asleep.

It's noise that awakens us – an incessant buzz of voices. Whatever is going on out there? Rousing ourselves, we look down through the window. Hordes of loud, brightly-dressed people are streaming up and down the narrow street, like noisy coloured liquid, flowing in opposing directions. Is this the main artery of old Palma? If we're going to eat tonight, we'll have to join that throng out there. Pity the café downstairs is closed in the evenings.

We find every space in every plaza is jam-packed with tables and chairs as we struggle to get by the merry diners in order to read the menus on the notice boards. The meals are all rather expensive for penny-pinching cyclists. Eventually we find ourselves on the edge of all this activity; somewhere much quieter, where we indulge in a budget pasta meal. Then we drag ourselves back to the hotel. As we climb into bed, we both have a sudden foreboding. "Do you think there's bugs in the bed?" we ask each other, in absolute unison – then burst out laughing. Sleep soon overtakes us.

* * *

Thursday morning dawns clear and promising. Hopefully we'll be in the monastery by tonight, for the peace and quiet we long for. But there's still the map to be purchased. Then there's another consideration – our cumbersome bags of pipe lagging will need leaving in a safe place. We don't want to be lugging those around.

We ask Señora where we can put them and she shows us to the cellar. It's weird down here. Not like a proper cellar at all but one with a sandy, undulating floor. In places you can stand upright, but in others you almost have to crawl. We clamber into a corner and hide them behind a hump. Then we realise that we'll have to come back to Apuntadores on our last night if we are going to retrieve them.

Riding round Palma looking for a map shop takes forever, but we must find a decent map that shows all the little lanes and tracks. It's afternoon before we know it and unbearably hot. At last we find a shop with just the type of map we need. To celebrate, we pop into a bar for a quick lager, then end up feeling hungry, so we have a snack as well. Our map shows all the twisty roads up the mountains and we can see it will be pointless to set off now; it's too hilly, too hot and too far. So we cycle down to the seafront where a sea breeze helps cool us down. There's a modern park on the other side of the boulevard, where we sit and pass the time of day, sweating. Another day gone!

Well, at least we now have time to visit the cathedral. It stands quite near to this park, looking spectacular. There are no tall buildings behind it or in front, to dwarf its Gothic magnificence and we approach it with enthusiasm. Inside, though, its splendour is lost amongst the profusion of decoration. This feels so oppressive to me. What I dislike most is the huge 'Crown of Thorns' installation, with light fittings around the circumference. It hangs in the chancel and I hate it blocking out the beauty of the architecture. In spite of my sentiments, we spend a long time in here. After all, Frank is not rankled by all these add-ons and why should I spoil it for him? It's nice and cool in here, anyway.

* * *

Our third day in Palma! We *must* get going. But there's something else we hadn't considered. Our flight home, in just over a week's time, will depart early in the morning. This will mean us leaving 'Hostal Apuntadores' around 4 am! So how on earth are we going to find that little road to the airport, in the dark? There's nothing for it but to retrace the route right now, while it's still fresh in our minds.

Since hunting for the map shop yesterday, we've become fairly familiar with the layout of Palma, so we don't have a problem finding the busy road that we arrived in on. But which turning did we come out of? The only way to find out is by cycling down each little road in turn. Then, by turning round to cycle back towards the city, we'll see if we recognize anything. Luckily we do, although we must make absolutely sure.

We follow the tiny road, retracing the route with the help of the map. When we finally reach the airport it's midday and boiling hot. Now, at last, we can set off for the monastery. It's a wonderful thought, that we'll soon be relaxing in the coolness and tranquillity of a sanctuary

Our map is proving to be extremely useful. Instead of cycling all the way back into Palma to pick up the main road, we are discovering an intricate route via small country lanes. There's a bit of trial and error involved, which is time consuming, but there's hardly a vehicle in sight. It's stiflingly hot though; we can barely tolerate it. They must be having a heat wave.

We pass a bar. Frank makes a sudden decision to stop and I manage to miss his back wheel. I'm keen to stop as well, but I don't think alcohol will do us much good. We sit under a shady porch, sipping our lagers and chilling out – well, sweating profusely might be more apt. And, no, the lager doesn't help. We have another. Now we haven't got the inclination or energy to do anything. So we just sit and drip.

Finally, when it's begun to cool down slightly, we push off. 5.30 pm already! Alas, we won't make it to the monastery after all. Yet another day gone! Where shall we stay then? We look at the map and see we'll be passing through a large town. It's called Inca. I thought all the Incas were on the other side of the world. Anyway, that's where we'll have to stay tonight.

Mercifully, it is not a hilly ride and we arrive sometime after seven o'clock. Seeing an out-of-town shop still open, we go in and enquire about hotels or hostels in the town. The two smart ladies behind the counter continue rolling up a large piece of fabric before addressing us. Then they shake their heads and explain. What are they saying? It can't be true. Hotels, hostels and B&Bs are only found on the coast. We're really stuck now!

All the same, we continue cycling into town, wondering what

the devil we can do. The town centre is looking quite festive and for a while we forget our predicament. In a large square, chairs are being set out in row upon row for some big event. Two young policemen stand at the side, taking care of proceedings. With the help of our phrase book, we learn that an enormous brass band will soon be playing here. Then we remember that we have nowhere to stay tonight. We tell one of the policemen that we have nowhere to sleep. He seems really amenable. Leaving his post, he takes us to the main police headquarters, where he asks his boss for permission to find us accommodation. The boss assents. We then follow him on a tour of the town. He enters each shop where he knows the owners in turn, to see if they can accommodate us. Eventually, in a boutique, a lovely lady called Anna consents to give us a bed for the night. She writes down her address and we arrange to meet up later, at her home.

After snacking in a bar, we arrive at the appointed time, at Anna's house on the outskirts of town. She welcomes us warmly. She's a most charming lady. We comprehend that her son and daughter-in-law are away for the weekend and therefore we can choose to sleep either in their double bed or in the two single beds in Anna's own room. We opt for the double bed. When we go up to the room later, she has made up the bed with beautifully embroidered sheets. We feel like royalty. Hopefully, we will have a right royal sleep.

Anna is going into town tonight and asks if we'd like to join her. But we feel too tired and that grand bed is beckoning us. We just crave sleep. Once in bed though, there is no sleep to be had. Folk are flocking into town, passing right under our window. Perhaps we should have gone after all. We close our eyes but sleep is impossible. All we hear are bass voices, "HOLA", soprano voices, "Hola", and kids voices, "*hola*." Even the toddlers are out tonight, whilst we wimps have gone to bed.

Maybe we do snatch an hour of sleep but well after midnight, all those voices return. Now it's "BUENAS NOCHES," "Buenas noches" and "adios" that's keeping us awake. The thin high-pitched voices of little children can be heard above the general cacophony of noise. Then at last – peace and quiet! Now we can drop off.

Suddenly, a terrifyingly loud noise jolts us awake: a horrendous whooshing, crashing sound, as a lorry load of bottles is emptied down a chute. In the same instant, a horrific 'YEEEOOOW' fills the air, as a frightened cat falls down the attic stairs and lands outside our bedroom door with a thud. We've got palpitations now. We'll never relax enough to go back to sleep. And we don't, for the next thing we know, scooters are buzzing into town. People are going to work already.

* * *

Anna greets us downstairs. She's convinced we've had a good night's sleep and after all her kindness we wouldn't wish her to think otherwise, especially as she won't take any money. So the first thing we do before setting off is to buy her a bouquet of flowers, which we take to the boutique. She's thrilled. Now we *must* get going. God willing, we'll reach our destination by this afternoon and, oh my, we're *really* looking forward to some peace and quiet. It's Saturday, so we've used up a whole week of our holiday and not yet achieved our aim.

As we head northwards the terrain begins to rise towards the mountains which have now come into view. In the little town of Selva we pass a yard where, out of the blue, we see marvellous slabs of shiny marble stacked against a wall. They display an array of lovely shades and patterns and I wonder what wonderful buildings they will grace.

After Selva, the climbing begins in earnest. Gasping, we loop backwards and forwards up steep slopes, passing ancient terraces built of stone, going up the mountainsides. It looks beautiful. The sweat running off my forehead is burning my eyes. Now I know why people wear those silly bands round their heads. But as we climb, the heat becomes less oppressive and the scenery is wonderful. Soon be there.

With one final effort we reach the gateway to the monastery and exhale with relief. Now we can have a whole week of perfect peace. We've certainly earned it, sweating up all these mountains.

Rounding the corner, we're surprised to see a coach parked on the driveway. What's that doing here? As we pedal on, there's a whole line of coaches in designated parking bays. "I thought this was supposed to be a retreat, not a damn coach park," grumbles Frank. Then further on round we are suddenly dazzled by bright sunlight, reflecting off a glass-fronted restaurant. "Are you sure this is the right place?" Frank asks, but I am unable to confirm that it is.

But now, the monastery has come into view at the end of a straight road, large and magnificent, as it nestles against a backdrop of dark green mountains and dazzling blue sky. Here at last!

We're still hoping to absorb some tranquillity in this splendid old building, where we can now make out rows of square windows on its stone frontage. I wonder which one will be ours? Then our ears prick up. Is that music I can hear? Yes it is. As we get nearer, the music gets louder. It's not monastic music or even hymns but loud, jolly music and it's jolly loud, blasting from speakers on the wall. And to add to all this inconsiderate incongruity, masses of children are dancing and prancing in a roped-off square in front of the entrance. We can't believe our eyes.

"This is it then, is it?" Frank says, dejectedly. "It's more like a theme park. We'd better book in." With a feeling of resignation, we enter the monastery.

Once inside, we find ourselves in a dark, wide corridor where we squint to look for the reception desk. Then a ghostly voice speaks to us from the wall panelling and we jerk round to see a little window in the wall. This, apparently, is where we book in. It looks more like an old-fashioned ticket-office at a railway station. Good, he's speaking to us in English. Was it something we said? We ask to book a room for one week.

"Oooh!" he says slowly and sonorously, "we are very sorry but we are fully booked until Tuesday". What! "Have you got a shed or a stable or somewhere we can sleep tonight then?" "Noo, but you will find accommodation in Port de Pollença," says the shadowy figure. That's on the east coast, we remember. It's five o'clock already. Panic is beginning to set in. Here we are, up in the mountains and we've got to cycle all the way to the east coast. How long will that take us? It could be dark before we get there.

"There are vacancies here from Tuesday to Thursday, if you like to book these," continues the deep voice from the window. Well, as our whole reason for coming to Majorca was to stay in the monastery, we may as well come back here, even if it's only for two days. Come on, hurry up, we're thinking. He's so slow. We need to get going pretty damn quickly.

Back outside, we look at the map. That's amazing. Port de Pollença is much nearer than we thought, in fact no more than 15 miles, but how arduous will it be? We try to ignore all the activity outside, which in retrospect may have been in celebration of a saint. Jumping on our bikes, we race off.

The ride proves to be spectacular. We twist and turn, rise and fall, full of adrenalin. Each time we emerge from a cutting or round a bend, a new panorama awaits us. Every mountain seems to have its own unique geology. Then the last few miles slope gradually downhill to Port de Pollença. Hurray! We're here already and it's still light.

We find a small hotel in a road behind the sea front, where we take one of the cheaper rooms for three nights. Before we go out on the town, I wash the chamois linings of our sweaty cycling shorts and lay them inside out on a towel, on a table in front of the open window.

While we're in town we meet an English cyclist called Barry and chat with him for a while. He tells us he does loads of touring and carries all his belongings in a compact cycle bag, behind the bike seat. He thinks we're mad, having two panniers each. So we ask him how he manages with so little. Apparently, he stays in hotels because they provide towels and he wears the same pair of shorts for cycling, swimming and sleeping! "Well," we think, "we'll stick to panniers!" We nickname him 'Barry One Bag'.

On our return, I check to see if the shorts are drying. Oh, horror of horrors! What's this? The chamois of my shorts is now a frenzied mass of tiny brown ants, hordes of them – my shorts, not Frank's. But where the devil have they come from? Aghast, we follow their dark trail backwards, down the table leg and across the floor to the panniers, which are propped against the wall. The line of ants goes into each pannier in turn, down to the bottom and out on the other side. Eventually we see where they are coming from – the electric socket on the wall. However are we going to sleep in here tonight, and how many more ants might there be behind that wall? We pull the bed right into the middle of the room and climb in, like we're climbing aboard a boat to escape piranhas. But who is going to get back out to switch off the light?

* * *

In the morning the ants have disappeared. When we go down for breakfast, we complain to the landlady and ask to move to a different room. Rather grudgingly, she lets us have a balcony room on the front. We discover later that it's our own fault, because ants are attracted to sweat and food. But we're really chuffed to have a balcony. Now our sweaty clothes can be draped over the chairs outside, along with any bags of food.

Because we're in the north of the island, we feel we must do some exploring. Last time we stayed in Majorca, the mountains were too far away to reach by bike. So today we head for Cap de Formentor, the rocky peninsula that sticks out on the north-eastern corner.

The mountain formations are stunning. We're compelled to stop at every opportunity. When we look down over the railings at one point, the drop makes us shudder. This peninsula is notorious for its strong winds, but today we are blessed with a cooling breeze. We finally reach the very end, where there's a lighthouse and a restaurant, but we're not tempted to go in; we're hoping to find a nice sheltered beach for a picnic.

On our return, we find the perfect spot. It's on the southern side of the peninsula, down a lane through dappled sunlight – the beautiful sandy bay of Cala Pi de la Posada. Here we idle away our time looking across the shiny sea towards another peninsula in the distant haze. We gaze absently at the lazy progress of boats crossing the bay. It's very soporific. It's been a glorious day. Tomorrow, perhaps, we'll explore that peninsula over there.

Later, while we're out on the balcony enjoying the evening air, a young German couple appear from the adjacent room. We have a stilted conversation with them and discover that they are also cyclists. We tell them that we've moved to this front room because of ants in the room at the back. But they also have ants in their balcony room, they tell us. It doesn't seem to worry them, so we don't bother to tell them what the attraction is. Now we'll certainly have to be strict with our clothes and food, because every room has an ant problem, it seems.

* * *

Today we're going to cycle southwards to that distant peninsula we saw yesterday; that is, after Frank has mended my puncture, which he does out on the street. Every passer-by gets into conversation with us. Frank's loving it, but I feel so frustrated. The morning has half gone before we set off. It's a pleasant enough ride but not spectacular like yesterday's. We follow the curve of the coast, stopping at the large popular beach of Alcúdia, where sunbathers flock in holiday time. It's empty now. We continue on towards the peninsula, looking forward to finding somewhere on the rocks to have our picnic. But alas, when we reach them, our way is barred. There are huge gates right across the road. It's a military base. Bah humbug!

* * *

Today's the day we get to stay in the monastery, albeit only for a couple of days. We'll have some serious relaxing to do then – if all those noisy people have gone. The ride back up to Lluc proves to be just as amazing as the outward journey, with the vivid blue sky providing a backdrop to the stunning spectacle of mountains. We reach the monastery by early afternoon. Thankfully, it's very peaceful now. Our room is up a stone staircase at the back of the building. It is simply furnished with no fussy accessories and feels very calm. The window looks down over a somewhat wild garden with tree-covered mountains beyond. Well, this is it! But how do we set about relaxing and perhaps meditating? We have no idea. Are we supposed to sit cross-legged on the floor, thinking nice thoughts or even trying to empty our minds of *all* thoughts – something I've never succeeded in doing? Ponderously, we unpack our panniers, then decide we can't stay in here a moment longer. Soon we're out in the sun, strolling round the gardens and wondering how we will fill our time.

As we return, we're surprised to see the German couple arriving. They didn't tell us they were coming here. After a brief chat, we leave them to settle in and go for an evening meal in the 'glasshouse', which rather resembles a restaurant in a garden centre. It's busy and quite noisy with its harsh acoustics but it's the only place to eat. In spite of its shortcomings, we enjoy our meal and the general atmosphere of the place, and stay there for quite a while, hoping, I suppose, that the Germans might join us. We're not too keen to return to that quiet room.

During the night the silence feels deafening. I almost panic. It's a good job we're only here for two nights, I think to myself.

* * *

The next day dawns just like all the others. After breakfast we go for a spin on the bikes, that seeming to be our only modus operandi. As we return in the early afternoon, the German couple are just setting off to ride the nearby Sa Calobra route, which is a breathtaking, looping, descent. It is known as the biggest cycling challenge in Majorca. Only this morning we'd stopped at the top of it to have an ice cream. We'd never heard of Sa Calobra until then but we saw a notice board giving all the details about it. According to the information, it comprises 26 hairpin bends in its seven-mile length and goes down the mountainside to a fishing village of the same name. It is, in fact only two miles as the crow flies from top to bottom, but is so contorted that it crosses over itself at one point. The Germans ask if we are going to try it. How can we resist such a challenge? "Later," we say.

We set off for Sa Calobra in the late afternoon. As we arrive at the start, the Germans are just puffing up to the top, hot and excited. They calculate how long it has taken them to cycle up from sea level. They are very pleased with their time. Can we match it? We wait for a coach to ascend before setting off.

What an exhilarating descent this turns out to be. The swoops and curves go on and on and on. You don't want them ever to end. But you need a strong stomach when you're near the edge. Some of the drops are truly scary. Frank is way ahead of me. I can't take corners like he can. When I see him coming back towards me on a big loop further down, I stop to take a photo. Now I'm even further behind. We're glad that no more coaches are coming up after that last one. It's scary enough to meet a car on a hairpin bend. Luckily we only pass two.

Finally I swoop down to the very bottom, feeling euphoric. Frank is waiting for me. We'd like to celebrate with a drink but the café is closed now. Anyway, we can't hang about – it will be dark before we know it. So, with a strong desire to get back to the top before sunset, we put every ounce of effort into our climb.

At last, puffing and gasping, we reach the top again. This time I keep up with Frank. We check our time and find we've taken 15 minutes less than the Germans. Wow! We're over the moon, especially as we're much older than they are. Pity we can't buy an ice cream to round off the evening.

On our return to the monastery, I stop several times to take photos of the mountains. The light is so atmospheric. But it's soon dark and we end up having to put our bike lights on. We're still on such a high. That was the most exciting ride of our lives.

* * *

It's a great relief when dawn arrives. In the blackness of the night, I've imagined ghostly monks coming at me from out of the walls. I'm not even sure if it was a bad dream or if it really happened.

When we're all packed up ready to leave, we decide we'll head back in the general direction of Palma, as there are only three days of holiday left. The last one of these must, of course, be spent at Hostal Apuntadores, in order to reclaim our pipe lagging. The map shows that Port de Sóller, on the north-western coast, is almost due north of Palma, so that's where we'll go. The road to take us there is a continuation of the same road that brought us from Port de Pollença.

We set off in brilliant sunshine, going eastwards through the mountains. After Sa Calobra, this is the most exciting road we will ride. It climbs, twists and plunges, disappearing into two tunnels before finally coming out at a dramatic viewpoint on a sharp bend. From the safety of a low wall, we pause to gaze down on the vast panorama, and what must surely be the bay of Port de Sóller in the distant haze. Then eagerly jumping back on the bikes, we swoop all the way down to the coast.

Port de Sóller sits in a most beautiful bay with a backdrop of mountains all around. There are palm trees along the promenade, which follows the curve of the bay and is just a step away from the beach. The sea has scarcely a ripple and rows of sailing boats are moored up in a sheltered corner of the bay, bobbing gently on the water.

We push the bikes right round the bay to where we can see a hotel almost on the beach. It resembles an office block, but they have vacancies and that's all we need. Inside it's very pleasant. Although we don't have a sea view, there are French doors opening onto a sunny rocky garden, which is part way up the side of a mountain. This is where we eat our picnic lunch. I'd be quite happy to stay here for a couple of days, but Frank has booked us in for one night only. He wants us to see a little more of Majorca before we return to Palma.

During the afternoon we don our bathing gear and head for the beach, looking forward to a fun frolic and revitalization in the sea. But it's a rather tame swim as there are no waves to speak of. We could just as well have been in a swimming pool.

Later, we explore the other side of the bay and find a variety of food stalls and restaurants. In one of these we enjoy a spicy Mexican meal as we watch the world go by. Then later, returning across the beach after dark, we almost tread on a rabble of rats running from under a bridge, searching for their supper.

* * *

There's no point in us lingering in Port de Sóller this morning if we intend to explore further afield. However we quite like it here and are reluctant to leave, especially as we don't have to be anywhere else in a hurry. So we easily fritter away our time, something we're so good at. Consequently, it's afternoon before we arrive in the town of Sóller, only a few miles inland. Now that we're away from the sea breezes, it's stinking hot once more. We sit in a cramped outdoor café near to tramlines that run through the centre of town, watching the to-ing and fro-ing of tram-trippers, close by our table.

We can't cope with all these crowds. There's barely room to open the map. Where shall we go next? The reverse side of our map shows pictures and texts of the places of interest to visit in Majorca. One of these is Valldemossa, further eastwards down the coast. It looks to be in a charming location, surrounded by mountains. But as the text is in Spanish we don't understand much about the place, apart from the fact that Chopin stayed here once. Perhaps that's where we should go. We can see on the map that there's a road running directly from Valldemossa to Palma. That should make for a straightforward return tomorrow. Actually, it's not that direct; the first part looks quite twisty, through the mountains.

Valldemossa is barely 15 miles away, so we don't rush to get going. But having thought this ride would be a cinch, we find we were sorely mistaken. There are so many short, steep hills on the rugged coastline that it takes forever. We have to keep stopping for a rest and a grumble. It's incredibly hot. Eventually, we roll into town at around 7.30 pm, having frittered away so much time sitting on rocky outcrops watching the waves. Now we must find somewhere to spend the night. But Valldemossa is a little way in from the coast. There are no beach hotels at our disposal. We wander round the town looking for accommodation, with a sort of sinking feeling in the pit of our stomachs. It's a bit of a déja vu situation. In the end, we have to admit defeat. We stand by a field gate and stroke the noses of some inquisitive goats, they being our only comfort as we watch the sun disappear. There is only one option left to us – we must ride back to Palma in the dark. I'm dreading it – it's only 14 miles to cycle but we'll have to go all the way in pitch darkness. Frank is being gallant.

I feel less tense, once the twisty mountain road begins to straighten out and we leave the mountains behind us. At least we've negotiated all those sharp bends without mishap. From now on, it's downhill all the way, so we can relax a little. Or so we think. But soon we become aware that there are major road improvements going on. In places, the surface of the road is just compressed stones. We bump along it, cursing. Then we realise there's a much worse hazard to cope with. There are no sides to the road. They just fall away into the darkness. Now we have to concentrate like mad to make sure we don't fall off the edge. It's absolutely nerve-racking.

With our heads buzzing, we arrive at last in Palma, where the nightlife is also buzzing. We make straight for Hostal Apuntadores and book in, realising that we've taken this place completely for granted. We've just assumed there will be vacancies for us. Goodness knows where we'd be tonight without it. We head straight for bed.

* * *

Today we have a spare day in Palma that we didn't really want. Another day in the mountains would have been much nicer. So as is our wont, we wander off along the coast. We go westwards this time, just using up the day. It's a disappointing ride, cycling through the, now empty mecca town of Megaluf with its myriad fish and chip shops but not a tourist in sight on this scorching mid-September day. We carry on through run-down suburbs to a small cove further round the bay. It's pleasant enough here but after all those mountains, it really doesn't float our boat. The heat wave hasn't relented and we're getting the full blast now that we're on the south coast again. We can't stand it for long. If we wished, we could explore further round the coast but we've lost all incentive and energy.

Our last supper in Palma is a fairly modest affair, although we manage to afford a little celebratory drink before our holiday money runs out. Then it's back to the hostel, where we retrieve our pipe lagging and head for bed, setting the alarm for 3.30 am.

* * *

In the early hours we find our little road to the airport without too much trouble, although the route seems totally different in the dark. We have very little time to prepare the bikes for the flight home and before we know it, we're zooming down into Gatwick.

Well, what a holiday that turned out to be, when we thought all we needed was a rest. It seems that those mountain rides were the pure tonic Frank was looking for, not incarceration in a monastery.

The Quirks of Norwich

August 1994

"Let's have a... quick look at the.... town centre first," I panted, as with relief we pushed on the pedals one more time to reach the crown of the hill and freewheeled down the other side. Frank nodded. "OK, then we'll nip round the cathedral. Ought to be away by midday."

We were glad to leave Norwich youth hostel, where all three courses of breakfast had been served together and the seemingly endless succession of narrow stairs and hard-to-open fire doors had greatly hindered us, with our arms so full of panniers. As if that hadn't been frustrating enough, we'd then had to push our way through hordes of children gathered for the junior chess championship who were blocking the entrance hall.

On reaching what we thought to be the centre, we found a

market in full swing. We turned to scan the rooftops below us, searching for the spire of the cathedral, without success. We were intrigued by a quaint old building which stood further up the hill. It was made from chunks of flint, like a patchwork quilt. It turned out to be the Tourist Information Centre. Great. Just what we needed!

We trudged up towards it, our laden bikes dangling wet socks, pants and flannels from our crossbars and panniers. They hung at various angles from an assortment of pegs. As we came level with the doorway, a smartly-dressed man jumped out and asked, "Are you tourists?" "No, we're just taking our bikes for a little walk to get the washing dry," I nearly said to him.

He told us he was a cathedral guide, but unfortunately his tours did not start until 2 pm, by which time he'd be delighted to show us around. "Sorry," I replied, "we haven't got time for a tour, we just want to know where the cathedral IS."

He went to great lengths explaining, pointing and waving his arms about, as the French do. However, he digressed so much, telling us about this famous building and that one, this famous person and that one, that by the time he had finished we were frankly flummoxed. We decided to go inside and get a map of the city.

Locking up the heavy bikes was not at all easy on the slope. We spent several minutes finding somewhere where they wouldn't roll away. Too long, it seemed, because by now another cathedral guide had accosted us (although we didn't realise that she was one at the time). Extremely tall and imposing, she breezed up and feigned an interest in our bikes. Her focus soon turned, however, to her own bike, which was a very good make, she told us. But she was worried about it because the chrome was coming off the wheels, and what could she do about it? "I've got the bike up here. Let me show you." It was a demand, not a request, and reluctantly we followed her further up the hill. She revealed her Raleigh, complete with sprung seat and wicker basket. (Well honestly, what else did we expect?)

There then followed a complete history of this bike. How it had once been parked against a building that was being cleaned. How Mr So and So from Such and Such Street said some harmful chemical must have dropped on it. She stopped to ask if we thought that this was what *might* have happened. But after a short pause in which we didn't give the correct answer in the allotted time, she continued; about how she'd complained to the judiciary but got nowhere and what could she do about it?

She obviously loved this bike with a passion. If we'd had the guts, we'd have said, "Madam, we think it's suffering from old age." But we didn't. I can't remember exactly what we did mutter but we realised that the hour and a half we'd allowed for a brief look round was fast slipping away.

We tried to make a quick getaway. But, oh no, she wasn't letting us go that easily. "No point in going into the TIC for a map. I'm on the way to the cathedral myself. I'm not on duty yet but I'll show you the way." We didn't dare argue.

Feeling like a couple of school kids, we were literally marched down through the streets of Norwich, running to keep up, then jamming on the brakes if she stopped unexpectedly – and all the time catching each other's eye and giggling behind her back. Short bursts of conversation along the way, revealed what we had suspected, that she was an ex-schoolmistress from a private school.

During this frogmarch to the cathedral, Frank was reprimanded twice, first for interrupting before she'd finished speaking and then for daring to step off the kerb before the 'green man' was flashing. He was lucky not to get detention, or worse!

We were zoomed, it seemed, via paths and alleyways, to a quiet car park at the back of the cathedral where we looked for some wall space to lock up the bikes. But, oh no, she wasn't having that. "These trees are quite strong enough," she insisted, whereupon she chose a young sapling and manhandled our bikes into precarious positions on either side of it. Then she told us how to lock them together and attempted to snatch the cable from us. *Get off*, we both thought. What we said was, "We can do it ourselves, thank you very much." She was really getting us down.

It was nearly midday and we were almost sick of the cathedral, even before we'd stepped inside. If she'd just leave us now, we'd have a really quick glimpse and be on our way. She had other ideas though and ignored our comments (half of which were whispered under our breath). We'd been reduced to the status of naughty children. She had a mission to fulfil, and fulfil it she would. So, hurrying us up, not because we were in a hurry but because Mrs So and So would be a third of the way through her tour, she commanded us to follow.

Everything began to feel unreal. This tall being didn't seem like a woman now, more akin to a poltergeist or a rush of ectoplasm, whilst we two defeated travellers followed her, not in control of our own bodies any more. In a daze, we were whooshed up this aisle, down that one, about turn, up these steps, through that chapel, then about turn, with absolutely no let up at all.

Until suddenly, she stopped dead. She had found them. For a moment, she became a charming tall lady, introducing us to the guide and asking if we might join the group, please. Then she wafted away in triumph.

The irony of all this was that we became so engrossed in our cathedral tour that we stayed there until 4 pm. Her will had indeed been done!

CHAPTER THREE

Aborted Ambition

August 1986

Pete peeling potatoes

There had been warnings on the radio for the last two days that Hurricane Charley was heading across the Atlantic. Having already wreaked havoc on the east coast of America, it was now Great Britain's turn to take the brunt. And so Charley arrived in time to wreck the Bank holiday weekend, bringing its fury to Wales and England. How fortunate that we'd hung on for a day or two.

We'd been eagerly preparing to go on a cycling holiday, kitted out with our newly-acquired camping equipment – the 'we' being myself and my two sons, Pete and Malc. I'd recently bought Pete a tent for his 14th birthday and, at the same time, one for his 12-year-old brother, even though his birthday was not until December. But we couldn't hang on any longer. I thought the boys needed some adventure in their lives – as did I!

I'd bought their two little ridge tents from a club book, where the items arrive straight away but are paid for in small instalments over a period of weeks. Last Christmas, I had bought them panniers from the club book, in order to start the ball rolling. As we never afforded proper family holidays, I realised that with bikes and camping equipment, we could go places under our own steam, on very little money.

Pete and Malc had begun their camping malarkey as soon as the tents arrived, pitching them in the back garden. This wasn't ideal with the lawn being on a slope, but that didn't seem to bother them much. So for the next two days the telly stayed off all day and they only popped indoors occasionally, to raid the food cupboard, to go to the loo, or fetch a puzzle book or a pack of cards from their bedroom. With their little camping stove set up on a piece of paving slab, they cooked themselves beans, sausages, boiled eggs, or whatever they could find, then sneaked the dirty dishes back into the kitchen when no one was about. What was most amazing was the harmony that ensued. Then on the third day it rained hard and everything had to be dragged indoors and dried. Anyway, it was high time the two of them came in for a wash.

The following week, we decided to go camping for one night only. We needed to know if we could manage without being close to home. We'd be silly to embark on a proper holiday, if we hadn't proved we could cope. So Lechlade was the town I chose for a 'one-night-stand', about 35 miles to the east of us, in an area of flat terrain. We would simply leave on the Saturday morning and return the next day.

The whole of the day before was spent in preparation. This would be a precursor for future cycling holidays. The bikes were checked over and our panniers carefully packed. We rolled the boys' sleeping bags around their tents, putting dustbin bags round the rolls to keep them dry. These would be tied across the top of their panniers with string. In my panniers I packed our cooking equipment, which simply consisted of a compact set of three small saucepans with a clip-on handle, a little camping stove with its gas canister, and a handful of cutlery, rolled inside a tea towel. Then I put in enough food to see us through. Pete lent me a drum-bag for my clothes, around which I wrapped my sleeping bag, with a dustbin bag on top. We ensured that all three loads were similar in weight.

And thus, on the Saturday morning, we set off on our very first trial run, with feelings of anxious excitement. It was not onerous, once we'd climbed out of the Stroud valleys onto the high plateau to Cirencester. We continued on in the same direction to Fairford, then Lechlade – a journey that couldn't be done safely on the main road today, with the increased speed and volume of traffic.

On the approach to Lechlade, we passed an open gate to a grassy field. "Let's camp in there, Mum, it'll be free," suggested Pete. We went back to have a look. It was a small field with high hedges. "Why not?" I agreed, so in true pioneering spirit we set up the little tents next to the hedgerow.

That one night away taught us some of the pitfalls we might

encounter. We were cold and uncomfortable during the night, sleeping on clumpy grass, or 'sods', as I soon referred to them. We therefore decided next morning that we'd buy some inflatable plastic mattresses when we returned home and three of those flimsy aluminium blankets that athletes are wrapped in after a marathon, to lay over our sleeping bags.

In a tired and more sombre mood, we ate our breakfast cereals, realising that camping was not always going to be fun. After our tents and belongings were packed, it seemed unfulfilling to just cycle back home. Perhaps, on our return journey, we could incorporate a place of interest to visit. We scoured the map to see what we could find.

"Hey, there's Kempsford," said Pete. "We could go and see Jenny and Colin, then come home a different way." These two were old family friends of ours; my husband Jim and I had been witnesses at their wedding. Recently, they had moved from their riverside home in Maisemore, where the River Severn often flooded the garden, to land-locked Kempsford. "Wouldn't they be surprised to see us?" added Malc.

Kempsford was southwest from here, at the bottom end of Fairford aerodrome. We might even get to see some interesting aircraft as we cycled round the perimeter. In the late 60s Jim and I had raced there from Cheltenham, to watch Concorde land on her maiden flight – if 'racing' is the correct term to use for a Standard van. Unfortunately we were just too late for the landing, but Concorde was still taxiing along the runway. Those were exciting days!

Jenny and Colin and their two daughters were *very* surprised to see us, and impressed that we'd been camping with our bikes.

We felt quite proud. They invited us to stay on, to have Sunday tea with them. They even rang Jim, to invite him over as well. It was ages since we'd last seen them, so there was much catching-up to be done and we had a lovely time. But we were tempting fate, knowing that rain was forecast later in the day, so Jim decided to take our luggage in the car, so that we could cycle home as quickly as possible and, hopefully, miss the rain. We didn't! We were soaked to the skin. It was a miserable journey but we were initiated. We were ready for a proper holiday.

Our holiday was going to be a few days on the south coast – a thrilling prospect for us, who rarely saw the sea. Jim would take us, with the bikes in the car, to the other side of Weston-super-Mare, from where we could cycle down to Taunton and stay with family friends on a farm in the Blackdown Hills. We would be able to reach the south coast from there the next day.

But just as we were about to set forth, we heard about Hurricane Charley and held our horses. It came with a vengeance, lashing rain at the windows and bending trees to their limits – thinning out the weaker ones. We were glad we'd hung on until it passed and, in retrospect, pleased we'd avoided the Bank Holiday traffic.

The storm abated and the weather settled into a gentle phase of late summer splendour. At last, it was time to go. We loaded up the car, (a spacious old Maxi), putting the boys in the back with the bikes. This was before seat-belt legislation. Jim was quite enthusiastic about going to Weston. He'd just acquired a metal detector from *Exchange & Mart*, a trading catalogue, and planned to spend some time with us on the beach, looking for lost coins. Quite an exciting prospect!

We parked up on the beach and patiently followed Jim as he did his detecting, trawling the sand around the edges of the pier, hoping to find lots of coins. Huh! The only objects he detected the whole afternoon were the little metal tops that you pull off drink cans. By mid-afternoon he conceded that this wasn't the best place to look after all. He bought us all ice creams, then we piled back into the car. All that time and lovely sunshine we'd wasted when we could have been cycling.

About five miles out of Weston, Jim pulled off the A370 and parked up in a gateway, where we unloaded the car and reassembled the bikes. Then he noticed something wrong with Pete's back tyre – it had a slit in it. We couldn't think when that had happened, but it wouldn't be safe to use. He looked at his watch. There was just time to buy a new tyre before the shops closed. He and Pete jumped in the car and sped back to Weston, leaving Malc and me abandoned on the roadside. It seemed an endless wait, not knowing when or if they'd come back.

Eventually they returned and fitted the new tyre. Then Jim said "Cheerio," wished us luck and drove home. He knew me well, and he knew that once I'd made up my mind to do something, there was no stopping me. And even though time was getting on, I'd work out some compromise.

It was far too late to head for Taunton now, so we searched the map for a campsite that we could reach by dusk. We found one on a farm – two miles back towards Weston! We'd hoped to be staying with our friends that night.

However, it was still fun, setting up the tents in a field close to a farmyard, with the low evening sunlight beaming straight into the tents. The boys cheerfully cooked beans on the stove, then boiled water for cups of tea. It was all such a novelty. I washed up under a cold running tap in the farmyard. Now it was time to blow up our new plastic mattresses. Boy, did that take a long time! We wished we'd had a foot pump instead of puffing all our moist breath into them. We had to keep stopping to give our mouths a rest, making sure we didn't lose any air in the meantime.

By now it was getting dark. I placed my mattress in Malc's tent, alongside his, while Pete had a tent to himself. Malc seemed quite happy with that arrangement. There was just enough room to squeeze down the middle. We took the aluminium blankets out of their tiny packets and laid them over our sleeping bags, because the nights had become quite chilly. Then we climbed in for the very first night of our cycling holiday, having cycled the grand distance of two miles!

* * *

The mattresses were wonderfully comfy, but we awoke to find our sleeping bags soaked with condensation. The undersides of the aluminium blankets were dripping wet. They'd kept all the moisture in. So that idea wasn't going to work for us. Luckily the day was warming up, so we could lay the sleeping bags out to dry before packing them away. The boys laid theirs over their tents, while I hung mine over the farmyard gate.

Deflating our mattresses was almost as protracted as blowing them up. It took ages. Never mind, the sleeping bags could do with more time to air in the sunshine. We bought half a dozen eggs from the farmer and had fried egg sandwiches for breakfast, followed by coffee in our red plastic beakers. Already we felt like old hands at this camping lark. Now we had to see if we could repack our panniers as proficiently as we had done at home, which wasn't that easy. But we weren't in a hurry.

By eleven o'clock everything was ready. We paid the farmer's wife the modest fee for our overnight stay and she wished us all the best. Then off we cycled down the A370, heading towards the A38 and Taunton. We'd been driven through Taunton before, so we knew how to get to Staple Fitzpaine and our friends' farm. But I made a complete idiot of myself at a roundabout in the town centre. It was on a rise and I was still in my top gear. After waiting for a gap in the traffic, I didn't have enough inertia to get the bike going and had to scoot round the roundabout with one foot while all the traffic stopped, patiently waiting. What an example to set my boys, who managed to cycle round perfectly.

By mid-afternoon we had found the farm and were welcomed by our friends, Charles and Tilly, whose son was Pete's godfather. We found it hard to adjust to their meal times, which were based around the milking of the cows, breakfast being at midday and evening meal late at night. But Tilly soon had a lovely plate of ham sandwiches and homemade cake set out in front of us, along with a large steaming pot of tea. Later on we went out with Charles to round up the cattle and the boys helped him move the electric fence further up the field. It was a pleasant stay, with really comfortable beds to sleep in.

* * *

We heard Charles get up very early to bring the cows in for

milking. He loved his cattle and had names for all of them. Tilly was up and working too, doing all her farmer's wife chores. Yesterday, she'd shown us how she skimmed the lovely thick cream off the top of the milk. She'd used some of it in the delicious sponge cake we were given the day before. Today she was preparing an earlier breakfast than usual, for our benefit. While we ate our cereals she had three fried breakfasts waiting for us in the Aga. What a multi-star hotel this was! We were full to bursting by the time we stepped down from the table.

Now for another bonus. She told us that if we followed a track up through the woods to the gate at the top, it would intercept the road we needed, to take us down to the coast. That would save us lots of messing about, trying to find a route from the map. We thanked them both and bade them fond farewells before pushing our bikes all the way up the hill.

We absolutely bowled along the top road over Staple Hill, then further on, down Stockland Hill all the way to Shute and onto the A358 into Axmouth, where there was a lovely flat campsite next to the River Axe. It had been an exhilarating cycle ride of about 40 miles and we'd reached the sea – well, almost. It was just a little way down the road and across the bridge into Seaton.

After booking in, we quickly set up the tents before going to explore. But at the first roundabout into Seaton, Malc jerked his arm in an awkward manner, trying to avoid a car that was accelerating towards him. We pulled onto the pavement to see what was up and he told us his arm was so painful he couldn't ride his bike. What a thing to happen so soon after our arrival. What should we do?

Then a lady passing by told us there was a surgery on the outskirts of town. We headed for it, up a long, steep hill, with poor Malc having to rest frequently because he could only push his bike with one arm. We were hot and tired when we reached the surgery, then had to wait ages to see the doctor, who diagnosed a torn muscle. He said it might heal within two hours, or it could take two days, or in some cases, two weeks! Well, what were we supposed to deduce from that? But wonder of wonders, by the time we'd eaten supper, Malc was chasing Pete round the campsite on his bike.

* * *

We'd slept without those aluminium blankets over us during the night but hadn't felt cold. As a consequence the sleeping bags were dry. Later, en route to the ladies', I peeped into the men's washroom because the boys had told me the floor was covered in excrement (not their word). They wouldn't go in for a wash. I could see what the problem was; the taps were so powerful that they shot water all over the floor. Then, with men bringing reddish-brown mud in off the field, the floor looked like the bottom of a cowshed. I explained this to them, but they still weren't convinced and I spent the next two days trying to coax them to wash in the sea, without success.

We spent a glorious day bumbling around Seaton and Beer. It was warm and sunny, although not warm enough to swim in the sea. We weren't doing anything exciting, just having a completely new experience. With every wave that lapped up the shore, the pebbles made a lovely swishing sound, which was quite soporific. Pete and Malc had never been on a pebbled beach before. They'd only experienced the vast, flat expanses of sand and mud at Skegness on the east coast, and Weston-super-Mare on the west.

Seaton was not bustling, now the Bank Holiday was over. With this pleasant weather, it seemed an ideal time of year to be there. We walked along the coast towards Beer, resting awhile on some red cliffs, which were unlike the chalky cliffs ahead of us, making for a truly two-toned coastline. Beer was a charming little village to explore. There were several fishing boats pulled up on the beach, which was also pebbly. We learnt that, in days gone by, it had been a haven for smugglers, probably because there were so many caves in which to hide smuggled goods. These caverns were the result of extensive stone quarrying, the stone being renowned for its ease of carving. Many famous cathedrals and buildings were listed as having stone from here.

Later on, in a café overlooking the sea, we enjoyed tea and scones with lashings of cream and homemade raspberry jam, which was an expensive luxury for us. I would have to be careful with my money now, so on the way back I bought a bag of potatoes. We'd be filling up on boiled spuds with a tin of mince tonight.

* * *

After breakfast we planned to pack up the tents and move on, even though we loved this campsite – that is, apart from the men's washroom, which the boys still refused to use. But we felt we should see more of the coast. Lyme Regis had a nice ring to its name, we thought. It was roughly five miles to the east. We aired the tents well before packing them and were ready to leave by late morning.

When we arrived at Lyme Regis, what first caught our eye was not the lovely long curved stone harbour wall, nor the beautiful wide sandy bay, but the masses of tree trunks, broken branches and scatterings of twigs that littered the beach. Of course, it was the work of Hurricane Charley. We'd almost forgotten about that. This coast must have taken a real bashing.

We were put off from going onto the beach, so turned inland to suss out the town first, soon tempted by the smell of meat pasties in a street close by. "Can we have one Mum, please?" pleaded Malc. We couldn't resist. Sitting on a low wall in the midday sun, we savoured their hot juiciness. They were too hot to hold and too hot to eat, but we couldn't wait for them to cool down, changing hands and puffing and gasping with each bite, as they burnt our mouths.

By now, money was going to be my biggest worry. There wasn't much left. Everything was costing more than I'd anticipated. I soon worked out that we couldn't afford to stay any more nights on the coast; we'd have to start heading back later on. When I told the boys this they were crestfallen. Just minutes before they'd been happily munching their pasties.

By mid-afternoon we began the return journey, fervently wishing we didn't have to leave this attractive seaside resort so soon. Now we were struggling up a daunting climb out of town on the B3165. However, half a mile up, we came to a cliffside park overhanging the sparkling blue sea. I gave the boys enough money for a game of crazy golf, feeling so guilty to be dragging them away after only two nights on the coast. It could have been three, if it hadn't been for Jim's metal detector.

The boys strung out their game as long as they possibly could, delaying our leaving. None of us relished the thought of cycling up the long, long hill. But it had to be done. Eventually, we were back on the bikes, heads down, slogging up this hill that went on forever. It wore us out.

Around 6pm we arrived in Crewkerne, where a chip shop was open. "Blow the money," I announced, "I'm going to get us fish and chips. We've got to keep our strength up." They were worth every penny, truly the best fish and chips we had ever tasted, but our money was ever dwindling. Too bad! We looked on the map for a campsite. The nearest one was near Yeovilton, which we estimated to be 10 miles further on.

After about five miles, Malc stopped. "Mum, I just can't go any further. I've got no energy left."

"Oh Malc it won't be long now," I pleaded, "can you just keep going if we go slowly?"

He pedalled a little way. "No I can't. I've gone all dizzy."

We stopped again and I found him a few biscuits in my pannier and made him drink some water. We didn't have much left. After that, he managed to pedal on for almost a mile before stopping again, worn out. It was dusk now. We had to reach the campsite somehow. I found a sweet in my handlebar bag and handed it to him – any little morsel we could find, just to keep him going. I knew I was pushing him to his limits, poor kid. He was nearly crying. By the time we found the campsite it was almost dark.

It didn't seem a very big site and we couldn't see much room for our tents, but with the small amount of light from the washroom windows nearby, we managed to squeeze them between two big tents. We worked quietly at our task, as all the campers seemed to have retired to bed. We didn't see a soul.

Pete and I put up Malc's tent, so that he could begin blowing up his mattress (if he could find the puff) while we erected the second tent. Because of our tiredness and the lateness of the hour, we only blew them half full, but at least we'd found somewhere to spend the night. With the lack of light we hadn't put the tents up very well. But as it wasn't windy and we'd soon be taking them down again, we felt they'd do.

I went into the washroom before settling down for the night and thought I was in the horror film *The Birds*. There were multitudes of moths flapping round my face, attracted through the open windows by the electric lights. A lepidopterist would have had a wonderful time counting all the different species, but I couldn't wait to get out. I thought it very sad that so many of them would die, either burnt by light bulbs or by being trapped inside.

* * *

Our plan was to rise at dawn and leave the site as quickly as possible because we didn't think it was fair for us to pay for a day's camping fee when we'd spent such a short time there. Anyway, we needed all the remaining money we had for food. This wasn't a good lesson to be teaching the boys, but food was my first priority.

We focused well on the job in hand, working quietly and

efficiently. When our rolls and panniers were ready, we carried them to the other side of the gate, then went back for the bikes. Outside, we could spend as long as it took to tie the rolls onto the bikes. What was so amazing was that we still hadn't seen a soul. Not only had all the campers been in bed by dark, they all seemed to be still snoozing – lucky beggars.

Now we had to find our way in reverse along the little country roads we'd struggled on last night. On reaching the first corner, we were confronted by scores of rabbits frolicking all over the road, used to having this time of day to themselves. They soon scooted into the hedgerows at the sight of us, but we felt privileged that we'd witnessed their early morning shindig. With the sharp morning air awakening our senses and filling our lungs, we felt fresh and optimistic about the day ahead, which was, as yet, unplanned.

Back on the main road we pedalled in a northerly direction, soon passing through Somerton, which I thought to be a very attractive little town. In the centre was a wide space, presumably a market square, with a lovely octagonal-roofed market cross, rather like the one we knew in Malmesbury, Wiltshire. Then I saw a sign saying that the town had Anglo-Saxon origins, my favourite era in history. But I wasn't able to stop. Pete and Malc were ploughing on ahead and I couldn't disrupt their progress.

We'd hoped the day's journey across the Somerset Levels would be a fairly flat one, but this was not the case and halfway up a very long hill our energy began to wane. We ran out of steam and pushed the laden bikes the remainder of the way, tired out already. Then came another long incline. We weren't feeling at all enthusiastic now. If we continued in the direction we were going, we would end up in Wells, a town we hoped to avoid because we knew there was a massive hill on the other side of it, having been taken there once by car. So we diverted to smaller roads, heading in a north-westerly direction. Now cycling was much more pleasant than being on the main road. Our spirits revived. Passing a small village shop, we stopped to buy crusty rolls and cheese, which we ate on the opposite side of the road, on a bench, beautifully bathed in sunshine. No wonder we were feeling the strain today. We'd missed having breakfast.

It was good to stop. We hadn't even discussed where we hoped to end up that day – somewhere in the direction of home, of course. We'd definitely have to camp in a field for the night.

When we'd finished our lovely rolls, we took a leisurely look at the map. Where should we go? Then Malc got excited when he saw Wookey Hole. He'd read about the huge caverns there, with a river running deep down underneath. "Please can we go there Mum, please?" What could I say? Pete was just as keen. But it would mean we'd have to negotiate some steep little Mendip roads to get there. They didn't mind that, they said.

We got back astride the heavy bikes, keeping the map on top of my handlebar bag, for reference. It was a tough ride and the only thing keeping the boys going was the expectations at the end of it. When at last we entered the visitors' car park, we were smacked in the face (metaphorically) by a signboard showing the entrance prices, something we'd been totally unprepared for. Naively, we hadn't realised how commercialised this attraction had become. We'd thought we would just walk into the caves with a guide, who would shine a torch around, to pick out all the wonderful formations, as used to be done in bygone days. We hadn't realised that the tours would be grand events, entailing music and light shows. The boys were devastated.

All the stuffing was knocked out of them now. They'd lost interest in our cycling tour. "Let's ring up Dad and see if he'll come and fetch us," they suggested. That seemed such a shame. One more day and we could have completed the whole ride back home. But I was tired too. I went to find a telephone box to phone Jim who, luckily, was quite prepared to come and take us home.

Well, we might as well spend the rest of our money on *something*. There was just enough for us to go on a papermaking tour. It was quite interesting really, and educational too; nothing like going inside the caves of course but better than nothing. Afterwards, with time on our hands, we got out the camping stove on the edge of the car park and boiled a saucepan of water for a cuppa, to the amusement of onlookers. It passed the time until Dad arrived.

And that was the abrupt end of our very first tour. Next year we'd try again – maybe even go abroad – God willing!

CHAPTER FOUR

When We Missed the Boat

September 1998

'Les Trois Ours' tucked against the Forêt de Brotonne

While Frank was chatting to his IT tutor, Louise, in the coffee break, he discovered that her sister had a holiday cottage in Normandy. Louise had a lovely pair of legs (so I'd gathered) and it was not uncommon for Frank to chat to her in the breaks. So now he was privy to this information about the cottage, where Louise and her cyclist boyfriend often went to stay. Would this sister, perhaps, rent it out to non-family members, if Louise could put in a good word for him, he inquired?

* * *

So here we were, taking our bikes on the ferry to Le Havre, heading for a holiday in Les Trois Ours (The Three Bears), a little cottage on the edge of the tiny village of Sainte Croix-sur-Azier, tucked against the Forêt de Brotonne. This forest is within a loop of the River Seine, somewhere between Le Havre and Rouen and north of the small town of Bourneville. We had booked it for two weeks and were planning to share the first week with a couple of cycling friends who were arriving from the ferry by car.

Getting out of Le Havre was more difficult than saying it. And as has happened to us in the past, as soon as we heard cars hooting and tooting, we realised we were on a motorway. Undoing the mistake and reversing your bike can be much harder than you think, and finding an alternative route can be even harder, if you find yourself having to go miles off course. But eventually we crossed the Tancarville Bridge over the Seine, which we knew to be the right way. A heavy shower had caught us out and our feet were soaked, so as we approached the first place of habitation, Quillebeuf, we found a café. Ostensibly we went in for coffee, but in fact we were more interested in changing into dry socks. As it was still fairly early in the day, we were the only customers. We made some convivial conversation with the proprietress, who was very pleasant and wanted to dry our socks for us. Indeed, all the older inhabitants of this part of Normandy, we were to discover, were very friendly and accommodating.

After finding Bourneville, we took a small road northwards. The countryside was criss-crossed with narrow roads across farmland and through tiny hamlets, and it took quite a bit of detective work to find the cottage. We arrived before our friends, Jill and Rob, who had been shopping for provisions to keep us going for a day or two.

We were all delighted with the cottage, which looked to be in the typical Normandy style of that area; of timber construction with wattle and daub walls. But on closer inspection it was more modern. Even so, the upper storey overhung at one end, with an outside wooden staircase leading to the first floor (or in this case, the attic), just as they did on the really old cottages. We noticed that the walls between the timbers were rendered and one of the windows was metal-framed, so it was not an authentic Normandy house. But it still looked cute and cosy and there was a huge stack of logs under the outside stairs.

The old-fashioned kitchen was at the opposite end to the overhang – not old, old fashioned; more like something from the 50s, as that's when it had been modernised, I surmised. There was a dated gas cooker and an old stone sink with a wooden draining board. Luckily, the last occupants had left a box of matches to light the gas. Against the opposite wall was a 50s-style metal-legged, Formica-topped table with four matching chairs, leaving just enough space for the four of us to wash up and dry the dishes (throughout that first week we had a rota going, for all the kitchen chores).

Next in line – for the rooms were in a linear layout – came the sitting room with its beamed ceiling and open fireplace, and also a heavy curtain over the front door to keep out the draughts. There was a sturdy ladder leading up to the attic bedroom; neither too steep nor too narrow. But as Jill and Rob were a little younger than us, they elected to sleep in the attic.

Next came the bedroom where Frank and I would sleep. The double bed looked reasonable enough but it proved to be quite hard with a slippery mattress, so that the bottom sheet would slide all over the place in the night. With that and the fact that Rob would wake us up each night on his somewhat noisy way to the toilet beyond, our sleep was regularly disturbed.

That first night we made a cracking log fire to keep out the evening chills of September and drank wine as we lounged in the comfy armchairs. There were numerous books and leaflets at our disposal to give us an insight into local places of interest. By the time we were heading for bed, we had made plans for where to cycle the next day. Jill and Rob were going in one direction and Frank and I fancied taking a ferry across the Seine. They probably slept like logs that night. We didn't.

* * *

For the first three days, we two couples did our own thing – exploring and getting to know the layout of the area. There were long straight roads through forests and winding roads down to the Seine, which formed huge loops between Quillebeuf and Rouen. Many roads terminated at a ferry crossing, so it was wise to learn the frequencies of the ferries.

On the Thursday, Rob took us in his car to Bayeux, to see the famous tapestry. The dual carriageways were excellent but we struggled to find a space to park in the city. It was well worth the effort though, because the tapestry is superb. It is in fact embroidery on a very long length of cloth that looked like linen. I suppose you could equate it to a newspaper article of today, made in the materials they had available in the 11th Century – literally, a timeline in history.

We wore headphones to get a proper sense of what was depicted, although it was obviously telling the story of William the Conqueror's victory over King Harold of England. But these commentaries helped us identify which were the French soldiers and which the British, by subtle differences of armour, hairstyle or moustache. But we found we couldn't loiter at any particular point of interest, as a whole line of visitors was following on behind and we didn't want to stop the flow.

To round off the day, not far from Ste Croix, we peeled south off the dual carriageway to the small town of Rougemontiers for an evening meal. On their travels, Jill and Rob had discovered a good-value restaurant here. It was actually a transport café with a good reputation for its food and we were able to verify this claim.

On Jill and Rob's final day, we set off together for a full day's cycle ride, which proved to be memorable. We fondly refer to it still as 'Three Weddings and a Still' as it was not long after the release of the film 'Four Weddings and a Funeral'.

We started off by cycling to Vieux Port, a quaint little village which is, as its name suggests, an old port on the river and only a few miles from Ste Croix. Here we popped in for a quick look at the church. Inside, an exhibition was taking place, showing local historic christening gowns and related ephemera. I was fascinated to find they had a baby's carrying cape in bright red woven wool, just like the one in the museum where I worked, made from the famous 'Stroud Red' cloth – a connection somewhere back in history, no doubt. Jill and I chatted for quite a while to the two lovely ladies who had set up this exhibition, although 'chatted' implies a free flow of conversation, which this was not. Even so, we were able to exchange information.

A while later, we found Rob and Frank slumped on a wall by the riverside, grumpily waiting for us and looking at their watches. Forgiven by the men for making them wait so long, our ride continued along a lovely high curved ridge around a large flat plain, probably flattened by flooding, which I later learned was called the Réserve Naturelle des Mannevilles. We saw many cottages in similar style to Les Trois Ours, one of which was for sale and which Frank wanted to buy, even though it was falling to bits.

At Quillebeuf we took a ferry across the Seine and headed north on quiet roads through small villages. In one of these we came across a typical Normandy-style house that had been converted into a restaurant, where we couldn't resist a bevvy and a bite to eat.

Soon after this, as we pedalled past a little church on a high prominence, the bells broke into a joyful peal and out through the doorway stepped a bride and groom. Following on behind came a large, jubilant and somewhat unruly entourage. We hung around to watch the shenanigans for a while, even getting confetti thrown over us in the mêlée. Then, leaving them to their pleasures, we cycled off down the other side of the hill and continued on our way.

In the next village, a shiny black beribboned car was waiting outside the church. Yet another wedding in such a short space of time! We were reluctant to carry on until we'd also witnessed this happy couple coming out of the church. But so many guests spilled out behind them that the churchyard and the road outside were soon full to choking. We, with our bikes, were getting in their way. So we moved on, not wishing to impede their celebrations.

Having set off westwards that morning, then northwards after crossing the river, we were now circling round in an easterly direction through small old-fashioned villages. In the middle of a village square, a group of men were standing by a queer-looking contraption with steam coming out of its metal chimney. We were so curious to see what they were up to that we couldn't pass them by. The jolly trio greeted us, and using few words and many gestures, conveyed to us that this was a still and they were making Calvados. The local farmers were not permitted to make it themselves, but they could bring their apples here, where it would be made collectively.

The men found plastic tumblers and gave us each a sample to try – not that we could tell its quality, never having drunk it before, or if we had, it certainly wouldn't have been hot Calvados, like this. Anyway, if these samples had been cold, they would still have warmed the cockles of our hearts – or stomachs, in this case. Soon we became quite mellow.

What an honour for these men, we thought. What a privilege, to be making and then sampling this spirit to test its quality. They poured more Calvados into our tumblers, enjoying the pleasure with which they were visibly providing us. Noticing that Frank's glass was filled to the brim, I remember thinking to myself, even in my rather inebriated state, that if we didn't get away soon we wouldn't be able to ride our bikes. So when we'd drained our second helpings, I was adamant that we should get going. Frank, being the merriest, was the hardest to persuade to leave.

To complete our circle back to Ste Croix, we would need to cross the river again, so were heading towards the ferry crossing at Caudébec, on the very top of a loop in the river. The little road we were on forked to the left, giving us the choice of cutting straight through a grassy park instead of the circuitous route that the road might take. There was no sign to say whether it was private or not and so, having a certain air of bravado about us since consuming the Calvados, we took the grassy option. This green sward seemed like a Capability Brown parkland, undulating gently through an avenue of trees. In the distance, a stately home came into view; or was it a château? Were we trespassing? We weren't going to turn back now, so we carried on, and as we drew nearer, could make out a large gathering of people swarming around the building. Would we get stopped? Then, lo and behold, we realised we'd inadvertently stumbled on yet another wedding party – this time at their reception. We pedalled by, feigning nonchalance and keeping our heads down. But then we realised that none of the guests was taking the slightest bit of notice, so we stopped to take in the scene and to see if this bride was as beautiful as the last two had been. Had we wished, I felt sure we'd have been welcomed into the celebrations. But we needed to push on, because the nights were drawing in now.

When we reached the ferry crossing at Caudébec the ferry

had just left, so, not wishing to be delayed, and noting on the map that there was a road bridge further on called the Pont de Brotonne, we took that route. Now all we needed to do was cycle round the inside curve of the river to our little cottage in the woods, stopping several times on the way to look at thatched cottages as we passed by. Some were empty and Frank expressed an interest in them. It was dusk when we arrived at the cottage. Three weddings and a still, eh? It had been a thoroughly enjoyable day, enhanced, for sure, by spirits!

* * *

Now we were on our own. Would we find the second week in the cottage as fulfilling as the first had been? There was surely plenty more to see, although sometimes fixed-point cycling holidays can get tedious, when you keep returning by the same known routes.

We toyed with the idea of sleeping in the attic. It was the first time we'd been up there since we'd arrived. It looked so inviting. But we were put off by the thought of coming down that ladder in the middle of the night to go to the loo, so we carried on sleeping in the bedroom. At least Rob wouldn't be blundering through in the dark. If we had been sleeping in the attic, it would have been us blundering through at night, so we couldn't hold it against him.

We cycled west to Pont Audemer on the River Risle, which flows into the Seine near Honfleur. Then afterwards, back at the cottage, we read a leaflet about this town and learned of its beautiful half-timbered houses lining the river's edge. But we didn't get to see anything very pretty there; in fact we were quite disappointed. We must have been at the wrong end of the town.

The previous week, we had cycled round the nearest northern loop of the river, having first taken the ferry across to Jumièrge. En route, we'd passed the Abbaye de Jumièrge, where we'd peeped through a hole in the massive wooden gates to view the ruins rather than paying to go in. (It wasn't open anyway). Now this week we went round a second northern loop, opposite Duclair, cycling past massive sand and gravel pits and observing large ferries taking lorry loads of gravel across the river. The flat roads around the river's edge are wonderful for cycling, with some amazing viewpoints.

* * *

It's now three days since Jill and Rob's departure and we are planning a trip to Rouen. It's going to be quite protracted, with four ferry crossings. But it's a lovely sunny day – just right for our venture. We set off fairly early, familiar now with many of the routes through the forest. As we pedal down a long straight and sun-dappled road, we're keeping a sharp lookout for wild boar. Jill and Rob spotted some running through the woods a few days ago. But all we come across is a dead deer in a ditch. The stench is nauseating and we hold our breath for ages.

When we reach Jumièrges we have to wait on the slipway until the ferry comes across. Once on the other side, we are able to pick up a ferry timetable from a wooden hut, which serves as ticket kiosk and shop. It's like a shed nestling under the trees and there's not much for sale. But we buy a bottle of fruit drink each to give us an energy boost, because we've just seen the steep rocky hill we must climb up through the forest. Once over the top we come swooping down several bends to our next crossing at Le Mesnil-sous-Jumièrge. When we've crossed the river here, we'll have cut across one whole northern loop of the Seine. We've never seen such a wide river as this, with so many meanders.

From Le Mesnil we cycle south-east along a designated scenic route through farmland until we're back into forest once more. We reach the river again, now flowing south, and follow its course down towards the next crossing point, on another scenic route. The views are wonderful and the tarmac surface superb.

A car comes past, followed by a racing cyclist in close pursuit – he's almost hanging onto its bumper. Quite a good training method, I suppose, unless the car makes an emergency stop.

We're heading for the town of La Bouille, almost at the bottom of the next loop, for our third ferry. What a bonus to have all these ferries at our disposal. It would be three times as far if we had to follow the course of the river.

After crossing at La Bouille we cycle round on the left-hand bank as the river flows north again. Our final crossing is halfway up this loop. As we wait for the ferry, we can see huge cranes and numerous factories on the other side. It doesn't look at all inviting. But once across, we find a road cutting straight through all this industry to bring us to a main road. Nearly there!

Here the fun starts. So far today, barely half a dozen cars have passed us. Now we're in the thick of traffic, heading north towards another crossing – this time a bridge into Rouen. We feel really threatened. There's not much room for bikes. In despair, we dismount at the next pedestrian crossing. Blow cycling! We'll continue on foot along a riverside pavement.

At last we are in the middle of old Rouen and out of all that manic traffic. The centre looks very antiquated, with tall timbered buildings and cobbled squares everywhere. We find a café in one such square and sit outside with our coffees and a plate of French fries, enjoying the ambience and sense of history that exude all around us. It's charming.

Afterwards, when we've ambled round for half an hour or so, we get a map from the tourist information office, then have another coffee in another square, while we peruse it. Frank sees a suburb on the map called St. Etienne, where he's heard of a very good cycle shop. He needs some new shorts. Perhaps we should try to find this place now we're in the area.

So that's what we do. The map helps us to avoid busy main roads. It's quite a distance south from the centre of Rouen but fairly flat, so we don't expend too much energy on cycling there. We'll need plenty in hand later, to get us back to Les Trois Ours.

Once in St. Etienne, the store is quite easy to find; a cube-like block of glass, set amongst modern lower-level shops. It is probably in suburbs like this that the inhabitants of Rouen do their shopping, as most of the city centre is dedicated to historic buildings.

There's so much cycling-related stuff in this store that we don't know where to start. At every turn, we're distracted from what we came to buy. Eventually we reach the clothes section, where Frank can't find any shorts that are suitable. After all that! He does, however, buy a pack of cycling socks – just to make this excursion worthwhile! We've wasted good time here, when

CHAPTER FOUR

we could have been exploring more of the sights of Rouen.

We cycle back to the city the way we came, keen to make up for lost time and quite eager to find some more places of interest. But as we dismount in the centre, a sudden realisation hits us. We've made an enormous miscalculation – we've left it too late to catch the ferries back to Ste Croix. No doubt we'd get the first two but then we'd be stranded in the dark in the middle of nowhere; lost in a forest perhaps, with wild boar running around. What stupid bloody idiots we are! We stand holding our bikes in the middle of a square, staring at each other open-mouthed and gasping in disbelief.

But we'll be even more stupid if we stand here bemoaning our bad luck. There's nothing for it – we're going to have to spend the night in Rouen, and the tourist office will be closed if we don't get a move on. It's so annoying to think we've already paid good money for the cottage at Ste Croix. It wasn't cheap,so we don't want to be paying through the nose to spend a night in this touristy place.

One consolation is that the tourist information office hasn't closed yet, although it's about to do so. A patient young lady with good language skills kindly finds us a cheap hotel, barely half a mile away, and books us in. We're so relieved. Anyway, if we try to forget that we're double paying for tonight, so to speak, this could be quite a novel experience for us.

The lady has put a cross on our map to show us where we have to go. Soon we find the hotel in a back street and are shown to our room on the first floor. I don't think they've had cyclists staying here before because they don't know where to put our bikes. In the end we leave them in a narrow passageway,

blocking the back door. Let's hope we don't need to get out in an emergency. Our room is small but comfortable enough, and it doesn't matter that the wardrobe door doesn't shut properly, or that the drawers are hard to open, because we've got nothing to put into them. At least we've got our own shower and toilet. There's no point in washing now though. We can't change our clothes. So we find a back street café for an omelette and more chips, before returning to take a shower and turn in for an early night.

* * *

After a continental breakfast, where we ask for seconds, as cyclists often do, we set out to enjoy a sunny morning in the city. Our plan is to set off for 'home' in the early afternoon. Our first port of call is the information office, because we want to fill our time wisely, not wander aimlessly about.

We're outside the office now, admiring a sturdy all-terrain cycle that's propped against the wall, loaded to the hilt. "It's British," I declare, just as the owner comes out of the door and finds us snooping over her bike. This young lady is built as sturdily as her bike, of medium height and quite chunky, with long curly straw-coloured hair sprouting from under her helmet. She looks the picture of health, her rosy cheeks glowing through her golden tan – just as I imagine Heidi would look in the old children's story. We jump away from her bike, slightly embarrassed at being caught out touching it. But she's really cool and rather pleased at the attention. She's also keen to chat and tell us about herself. Her name is Mel and she's cycling round the world. There's a pause while we take in this impressive

60

news. Wow! Fancy actually meeting someone in the process of cycling round the world. We feel somewhat honoured. But as the one-way conversation progresses, she admits that she doesn't know where to go next.

When she's told us everything we need to know, she asks what we're up to. We tell her about the little cottage in the forest and how we had to cross the river on four ferries to reach here but left it too late to catch them all back. She seems quite intrigued. As she doesn't know which direction to take next, we invite her to come back to our place for the night. After all, there's a big lawn for her to erect her tent and as we were helped last night, we can surely offer a favour to someone today. Mel jumps at the chance. We arrange to meet her outside this office at midday, earlier than we intended, but with all that kit she's dragging around, the journey is bound to take longer than it took us to get here. We just hope she's as strong a cyclist as she looks.

We set off to look at more places of interest, including the magnificent cathedral. But our minds are not really focused on sightseeing now; not after asking Mel to cycle back with us. We're not really taking in the wonder and beauty of anything around us - we're just passing the time of day. Perhaps it would be better to spend our time at a café, relaxing in this beautiful September sunshine that we've been blessed with, and save our energy for the journey back.

Mel is eagerly waiting for us as at midday. Frank and I discuss which way to get out of Rouen – definitely not the way we came in. She doesn't take part in this discussion, because she didn't enter the city from the direction that we did.

We decide to follow the inside curve of the river westwards, right round the top then straight down through the dockland. Then we wonder if we might have made a bad decision. But it is, in fact, a wonderful choice. Once we've rounded the curve, the road cuts straight down through the industrial area and instead of being threatened by heavy trundling traffic, the road is almost devoid of lorries – they're all parked up, being loaded or unloaded. We have timed this just right.

Halfway down the loop, we come to our first ferry. This is a new experience for Mel, although she hasn't told us what places she has already cycled through. She's less chatty than when we first met her but quite cheerful. Perhaps she's pondering on which way she'll be going round the world. Or maybe she's got nothing else to tell us.

Our ride becomes scenic, but then the panoramic views disappear as we head into forestland. We reappear at a different aspect, emerging from the trees at yet another point on the river's curve. We're enjoying showing her how beautiful this part of Normandy is. But poor Mel is struggling to keep up with us, even when the road is flat. Maybe she's used up too much energy, too soon. It doesn't matter. We don't mind waiting for her. It's not as if the weather is cold or wet.

Somewhere around the halfway point, we stop at a village café for a rest and refreshments. While Mel is at the toilet, Frank asks me if we should let her sleep in the attic. It seems mean that we can just get into bed, while she'll have all the paraphernalia of putting up her tent. But I'm not sure if we should. After all, we don't really know what she's like. She might trash the place, for all we know, or steal from us. I'll just consider his suggestion.

After the ferry crossing to Les-Mesnil-sous-Jumièrge, poor Mel has to push her great load up the steep winding hill. How she'll cope in mountainous countries, God only knows. But we admire her pluck. Neither of us would consider going off on such a tour, alone. We're wimps, I suppose.

Once we've crossed at Jumièrge there'll be no more hills, we tell her. Then we come to the dead deer in the ditch and Frank and I race past to get away from the smell. Mel is miles behind, probably thinking we're trying to lose her. But when we're clear of the deer we stop to wait again. She's encouraged to know that we only have a few more miles to go.

At last, we reach Ste Croix with plenty of useable daylight left. Mel is as delighted as we are with the cottage. She can relax now while I rustle up a quick meal. Frank makes us all a coffee and they drink theirs at the garden table, enjoying the evening sun. We still haven't decided whether to offer her the attic or not.

I call them in when the pasta is ready. We haven't invited her in until now. As she sits next to me at the kitchen table, I explain the layout of the cottage. I tell her that the shower is right down at the far end.

"Oh, I don't wash," she says casually, and Frank and I catch each other's eye. I find myself surreptitiously sniffing her, to find out what she smells like. I feel uncomfortable now, sitting shoulder to shoulder with her, even though I can't smell any body odours. But that's decided it for us. She's welcome to put her tent up in the garden.

* * *

Next morning Mel breakfasts with us before taking down her tent. Good, she's not planning to linger here any longer. When she's all packed up and ready to go, we have coffee together in the garden. She doesn't seem to be in a particular hurry – quite aimless, in fact. It's then that she tells us she's not going round the world just yet; she's decided to go to Ireland first. What a turnabout. A really mixed-up young lady she must be.

We wave goodbye to her as she sets off down the lane, and wonder if she'll even find her way out of Ste Croix. We haven't witnessed her consulting any maps. Perhaps she just sets a compass point and heads in that direction. Anyway, she's added another dimension to the second week of our holiday and made it quite memorable, to say the least. We're rather glad we missed the ferry.

The Geological Wonders of Lydney Cliffs

July 2000

Heading back to Lydney harbour

Oh lucky me! Today is just right for this particular cycle ride; not too hot, nor yet too cool and with just a slight breeze. It's ideal for us to bike up to Gloucester, cross the River Severn and continue down the other side to Lydney harbour.

A few weeks ago, at a committee meeting of the

Stroud Cyclists' Touring Club, we members worked out a list of cycle rides to cover the next three months. Each of us is expected to suggest one or two rides and also, to lead some of them. For quite a while I've had a burning ambition to do a certain ride. But the timing has to be just right. And this is the day I have chosen for it.

* * *

I work at a museum which five years before this had closed its doors to the public. A big change was afoot. Its closing had caused an outcry in the community and the curator received many letters of complaint. But if the museum were to be improved and brought into the 21st Century it would need moving from its Victorian Gothic building in the town centre to new and bigger premises. This would not be an overnight job. Behind closed doors, for the next six and a half years, the staff steadfastly slogged away, cataloguing, photographing, packing and writing grant applications, in preparation for this momentous event. And just to appease the public, an open day was held once a month, so that people could come in and see what we were up to.

The artefacts in their entirety were to be put onto a database. We staff were kitted out with computers and ergonomic chairs, to avoid getting backache, then each allotted our various tasks. My initial task was to catalogue drawer upon drawer of fossils from the solid Victorian chests that lined the walls of those high-ceilinged galleries. As we shivered through that first winter, my interest in geology was born.

What a wonderful opportunity this was for me. What a learning curve! I began to learn about ammonites, brachiopods, crinoids, trilobites; the list was endless. I became so interested that when I heard about a geology class in my parish of Rodborough, I immediately enrolled. The course was titled 'Geology of the Cotswolds for Beginners.' Ha! When I got there I found that half of these mature students were doing 'A' levels or even degrees, albeit in other branches of geology. Slightly daunted, I set myself to learn. Now I was hearing about eons, eras and epochs, and the Jurassic limestone that makes up our Cotswolds.

There were also field trips to go on. So exciting! One such trip, and my favourite, was to Lydney cliffs. It was on a grey November day and we had parked our cars near Lydney, on the Welsh side of the river, then changed into suitable footwear. Wearing my newly-acquired boots, I clumped down the long straight road to Lydney harbour. In my haversack was a flask of coffee, a packed lunch, my hard-backed geology notebook, pencils and a few crayons. We were all done up in coats and scarves to keep out the chill.

At the harbour's end, where the canal enters the river, we turned upstream and headed towards the riverbank. Nick, our tutor, had checked the tide times, so we knew we'd be safe. In our sensible footwear we had to cross an area of muddy grass before reaching the shore, which was still wet from the ebbing tide.

Soon we were brought to the first place of real interest; a south-facing cliff, not far from the harbour. As we drew nearer, we could see white translucent lumps and lines embedded in the rosy rock. On closer inspection, these lumps looked like semiprecious stones set into the cliff face, which Nick told us was Old Red Sandstone.

Now he explained to us how this sandstone had been formed. Going back 420 million years, towards the end of the Silurian era, this rock had initially been formed by layer upon layer of silt deposited on a flood plain. His enthusiasm infused us and he went on to tell us that, in those times, this part of the earth would have been about 20 degrees the other side of the equator, when most of the continents were closer together, many still joined into one big mass. He said the climate then would have been arid or semi-arid. This all seemed mind-bogglingly incredible to comprehend. He told us that in time, simple plants would have begun to colonise the top layer of the deposited mud, breaking up the surface. Then, during the next period of flood, the silted water, which was rich in calcium, would percolate underground into the spaces made by plant roots. When arid conditions returned, these calcium deposits would dry out into pockets below the surface. Nick said there must also have been a presence of magnesium in the water because these two elements together would form the translucent nodules that we were now looking at. They were called dolocretes and would have taken thousands and thousands of years to form, with the same sequence being repeated again and again. It was fascinating.

Leaving the cliff behind us, we carried on up the beach. At times the going was very dicey – slippery boulders strewn all over the place, with sticky mud in between. We came to a sandy area and paused for a while; a chance for Nick to explain and show us the evidence of river terracing. We made more notes and diagrams. I hoped I'd understand all my sketches and rough notes when it came to revision.

On we trawled up the beach until we came to a cliff facing up-stream, probably north eastwards. By now we'd walked a good mile on this tricky terrain and had come to the spectacle I'd been waiting to see – the 'pseudo anticlines', or the Christmas tree effect. Wow! As promised, it really did look like rows of Christmas trees. Now we needed to know how these had been formed. It was all so very interesting.

We learned that the process was similar to the way the nodules were formed on the first cliff, except that here the layers of silt laid down in the flood plains were of a certain type of clay, capable of great expansion and contraction. In dry periods this clay would crack, curving up at the edges. Subsequent floodwater, full of calcium and magnesium, would have filtered into the gaps. These resulting dolocretes resembled a succession of swooping curves. And with more curves forming on top, over and over again, the appearance was like a continuous line of Christmas trees. It was just amazing.

* * *

So today I am leading the cycle club there, to show them what I saw back on that late autumn day. I have estimated that the whole ride will be about an 80-mile round trip, returning over the Severn Bridge and back up the other side of the river. Some of our members have elected to start from Gloucester Docks. This will cut ten miles off their distance. We stop to pick them up, increasing our numbers to ten.

From the docks we pedal westwards to cross the River Severn, then continue for a while on a cycle path parallel to the A48, which runs down the other side. But I don't keep to the main road for long. Intrigue is the name of the game, if you want to make a ride memorable and not merely 'run-of-the-mill.' One of my surprises is to be a new venue for our morning coffee stop. So we turn right off the main road, heading towards the eastern edge of the Forest of Dean. We soon find ourselves on a very minor road, puffing and gasping up a steep climb, which brings us to our destination, perched on the top of Popes Hill – a HOTEL. Not the usual type of hostelry for a bunch of sweaty cyclists! But just a week ago I'd sought permission to bring the club here. The proprietors were extremely obliging but explained that they didn't *do* cakes. However, sitting outside on a terrace looking out over the magnificent view of the River Severn with the Cotswolds beyond, none of my companions seem bothered that we have only biscuits with our coffee instead of the usual choice of cakes that we might get in a café.

Suitably refreshed, we set off on the next leg of our journey, keeping to the hilly roads of the forest until eventually we rejoin the A48 at Blakeney. After continuing southwards for another two miles, we notice a track on our left and stop to study the map. Yes, this concrete track will take us all the way to Lydney harbour, by way of a golf course. It wasn't on my itinerary, but it has advantages. It will cut off a big corner so that we won't have to go through Lydney town. We can't afford to waste time. None of them know what my second surprise is going to be and I can't wait to show them.

Packing the cycle map into my handlebar bag, we set off

down the short-cut concrete track, in a peloton-like bunch – rather too close for my liking. When the track narrows through a gateway, Jim gets squeezed out and brakes sharply. His wheel skids on the metal cattle-grid, throwing him and his bike to the ground. As he falls, his head hits the gatepost. Good grief! I don't want anyone to get hurt, in my enthusiasm to show the wonders of Lydney cliffs. Jim gets to his feet, adjusts his helmet and assures us he's OK. Thank goodness for that.

We carry on down the track. I'm sure they're all going to be amazed at what I'm taking them to see. If I hadn't joined that geology class I wouldn't have known they existed. We lock our bikes against the harbour wall. Good! The tide is going out, as I know it should be. I'd checked the tide-times weeks ago. There's plenty of time before it turns.

As we set off across the muddy grass there are moans from some of the group. Of course, I'd forgotten; lots of them are wearing special cycling shoes with cleats. They don't want to get those all muddied up. (A cleated cycle shoe has a metal plate embedded under the sole with a hole in the middle, which fits neatly onto a small pedal with a knobble on top. These give cyclists more momentum as they can pull up on one pedal while pushing down on the other. It makes hill climbing more efficient but walking is a tad more difficult.) I, however, still have old-fashioned toe-clips on my pedals. I can adjust the straps to accommodate any width of shoe. Today, I'm wearing a stout pair of old trainers. I could be feeling smug but actually, I'm a bit concerned now. Should I have given my companions more information, so they could have been prepared, instead of having all this surprise stuff?

I assure them that the going will soon be better and, trying hard to be bright and encouraging, lead them onwards. I know that the first place of interest isn't far beyond the grassy bit. It's the south-facing cliff we're heading towards. We reach the place where I know it should be, but there's nothing to see at all. Instead of that rosy cliff-face smothered with jewel-like dolocretes, there's just a nondescript greyish rock-face. What's happened?

I try not to show my disappointment, although I'm gutted. The others didn't know what to expect, so I bluff a bit to hide my embarrassment. It wasn't *so* long ago that I came here on that field trip. What's wrong with my memory? Oh well! We still have the *pièce de resistance.*

We continue onwards and as promised, before long, we reach the hard wet sand. Unfortunately, this doesn't last for long. Soon the going gets tricky again and we must choose whether to step from one slippery boulder to the next or tread between them in the mud. I can't be very popular now, I'm sure. The ones wearing specialised shoes are lagging. I hear a yell from behind and spin round to see one of them slipping off a boulder. He twists his ankle as he falls in the mud. Now I'm feeling really guilty. I try to hurry back to assist him but already he's on his feet. He tries out his ankle and finds it still bears his weight. Once again I've been let off the hook. From now on, he decides, he's going to walk between the boulders for his own safety, even if his shoes will get caked in mud. His clothes are muddy anyway. These cyclists are such a good bunch; so forgiving.

I carry on, now walking at the pace of the laggers. After all, there's no rush. It's not as if rain is imminent, nor is the tide due to come in for several more hours. It's just that in my eagerness, I have been pushing the pace a bit. I estimate that we have another quarter of a mile to go. When I look across the river, Sharpness docks are in view. When we're directly opposite, we'll be in the right place – I think. But it's hard to judge, as the river is a mile wide at this point.

A feeling of excitement is bubbling up inside me now. I'll soon be able to share the spectacle that filled me with wonder, back on that November day. Yes! This must surely be the north-facing cliff that I've come to find. My enthusiasm is beginning to rub off on my companions, so I tell them what we are about to witness.

We round the corner of the cliff. "Wha' pink rock?" says one. "Where's these Christmas tree thingies then, eh?" says another. "Aah, yer 'avin' us on. Can't see a thing." They all agree, and it's true. The rock isn't pink and there's no Christmas tree effect to be seen. I'm dumbfounded. Where *has* it all disappeared?

I certainly have egg on my face now. Everyone is teasing me as we pick our way back to Lydney harbour. At least none of them is annoyed or miserable, bless 'em! We unlock the bikes and pedal up to Lydney to find a pub. We could all do with a stiff drink, and lunch is long overdue.

But this is such a mystery. Maybe the rocks dried out in the summer months, masking everything we've come to see. Or was I, perhaps, wearing rose-coloured spectacles when I first came here? I *so* wanted to share the geological wonders of Lydney cliffs.

Not to be Repeated

June 1998

Repairs in a layby, coming down from Madonna

Frank unfolds the map and smooths it out across the table while outside, the sunny Surrey countryside whizzes by the windows of the train – hedges and gaps, hedges and gaps, flickering intermittent shade and light, shade and light across the page. Only an hour or so ago, we had arrived back at Gatwick airport from Verona, after two weeks of wonderful cycling in the Dolomites in northern Italy. We want to retrace our route and relive the memories while they are still fresh, before they get lost in the humdrum of daily life.

* * *

Back in springtime, when my cycle club friends had been preparing for this holiday, I was not amongst them. This was because my first grandchild was due to be born on the very day they planned to set off. Although I was really envious of my cycling companions, there was no way I was going to miss my big family event. However, Ben, my lovely grandson, arrived two weeks earlier than expected and, thrilled to bits at becoming a Grandma, I hurried to make my acquaintance with him.

It was only when I'd returned home that I realised I'd be able to go on the cycling holiday after all, if I got my act together. Rushing to a local travel agent, I managed to book a last-minute flight to Verona. Most of the club members were planning to travel on the European Bike Express for the first time, but my partner Frank and two others from our group had chosen to fly there. My plane would be taking off just one hour before theirs.

I was elated to be going on this holiday. The route would take us up the eastern side of the Brenta Dolomites, round the northern end in a big loop and back down the other side to Lake Garda, where we planned to spend three nights on the lakeside before returning to Verona. For a final treat, we had planned a day trip to Venice by train. However I hadn't appreciated that Sheila, the person who had organised this trip, had been obliged to ring all the hostels and hotels that she had previously booked to add me into the equation at the eleventh hour. It was years later that I found out what a nightmare this had been for her.

* * *

With his sunburnt finger, Frank traces our route across the map. The motion of the train gently rocks us back and forth, as I peer down to where he is pointing. Ah yes, Verona!. Our first night was in a hostel that had formerly been a nunnery. It stood on a hill somewhere on the outskirts of Verona. I remember the four of us crossing a many-arched Roman bridge called Ponte Pietra to reach the hostel. Frank and I were so tired we could barely keep our eyes open, having spent a sleepless night at Gatwick Airport. After registering and finding our respective dormitories, we'd slept like logs until the rest of the gang, arriving by coach, had woken us up in the late afternoon. That evening, after a convivial meal in a tiny restaurant nearby, we had all crashed into bed. And I, in spite of having slept the whole afternoon, had the best night's sleep I can ever remember,

We follow our route due north up the map, squinting to pick out the little road that one of our group had discovered. It ran alongside a river and had made for a quiet and traffic-free day of cycling to get to Roveretto. This is where we spent our second night. It was a youth hostel that seemed more like a large café with sleeping accommodation above. The wardens were a friendly couple with a cute toddler son. He would come and chat away to us in his own special language and although we didn't understand a thing, we found him very endearing.

I remember how busy the town was the following morning. The streets were crammed with market stalls and bustling with shoppers. It was hard to push by them without banging their bottoms with our panniers.

The train stops at a station. We don't bother to look out of the window to see which one it is; we're too engrossed in reliving this holiday before our memories fade. Frank gets out his diary to check the name of the next place we'd stayed, on that third night. It was difficult to remember. Ah yes – Calceranica Al Lago!

Here we stayed at a posh hotel with its own beach, next to a lake. Most of us had taken a refreshing plunge as soon as we'd unpacked. I have to admit that I prefer swimming in the sea. I like salt in my swimming water. But it was a huge lake. You could almost imagine you were in a bay of the sea, with distant mountains in the purple haze of evening, on the other side.

That day, we had headed north eastwards from Roveretto, stopping for coffee on the teetering terrace of a café on a steep mountainside. A little later we had picnic lunched on a slope overlooking a distant village, where the church bells began to ring out over the plain. Everything felt so Italian, from the pointed cypress trees and the Roman-style pan-tiled roofs to the wafer-thin slices of *prosciutto crudo* that we bought each day to put into our crusty bread rolls, for lunch.

Suddenly, remembering our laden bikes are at the far end of the carriage, we look behind us to ensure they haven't been nicked. It's stupid of us not to have checked sooner, while people were in the process of getting off the train. But all is well. The bikes are safe. So, readjusting our eyes, we trace our route north westwards up the map towards Molveno. Ah, there it is, at the top end of Lago di Molveno. We can see the ski slopes marked on the mountains behind it.

We spent two nights in this rather upmarket town. This was to give us a chance to see the 'Giro d'Italia' (National Italian bike race), which was due to come by here, the very next day.

En route to Malveno, we had to get through the city of Trento, in the province of Trentino, which proved to be a bit of a nightmare. We found ourselves high up on a huge unfinished road, which terminated, for us, at a big blockage of mechanical road-building equipment. A trio of tanned workmen were standing by, grinning at us in our dilemma. Sheila began talking to them in Italian, to ask which way we should go, only to find out they were all English, from 'oop' north. It was like being in an episode of *Auf Wiedersehen Pet*, except that we were in Italy.

After we'd manoeuvred ourselves past that obstruction, there was a tunnel to get through. Normally it wouldn't be a problem, except when you are in the very middle and all you can see is a dot of light at the end. But we'd noticed that there were cables running along the ground, going through the tunnel. As we progressed into the darkness, it was harder and harder to see them. If our wheels had run onto them, we might have been thrown into the road. And with Italian drivers whizzing by us, that was a very scary prospect.

Further on, there was a slightly shorter tunnel, which also had cables running through. It was good to come out on the other side to enjoy the countryside once more, especially when we found a track through woods and wonderful flower meadows which brought us right down to the lakeside, opposite Molveno.

Frank and I had a fabulous room with a balcony overlooking the lake. If we'd been booking this holiday ourselves, we'd have opted for something much cheaper. But the holiday was all paid for up front, probably with a discount for a group booking, so we made the most of it, jacuzzi and all.

The next morning, after a multi-choice breakfast, the rest of the group set off on their bikes to intercept the Giro d'Italia at the top of a steep climb where hopefully they would be able to spot famous riders coming up the hill. We were not avid followers of cycle racing, much to the surprise of our fellow cyclists, apart from watching the scenery during the Tour de France. We had decided instead to go up the two ski lifts, right to the top of the mountain.

When we reached the top it was pretty cold. A sudden storm blew up, whizzing in on a turbulent wind, bringing an unexpected thunderstorm. We rushed to take cover, glad to find an open café at the summit. There we sat out the storm, watching the lightning and listening to the hail and thunder from the complacent security of our refuge. But it was soon over and we were descending back to base in sunshine. The lift from the top to the halfway station was merely a stand-on affair, having a pole in the middle with a handle to hang on to. I had the heebie-jeebies coming down but felt extremely brave!

For a while we meandered around a park on the lakeside

opposite the hotel, taking photos and enjoying the tranquillity. But as soon as we stepped out onto the street, we were forced to jump aside and pin ourselves to the wall because, whizzing down the hill towards us, was a noisy cavalcade. Right behind, with pedals spinning furiously, came a manic peleton of cyclists. What a shock! We could have been splattered because there was no room for spectators here. We'd had no idea that the race would be coming *through* Molveno and only recognised one cyclist, who was wearing a bandana. It was Pantani and he was in the lead. Within seconds they had whooshed out of sight. We felt quite chuffed to have glimpsed the race, considering that we'd also been to the top of the mountain. Apparently, Pantani won both the Giro d'Italia and the Tour de France that year.

The train has stopped again – lots of people are alighting and more getting in. We check that the bikes are OK. Gosh, we're at Guildford already. That's about halfway to Reading, we reckon. Soon be there. The sun is streaming in the window on our side of the carriage. It feels almost as hot as Italy. Back to the map again, where we trace our route to Cles, the most northerly overnight stop of our trip. The day we left Cles, I had volunteered to lead the group. I had diligently worked out my route the night before. There weren't many routes to choose from, as there were few roads through the mountains. But the more 'off road' tracks one could find, the more enjoyable the ride was likely to be.

This day we would be cycling in a big loop, going even further north; right round the northern extent of the Brenta Dolomites and not far from the Austrian border. Firstly, we'd crossed a small bridge at the bottom end of a lake near Cles and accessed a quiet road on the opposite side. Later we cycled alongside a churning, icy mountain river, where a group of brave rafters came by, pitching and tossing in an inflatable.

For lunch we picnicked on a sunny grassy bank in a quiet valley, dallying far too long as we mustered up the strength and willpower for the climb ahead. Then, turning south, we began our long slog up the Carlo Magno pass to the ski resort of Madonna di Campiglio at the top. It was a tough climb.

At Madonna, we stayed in the Hotel Diana for three nights. The resort seemed pretty dead in the height of summer. Unfortunately for us, because we had planned two whole days of walking in the mountains, it rained on both of them and was quite miserable, with low cloud cover. However togged up in our cycle waterproofs, we still did our walks to various waterfalls, spending some time in refuges and finding rare wild flowers on the way.

On the third day the sun reappeared in all its splendour as we bowled down from Madonna, past meadows resplendent with wild flowers, all the way to Lake Garda. Here we had two whole days to do our own thing. Frank and I fell in love with Malcesine, a gorgeous, steep little town on the eastern side of the lake.

We've had to stand up slightly now, to lean over the table in order to trace the most northerly extent of our route. It's almost at the top of the map.

"That looks interestin'," comes a voice from the other side of the table. "Is that where yer've bin on 'olidy?" My head jerks up to see an elderly lady is sitting opposite us. I am almost in her face. When did she get on the train? I'm embarrassed that we've monopolised this table ever since we left Gatwick and have been almost oblivious of fellow travellers. But something has struck a chord in my head. I recognise her accent.

"Are you from Lincolnshire?" I ask. "Yis ayam, achly," she replies, "Skegness."

"Skegness!" I exclaim. "I spent all my childhood holidays in Skegness. My Mum lived there for a while when Dad was away in the war. In fact my brother was born there." I gabble on and on, thrilled to find someone who comes from 'Skeggy', as it formed such a large part of my childhood. "We went to Skeggy every single summer," I continue, "until I was about thirteen, I think. We stayed in the house of some friends of Mum's. While they went abroad for a couple of weeks, we would take over their house. It was great."

"An' whear wuz this 'ouse?" asks the elderly lady.

"Well," I answer, "it was on the south side of Skeggy, somewhere off Drummond Road."

"Wuz it Derby Avenue be any chance?" she queries.

"Yes that's it. The house was about halfway down on the right. The road just petered out onto the beach. It was ever such a long way to get to the sea. I remember that after the great floods of 1953 they built those big sand dunes right the way along, in case it happened again. We used to cut ourselves on that horrible grass they planted on them. It was really sharp. But we had wonderful holidays there." I ramble on excitedly. "It was a big house and my widowed aunty and three cousins always came with us; sometimes we'd take a few more cousins as well."

"It wan't Ethel Johnson's 'ouse wuz it?"

I was astounded. How did she know that? "Yes, that was her name," I reply, "I'd forgotten."

"Well blow me, she's me best friend," the old lady admits. "She's blind nah yer know and she lives in un old peepuls' 'ome near the golf course, dahn near Gibralter Point."

By now I've completely forgotten about our holiday in Italy. I'm just flabbergasted with these coincidences. We are nearly at Reading now.

"I've got to git ter Bristol," says the lady. "You don't know what platform the train guz from, de ye?"

"We're going to Bristol as well, and no, we don't know which platform it is. We'll have to ask."

As we draw into Reading station, we make our way down the carriage to retrieve the bikes. There isn't room to turn them round so we push them backwards off the train. My back wheel thuds onto the platform, reminding me of all the extra weight I'm carrying in my panniers. I'd had quite a few Italian lire left over at the end of the holiday, so I'd splurged it all in the duty-free. I'd bought a rather lanky and over-priced 'Donald Duck' for Ben, plus two blue-painted eggcups. There was also a matching teapot in the same pattern – the only things 'Italian' that I could find in the duty-free. They were made in Poland and painted in Italy, or vice versa!

Then I'd indulged myself with three large bottles of liqueurs, one of which was limoncello and all of which I realised later, I could have bought in English supermarkets. Anyway, the 7lbs weight I allowed myself per pannier, must be almost doubled by all this stuff. I can hardly lift the back wheel off the ground.

On this very crowded platform we see the old lady hovering behind us. She needs to know where to go. We must quickly find which platform we need, because there are less than ten minutes to spare. Neither Frank nor I are very tall, so it's hard to see if any porters are about. (This was before train times and platform numbers were displayed on digital screens, and also when Reading station had three platform 4s). Anyway, there isn't a porter in sight.

We're getting anxious now. Then we hear someone say "It's platform eight", so we turn towards the escalators. "I'm not goin' on an eskilater" says the old lady and toddles off towards the lift. I follow Frank, who is already halfway up. I catch him up on the landing and we descend with our laden bikes, one behind the other, to platform eight. We arrive slightly puffed, only to be told by someone else, "Oh no, it's not this platform, it's platform four." That's where we've just come from.

Frank lifts his bike around and races back to the escalators. As I follow, I see the old lady's case on wheels coming out of the lift, followed by the old lady herself. As she approaches, I tell her it's all been a mistake and we have only four minutes now to get back to platform four. I advise her that she won't have time to go by the lift. "Don't worry," I say. "I'll help you on the escalator. If you get onto one step I'll put your case on the one behind you and then I'll follow you up." She trusts me and does as I've suggested and I lift her case onto the next step. My bike is on my left side now. I usually hold it on my right.

The bike goes up a little way, then the back wheel slips down two steps and the bike skews a bit. It goes up a few more steps. Again it slides down. Crikey! It's skewed so much, it's jammed solid across the escalator and I'm desperately trying to get back down before I'm minced up in the gap between my bike frame and the escalator steps.

Now I'm on my hands and knees, crawling like a mad thing away from my bike and trying to get off at the bottom. Every time I reach the end, I can't quite get my hands onto terra firma. However hard I try, I'm carried back to where the steps separate, exposing sharp edges that dig into my shins. I make another frantic effort, only to fail again. Now I'm in an absolute panic, like someone possessed. On all fours, my hands and knees are a blur. I can't work them any faster. The mincing machine is waiting for me.

Suddenly everything halts. All I can hear is my rasping breath as my chest heaves up and down. Then I become aware of a pair of neat shoes in front of me. I lift my head to see a smartly-dressed lady before me. She's a smart thinker too. She's pressed the 'stop' button. I crawl off weakly and pull myself up to thank her profusely. She has probably saved my life. I'm just in time to look back up the escalator to see the old lady stepping off. What has seemed to me like an hour of trauma has probably lasted for only a minute. That old lady is totally unaware of what was happening behind her back and I never see her again. But I hope she catches her train. Frank is nowhere in sight. He's probably getting on the Bristol train with our elderly lady. Then I see him coming down again, searching for me.

Frank and I are now looking down at my damaged legs. There are rows and rows of horizontal teeth marks, all the way up my shins and over my knees. The upward points are as white as white; pressed right in. Slowly, slowly, as we look, a red teardrop forms from each point. I don't know why – I think of the Madonna's tears. Now the tears begin to trickle down my shins. My legs are crying! We go to find a first-aid point, which proves to be rather pointless on this late Sunday station.

It's a girl from Pizza Hut who provides us with some absorbent paper towels and I clean myself up in the ladies'. I'm really shaken and sore but not in any pain. We go back and have a pizza while we wait for the next train.

My misfortune hasn't ended yet. In my state of shock, I have left my bum-bag on the Bristol train. I'm convinced that the dubious-looking fellow sitting opposite us has nicked it. But how wrong I am. He is probably the person who handed it in, complete with money and passport. I receive it back by courier van within the week, all the way from Swansea.

* * *

When I return to my museum job the following week, the Curator asks me if I've had a good holiday. I lift up my trousers and show her my shins. Yes, I've had a wonderful holiday, but it's all in the past now. And I won't ever take my bike on an escalator again.

Topsy-Turvy in the Tarn

June 1999

A well-earned rest by the Tarn

The mini bus turned off the main road, creeping carefully down a sandy lane towards the river's edge. The trailer carrying our canoes jolted along behind us. There was a buzz of excitement as our two-seater Canadian canoes were unloaded. Then, two by two, we were put into a lovely wide part of the River Tarn, where we paddled around waiting for everyone to be launched. A barrel was strapped securely into each canoe, containing all the belongings that we would need for the next three days.

Colin, who had organised the whole holiday, was in a kayak, with the remaining ten of us in the five double canoes. We were all members of a cycling club, spending two weeks touring the Cévennes, in the south of the Massif Central in France. This three-day canoe trip through the Tarn gorge was to be the highlight of our tour. This group was made up of three couples: Jill and Rob, Thelma and Jim and Frank and myself, plus two young men, Phil and Dave, and two mature single women, Sheila and Daphne, not forgetting Colin. The three other members from our cycle club, Maurice and Maurice and Marion, a couple of semi-professional photographers, were slightly more mature and not at all keen on the water. They had opted to continue cycle touring until we all met up again at Le Rozier, three days of canoeing downstream.

Earlier in the year, we'd had several day trips down the river Wye on the English-Welsh border, honing our skills while enjoying the wonderful tranquil scenery. We'd seen sand-martins disappear into sandy holes on the water's edge and bemoaned the encroachment of sickly-smelling Himalayan balsam along the banks. Where the water was deep enough, we'd practised capsizing and swimming to the bank, clutching on to our precious paddles, without which we would be stymied – assuming our canoes had not floated away, of course. The only rapids we'd encountered were a few bubbly stretches near Hay-on-Wye, when the water was low. But we were fairly confident we could handle the rapids on the Tarn. After all, they were only classed as Grade 2 – 'easy rapids with a bit of excitement'.

We had arrived in the Cévennes by means of the European Bike Express, a coach carrying all the bikes in a trailer. It is a great way to bring bikes to Europe without the hassle of airports, where sometimes you see your bike being dropped from the cargo hold onto the airport tarmac. However, because it had been such a hot day when we'd boarded the coach, my partner Frank and I were wearing shorts and sandals. During the night we'd frozen because the people at the back of the coach had demanded that we keep the front windows open, so those of us seated near the front were feeling more than our fair share of fresh air. Frank and I ended up borrowing newspapers, which we wrapped round our legs and feet to keep warm. The rest of our group were more adequately dressed.

Early the next morning we were dispatched somewhere below Orange, not far from the Pont du Gard, a spectacular three-tiered Roman bridge spanning the River Gard. Here we had coffee by the riverside before climbing over the ancient bridge, marvelling at its enduring structure. From a height, we'd gained an idea of the sort of terrain we would soon be cycling into. It was a fabulous introduction to our holiday.

Now, after two hilly days of cycling and one rest day in Florac, we were about to set off down the River Tarn. Jill and husband Rob paddled by us. Jill remarked, "Why are you looking so nervous Fran, you love canoeing? Well I didn't know I was looking that way, but I admit I had slight reservations about my ability to steer. Frank would normally be sitting at the back of the canoe having main control over the steerage, while I'd be in the front, merely aiding and abetting. But due to Frank's high spirits on leaving our very first B&B, he had thrown his panniers to me from an upstairs window (just for a joke) and had cricked out his back and could barely stand. The rest of the club had left us, hoping we'd catch them up at the coffee stop. They were used to Frank's pranks and his occasional back problems. But Frank's back was pretty bad, and I have to admit we felt they had abandoned us. We feared we might not even be able to catch up with them.

However, determined not to spoil our holiday through his own stupidity, Frank gritted his teeth and gingerly lifted his leg over the bike. Then, turning the pedals very, very gently, we set off. We eventually reached the planned café stop to find our companions anxiously looking out for us. When they saw the state Frank was in, they were most patient while he lay on a path outside with ice packs on his back to ease the pain. Thankfully, their patience paid off, for luckily, he was able to continue. Now, after a couple of days of cycling, resting and ice-packing, we were hoping he'd be ok for this canoeing. And I, as a consequence, was in pole position at the back.

The sun beamed down on us as we set off down the gently-flowing river, following Colin in his kayak. With the paddles dipping rhythmically in and out of the water, I began to relax, realising how privileged we all were to have this wonderful opportunity. The river was as clear as spring water and we could see between the waving fronds of bright green weeds, right to the sandy bottom. It was magical. Almost in silence, apart from the birds singing on the banks and the splishes and splashes of the paddles, our canoes slid through the water towards a big curve in the river. As we paddled round, the scenery unfolded in front of us, with the banks rising gradually towards the cliffs that make up the Tarn gorge. We gazed ahead in eager anticipation.

Continuing on round, our canoes seemed to speed up, as if pulled by invisible cords. Then, horror of horrors, we found we were being rushed towards a huge tree lying semi-submerged ahead of us. The river, now narrowed to half its width by a large sandbank on our right, had become a churning channel blocked by this uprooted tree. There were in fact two trees, one behind the other, and what looked like their massive branches were actually their roots.

There was no get-out clause – hardly time to panic. We were thrust forwards into a bubbling cauldron of confusion. I have little recollection of what was happening to the others; all I remember is our boat being lifted up and over a huge root while the one above just skimmed Frank's head. I made the unforgivable mistake of grabbing hold of that root, which was coming straight at me. I forced my head underneath it, to avoid being knocked into next week, but it was a sure way to capsize the boat, and over we went, thrown out into the turmoil of racing water. We were whooshed downstream, the submerged branches bashing our legs as we swept through them. I panicked when Frank disappeared from my side. He bobbed up again spluttering and floundering, trying to keep his head above water. His glasses had gone and he couldn't see much and was confused.

Soon the trees were behind us, but the strong current carried us onwards, with our boat bobbing up and down before us. Miraculously, the barrel was still strapped in. What a pity *we* hadn't been!

I remembered a tactic we'd been told to try in a situation

such as this; that was to lie on our backs with our legs stretched in front of us and our arms extended sideways. I tried it. It worked. I actually enjoyed it for a moment or two. Then, as we were carried round a left-hand bend, we sailed by a group of canoeists sitting on the bank, looking forlorn. We struggled towards the edge, where they ran to help drag us out. We felt all limp, gasping as we flopped down on the bank to recover. Frank was relieved to find his glasses were still hanging round his neck on a cord.

By now our boat had become jammed on the other side of the river, a little way ahead. One of the young men, who were German, jumped into his canoe and crossed the current to retrieve it. No sooner had he done so than it was swept away again. Damnation. We would have to go after it. Already we were too far from our friends to know what was happening to them. Reluctantly, we eased ourselves up off the ground, thanked the Germans for their help and began plodding onwards.

The riverbank was strewn with stones that wobbled when we stepped on them. It was slow progress as we stepped from one insecure stone to the next, with our feet hurting through the thin soles of our plimsolls and the constant worry of twisting an ankle. By now our canoe was out of sight round a distant bend. Would we ever see it again? But when at last we reached that bend, we came across another group of washed-up foreign canoeists. And we could see our canoe, stuck on the other side again, trapped in the weeds.

Just as before, one of the canoeists offered to fetch it for us. And the self-same thing happened – no sooner had he freed it than off it went on its merry way, further down river. Grumbling and cursing because our ankles were aching, we followed on after it. What else could we do? All our belongings were in that barrel. But the distance between us and our friends was getting greater and greater, and we had no idea what state they were in.

When we rounded the next bend, we were glad to find that our canoe was nestled into the bank on *our* side of the river. What a relief! We also found two paddles which we thought must be ours, since we'd let go of them in the panic. The river was now flowing at a steadier pace.

We dragged the boat onto the bank, which was sandier here, then sat down heavily, in need of a well-earned rest. It was good to remove our lifejackets. They'd made us so hot and sweaty. The sun was high in the sky and our clothes dried quickly. But no sooner had we begun to relax than Frank spotted another canoe coming round the corner. "Quick, don't let it go past," he shouted and we jumped up and caught it in the nick of time, pulling it in alongside our own. A paddle soon followed and we grabbed that as well. Whatever was happening to our friends back up river? Now what should we do?

We waited and waited and waited, but nobody came. I likened us to Robinson Crusoe and Man Friday, stuck on a tropical island with no means of escape. It seemed a pretty hopeless state of affairs. "I can't stand this," complained Frank, after we'd been sitting in silence for ages and ages, "lets climb up the bank." That sounded like a feasible idea and we walked over to the trees, which grew thickly up the steep side of the river. But it was a fruitless struggle as, clinging on to branches, we attempted to haul ourselves up, only to slither all the way to the bottom again after making hardly any progress at all. We tried and tried but were burning up in the heat by now and our hands were so sore. Then I remembered that our packed lunches were in the barrel, provided by the hotel in Florac. We retrieved them and, forgetting for a while that we were stranded, we happily munched through our lunches. There was no sign of our water bottles, so an apple each would have to suffice.

We couldn't remain here a moment longer. We would have to make our way back and find out what was happening to the others. It was a daunting prospect, but this interminable hanging around was just as bad.

Our slow, painful progress was only highlighted for me when I found a ridged and age-rounded piece of rim from a terracotta pot. It must surely be Roman, I felt. I put it carefully in my shorts pocket and caught up with Frank.

We passed the place where we'd encountered the second group of shipwrecked foreigners, but they weren't there any more. What a mystery! We couldn't see how they'd been rescued without coming past us. The German group had also disappeared. We were even more mystified.

Then at last we reached the bend that we'd first been swept round. And there, upriver on the other side, we saw a cluster of busy people on a sandbank. They looked like Lilliputians. We got as close as we could. Yes, it *was* our friends. We shouted across to them and waved frantically. They didn't notice us for a while, as they couldn't hear us from that distance, but when they did see us, they waved back vigorously, obviously delighted to see us. Again we shouted, more hoarsely this time as our throats were so dry, to tell them that we had two canoes, two barrels and three paddles. Still they couldn't hear us. Tempting fate, we waded into the river on the inside bend until we were as far across as we dared to go without being caught in the current – up to our waists in fact. We shouted again as loudly as possible. But still they were too far away to hear. Whatever were they up to? We couldn't see them all, but the ones we could seemed very busy at something. As nobody was lying on the ground or sitting with their head in their hands, we could only assume they were all OK. It was pointless to stand there forever in the river, struggling to keep our footage and feeling useless to the cause, whatever that was. So reluctantly we waded back out and headed, dejectedly, down the way we'd come.

Then, up on the high roadside on the opposite cliffs, we noticed three people waving like mad. When our eyes adjusted, we could see that it was Maurice and Maurice and Marion with their bikes. What a stroke of luck! We could tell them we had two canoes, two barrels and three paddles. Maybe they could get close enough to the others to let them know. We shouted several times as loudly as we were able, but they hadn't a clue what we were saying. All our efforts were in vain, so we waved cheerio and, even more dispiritedly, carried on across the stones.

* * *

We found out later what had happened. Jill and Rob had capsized in the Hellespont, as had Daphne and young Phil. Although they had been just in front of us, we hadn't seen them go, nor did we remember passing them on our turbulent journey down the river. Jill and Rob had ended up one on either side of the trees, and Rob admitted later that he thought he'd lost her forever as he couldn't see her at all. But she was hanging on to a tree root on the opposite side and eventually managed to haul herself up into the tree. Daphne had done something similar, although she didn't relate the full details. But both she and Jill were up there in the tree, desperately hanging on. Rob, meanwhile, had worked his way round from root to root and branch to branch, right to the very end of the first tree. Here he'd found a rope tied to a branch with which he'd managed, somehow, to reach the sandbank, probably helped by Colin, who had skilfully made it to the sandbank in his kayak. Thelma and husband Jim had realised in time what had happened to those in front of them, and to avoid coming to grief had steered their canoe into the right-hand bank. Young Dave, who was sharing with Sheila, had done the same with their canoe. Once out of the current, they'd beached their boats on the sandbank. It was fortunate for Thelma because, just a few days later, she realised she was pregnant.

But Jill and Daphne were stuck there in the tree, in the middle of all that turbulence. From the sandbank, Rob had gently coaxed Jill into making her way down towards the branches, from which she could jump into the water and grab hold of the rope. Easy to say but terrifying to do! Sheila, meanwhile, saw a long, strong stick on the sandbank, probably part of the tree and, thinking it might help in the rescue operation, grabbed it and ran, dragging it to the river's edge. Here, she held it out over the water towards Jill, who was mustering up courage to take the plunge. Sheila was tall, strong and wiry, and very level-headed. Her long stick reached well out into the river, which undoubtedly gave Jill some encouragement. Jill jumped and caught the rope, hanging onto it with all her strength, with the strong current pulling at her all the while, trying to force her to let go. But slowly and carefully, hand over hand, she worked her way down to a big knot that someone had tied at the end of the rope. Now for the hardest task of all, to let go with one hand and grab hold of Sheila's stick. She went for it. And hanging on for dear life, she was dragged to safety, over all the stones and shingle.

Now it was Daphne's turn. She jumped into the water but missed the rope. Off she went, through the submerged branches where, somehow – and she can't remember how – she got close enough to the sandbank to be pulled ashore. A few feet further and she'd have missed the sandbank altogether. Amazingly, Daphne wasn't as traumatized by her ordeal as were Jill, Frank and myself. Such a tough cookie! But unfortunately she lost her spectacles in the mayhem.

None of them knew what had happened to us. They had last seen us disappearing round the bend, but at least we were floating. They did know, however, that two canoes were submerged in the river, wrapped around the bole of the tree, one above the other. The power of the water was bending them into right angles. The one on top belonged to Rob and Jill, while the one underneath must be Phil and Daphne's. Before anyone could go anywhere, they would have to retrieve these boats.

Rob and Dave were both tall, strongly-built chaps, and between them they managed to release the upper canoe from the clutches of the current and somehow, haul it across to the sandbank. The barrel was still in the boat, which seemed remarkable, considering all the forces it had been subjected to. The canoes were plastic, so they could withstand being bent double. It was just a matter of standing on the creases to straighten them out – just like that!

It was probably around this time that we'd appeared on the scene. They'd obviously been relieved to see us but had other pressing concerns to attend to, for they now had to retrieve the second boat. This one was deeper in the water and more firmly trapped than the first.

It was Dave who proved to be the hero of the day – Dave, who always reminded me of 'The curly-headed ploughboy who whistled o'er the lea', the first tune I learned to play on the piano. He was the calm one who took charge of proceedings. First they would need a long rope. So Dave climbed the steep riverbank to reach the road, then a steep hill on the other side, where eventually he found a farmhouse and borrowed a goodly rope. Whatever they did with this rope and by whatever means Frank and I don't know, but it was almost five o'clock before they had freed that second canoe from the river's tenacious grip. And after all their tireless efforts, they found that it didn't even belong to our group at all. It had a German name on it and there was no barrel.

Daphne was distraught. She had valuable and treasured items in her barrel, along with her changes of clothes of course. Phil, no doubt, was feeling equally upset. Anyway, they couldn't hang about any longer. It had taken the best part of the day to retrieve that last canoe and we were booked into a riverside hotel some miles downstream, in the little town of St Enimie.

* * *

In the silence of the late afternoon I heard the crackling of sticks somewhere in the trees on the steep bank opposite, which was now bathed in sunshine. "What's that?" I exclaimed. We listened intently. Then we thought we could hear the sound of a motor, getting closer. And then, to our great astonishment, a white van pulling a trailer appeared in the dappled sunlight and halted near the riverbank. A man jumped out and called across to us. It was the boat hirer. Hurray! Now our friends were climbing out of the van, one by one; all nine of them. Thank goodness. We were so glad to see them that we didn't even question how they'd been rescued.

When Daphne saw we had an extra boat and barrel pulled up next to ours, she burst into tears. Frank and I could almost have cried too, after all that waiting and uncertainty.

We two now had to put on our lifejackets and each take a canoe downstream and across to the other side. We felt quite fazed about doing this. After spending so many hours with nothing better to do than mull over the traumatic happenings of the day again and again, we'd really lost our bottle, as had some of the others, we later discovered.

We duly arrived at our hotel in St Enimie, where, over copious cups of tea on the veranda, we could tell each other the details of the day's dilemmas and get them out of our system. We wondered why the hirers had put us into that part of the river, surely knowing of the danger that lay ahead. We found out that the river had been in flood only a fortnight earlier; four metres higher in fact.

By next morning we braved ourselves to continue, none of us wanting to seem wimpish, even though we might have felt like wimps. Unfortunately, Jill bottled out when an incident occurred which brought back the horrors of the previous day, so Phil took her place in Rob's canoe, while Daphne kindly volunteered to quit canoeing and accompany Jill to the shore. When the hirers came to pick up the spare canoe, they took the 'girls' to the next hotel, in Les Vignes.

Meanwhile, we canoeists got really into the swing of things. On the second day, with Frank now steering us from the back seat, we became well and truly wedged against a huge rock, right in the middle of the river. We were held fast by the strong flow which whooshed round the rock on both sides of us. Our only way off was to go backwards down the rapids, avoiding other rocks on the way. It was as hairy as hell, but we were so elated to succeed that we gained lots more confidence. On our final day we all boldly canoed down a weir, but were then gutted to find that this was the last challenge of the trip.

The second week of cycling, however, proved to be just as rewarding, although less hairy than the canoeing had been. One day we cycled to the top of Mont Aigoual, the highest point in the Cévennes, and the next we went down on a funicular railway to the depths of Aven Amand, a cave between the Tarn and the Jonte gorges, which was the most spectacular any of us had seen.

For me, the *pièce de resistance* was the Cirque de Navacelles, a huge bowl in the mountainside, geologically called an 'incised meander' and formed by the wanderings of the River Vis. The oxbow lake, which had formed thousands of years before, was now dried up, leaving a circle of arable land at the bottom of the bowl, with a pyramid of rock in the middle, next to which nestles the little village of Navacelles. And down at the far end, right against the mountainside, was the most beautifully clear, fast-flowing little river I had ever seen, which disappeared over a ledge in a waterfall. By climbing down the side of this, you could have a wonderfully refreshing swim in the swirling pool below. And some of us did. The ride from the top to the bottom was equally invigorating, swooping and looping all the way down, causing a breeze that cooled us. But the coming back up, with heat radiating from the cliff sides, proved to be almost beyond us. Wherever there was any hint of shade, and there was very little, we tried to shelter for a while, finally making it to the top in a panting lather of sweat, gasping for water. How we wished for a swim in that swirling pool once more.

Our fabulous tour ended on the outskirts of Montpellier, where we caught the bike bus back to England.

* * *

When I returned to the museum the following week, the Curator asked me if I've had a good holiday. Before I asked her about my shard of pottery, I drew up my trousers and showed her my black and blue legs. So much for grade 2 – 'easy rapids with a bit of excitement'!

A Week in Paradise

June 2000

The author about to board the hulking plane to paradise

Quite frankly, this is not a story about cycling but the tale of two cyclists embarking on an uncharacteristic holiday in the tropics.

Back in January 2000, Frank's son Ben and his long-term girlfriend Kerri made a shock announcement. They were planning to marry in June of that year, in the Caribbean. They told us it would be a much cheaper option than getting married in England – except for the guests, who, of course, would have to pay their own way.

Frank's first reaction to this out-of-the-blue announcement was, "Huh, I'm not going all that way for just one piddling week. It's ridiculous. Fancy getting married in the Dominican Republic! They must be nuts." But after we'd talked it over, we realised what a very good package it was (£650 all inclusive). We gradually warmed to the idea. But would *I* be able to save up that amount of money before June? Then Frank made me a generous offer; he would pay for all my trips and treats while we were out there. Could I refuse? I could not! So now we were anticipating a blissful week together in paradise.

* * *

Coming in to land at Puerta Plata airport, in this huge, no-frills aeroplane, is a scary experience. I'm sure we're going to land in the sea. Then, at the last minute a field appears with a runway down the middle. Phew! Saved! But hey, is it going to be long enough for this hulking plane? Help! I close my eyes tightly. My heart is pounding in my chest as I wait for my inevitable doom. Then the passengers start cheering and clapping and I open my eyes. We have landed safely.

Surprisingly, although we've been packed in like sardines, Frank and I have enjoyed the flight. We were astonished that we could actually see waves way down on the sunny Atlantic, and could discern ships sailing across the ocean.

As we make our way down the canvas-covered walkway to our waiting bus, the heat hits us. We are hassled by men who want to carry our luggage and earn themselves a quick buck. We tighten our grip on the handles and keep walking. On both sides, hawkers are trying to sell us brightly-coloured wares: paper flowers, straw hats, paper fans, straw flowers – anything that might catch the fancy of us 'rich' visitors. In spite of their beautiful, hopeful smiles, we don't stop.

Our bus is quite old-fashioned. There are floppy, printed cotton curtains at the windows, like the ones we might have hung in our kitchens in bygone days, except that these are to shade us from the sun. Quaint! I hope the hotel will be of a higher standard than this. Now our courier is making herself known to us, over a malfunctioning microphone. She fiddles with the knobs before managing to introduce herself and tell us how far it is to our hotel. She would like us all to meet up in the hotel theatre at 2 pm today, so that we can choose which trips we would like to go on. It's stifling in here. Let's just get there!

The journey is an eye-opener. We've pulled the curtains aside to see where we are. When we stop at traffic lights in Puerta Plata, our bus is jostled from both sides by motorbikes – multi-passengered motorbikes. It's incredible. There are whole families on bikes – dad and mum with several children squashed in between. When the lights change to green, our hearts are in our mouths as they race off with a manic, roaring buzz. This is probably the school run!

After weaving our way through the chaos, we reach our hotel in less than half an hour. The hotel, the Riu Merengue, is on the north coast, towards the border with Haiti, and is the best hotel in the Dominican Republic. That's what we've been told and we have no way to refute this fact, although the state of this bus doesn't augur well.

Ben and Kerri are there to greet us as we pull up outside the impressive entrance. They arrived a week ago to attend the joint weddings of two of Ben's workmates, who have married identical twins. Now these four will be attending Ben and Kerri's wedding on Monday, and one of his mates will be Best Man. There are nine of us arriving today: Kerri's parents, Ginny and Vince, Ben's Mum, Kath and two of her close friends, Marie-Ann and Dave. Also there are two of Kerri's friends, Helen and Lucy, who will be her bridesmaids. So, with Frank and me, there'll be plenty of us to celebrate this forthcoming marriage.

The accommodation is not in the hotel itself; it's out in the garden, which is vast. The apartments are built in groups of eight – four at ground level with four identical ones on top, each with a corner balcony. To reach these blocks there's a minefield of pathways to negotiate, through lush tropical gardens. Our apartment is near the perimeter. It takes quite some time to find it. Together with Ginny and Vince, who will be in the same block as us, we make our way through palm trees and bushes. We must remember where that banana tree is growing by a balcony, which apartment is next to a pineapple tree and what path goes under an arch of Bougainvillea. It's very confusing, but these are the only markers we can use to remember the way.

Both our apartments are on the first floor. We have no idea where the rest of our party is housed. On the shiny grey marbled landing, we two couples separate and unlock our opposing front doors. The bathroom is the first room we encounter. It's large and lavish, with more mod cons than we could wish for. But rays of sunshine draw us quickly towards the bedroom, which is very spacious, light and airy. The bed is enormous, covered with a shiny, brightly-coloured bedspread on which sit two graceful white swans adorned with fresh flowers. 'Towel sculpture' I suppose you would call it. For us, who usually embark on low-budget cycling holidays, this is indeed a fascinating first.

Above us hangs a huge fan, which we are going to appreciate in the coming nights. Opposite the bed, the right-hand corner of the room is cut off at an angle with glass doors across. These lead to our balcony. We pull back the pretty beige curtains and open the doors. We'll be able to lie in bed in the mornings and look out over all the sunny greenery. There's a fridge under a marble-topped counter on our left. We take a second look. Wow! There are bottles of spirits hanging upside down on the wall. It's like a pub. Finding glasses in the cupboard above, we both decant a measure of, in turn, rum, whisky, brandy and gin. Frank says, "Crikey, this is all free. We could drink it all day long if we wanted to." Steady on, I'm thinking, we've got the rest of the day to get through yet, and we're jet-lagged. We're also really thirsty. There's bottled water in the fridge and we down a bottleful each. Ah! That's better.

Actually, we're not feeling very jet-lagged yet. Maybe there's just too much to discover to allow for tiredness, or perhaps the drink has given us a great feeling of bonhomie. After we've unpacked and hung our clothes in the walk-in wardrobe we're keen to get back to the hotel itself – if we can find the way. We keep leading each other up the garden path, so to speak, saying, "No, I'm sure it's this way," but finding it's not. "Well I'm *sure* that was the pineapple tree we passed," says Frank, but it wasn't. We get there, eventually.

Outside the hotel entrance is a large and beautiful swimming pool. Not many people are swimming; most are roasting round the edge on sun beds. If they so desired, they could lie under a straw-roofed canopy in the shade – there are circular ones all around the pool. The hotel building has a Spanish look about it, which I suppose is quite natural for a Hispanic country.

We mount the canopied steps to the wide entrance and head for the reception desk. Everywhere we look there is carved, polished wood. It's fabulous. The receptionist informs us, in well-spoken English, that we may go through to the dining hall and help ourselves to food, if we wish. Another eye-opener awaits us here– there is food for all nationalities. The choice is phenomenal. What shall we try? Well, for now, we stick to what we know. We don't want any upset tummies on the first day. We take our food over to a table and find other members of our party are already here. None of them has seen Ben or Kerri since our first arrival. It seems there is so much one can do that you may not see your friends for a whole week. But one of our group informs us that Ben and Kerri want to introduce us all to their mates before we attend our meeting this afternoon.

We set off to look for the bar they're supposed to be in, which apparently is adjacent to a second swimming pool. We hear loud music blasting through an open door and guess this must be the place – very much a young people's bar. As we step into the gloom, lit only by flashing gaming machines, Ben jumps out to welcome us. A drunken voice from behind him shouts, "Who's this then, shag?" (a Bristolian term of endearment). "It's my dad," says Ben. "Papa Shag" they all chorus, and unfortunately, this name sticks throughout the week. After a couple of drinks in this raucous atmosphere, we're glad that it's time to attend our meeting in the theatre.

The courier is standing centre stage wearing very high heels, a very tight dress and very red lipstick, enjoying her moment of glory. She hands out sheets of paper to pass around the packed auditorium. On these we must tick the boxes for the trips we would like to go on. We listen to all the details. There are so many options to choose from and really too much information to absorb in one go.

Now then, we *must* remember to keep Monday free for Ben and Kerri's wedding day. After much perusal, we make our decisions. In Sunday's box we tick the safari trip to some waterfalls, where we'll be able to swim if we want to; for Wednesday we choose snorkelling on coral reefs, and on Friday it's the pony trekking we've chosen. Very exciting! What an action-packed holiday this is going to be. But now we just want to get back to our apartment and change into swimwear. We haven't seen the beach yet.

It's not far from the hotel to the beach; down by the swimming pool, where colourful bougainvillea smothers the trellis fence, then along a sandy track through tall shady trees, and hey presto, we're on the beach. The sand is fine and soft, the sea glistens in shades of turquoise and pale blue and palm trees stretch their fronds above us, shading groups of sun beds that are set at our disposal in little groups. What more could we possibly wish for? And to top it all, the sun is shining constantly from a blue, blue sky. It's absolutely idyllic and better than we had ever imagined.

We race each other into the sea like mad young teenagers. The water is so warm that you can hardly tell when you're wet. As the shore slopes very gently, we have to strike out a long way into the sea before it's deep enough for a swim. We've been cooped up all those hours in that plane, then in the noisy bar and after, in the theatre. Now at last, we feel free to properly enjoy ourselves.

* * *

On Sunday morning we awake to the sound of birdsong, plus the whirring of the fan. It's been going all night long. We didn't dare leave the balcony doors open, in case we let in mosquitoes or other biting insects. But any thoughts we had of lazing in bed are dashed, because we haven't the time. If we don't get over to breakfast soon, we'll miss the safari. Blimey, I haven't even decided what I should wear; perhaps just my swimming costume under my shorts and top.

Last night, although all of us felt ready to flop, we enjoyed a lovely dinner, entertained by three guitarists, who went from table to table, serenading us with their gentle music and soft voices. Afterwards we headed straight back for bed – although it wasn't quite that straight. We had a hell of a job finding our way in the dark, in spite of the lamplight.

At nine o'clock we're all assembled outside the hotel, waiting for our safari trucks. Three open trucks arrive and we clamber into the back of one of them, together with Ginny and Vince, Kath, Marie-Ann and Dave, as directed by our guide, Gerald. Gerald is a big man with a big personality. We warm to him immediately. Ben and Kerri and their friends are in another truck. The blond twins are not coming. We've hardly seen them, but we've heard that they're enjoying the free rum.

Our trucks rumble down to the main road on their big, chunky wheels, which elevate us high above the ground. Soon we turn off onto dirt tracks with Gerald standing on the back steps the whole time, hanging on as we jolt over rough ground. He's a laugh a minute, making jokes and throwing his head back in fits of mirth, displaying perfect white teeth. He tells us he loves to dance the 'merengue' and wiggles his chubby hips to demonstrate. We've never heard of it.

When we pass little homesteads, children run out shouting "Menthe, menthe." They seem mad on mints, but we've been told not to give them any sweets. If we wish, we can give them exercise books, pens and pencils. That's what they really need. Some of our group have remembered to bring these gifts, and the truck stops to allow us to hand them over. The children's faces don't show much appreciation – maybe a few sweets would make them smile.

In the late morning we pull up under a copse of tall trees. This is obviously a pre-arranged stop, to help boost the local economy. Makeshift stalls are spread with locally-made souvenirs, mainly animals carved from soapstone. I rather like them and buy a pair of frogs. They'll make a nice present for my relatives. When we look up from all this display, we see a real animal close by – too close for comfort, I fear. It's a large brown snake and it's wrapped around a man's body. We step back in horror then, one by one, draw closer; rather as timid cows do when you hang over a field gate. The man assures us that it won't bite and encourages us to touch it. I'm amongst those who try. Its skin feels warm and dry, not cold and slimy, as I was prone to believe. For a fee, we can hold it. Frank withdraws from the front line. Kath and I remain. We're going to have a go. She goes first, looking as cool as cucumber. It's a big snake. It may not bite, but it could squeeze you to death if it wanted to. Then it's my turn; God help me. I'm not as relaxed as Kath, but if she can do it, so can I. Frank is in the background taking photos of us.

We climb back into our trucks and set off again. Lunch stop will be next. We are now in open countryside with animals grazing on the hillsides, mainly cattle and horses. There's lots of fencing around. Is it to keep the animals in or to keep the natives out? We trundle up a dusty track and stop while one of the drivers unlocks a gate, then continue uphill. Gerald tells us that this vast estate belongs to one man. We learn that a large portion of the Dominican Republic belongs to just a few wealthy people. All this fencing reminds me of *Bonanza* on TV, where the Cartwright family had to continuously defend their big cattle ranch.

We're now heading towards an oasis; there are palm trees, bright flowers and succulent leaves sprouting from the dusty ground ahead. As we draw closer we can see that it's an ornate swimming pool, surrounded by lush greenery. "Here you are," says Gerald. "You can have a nice swim before your lunch." But only Frank and I jump out enthusiastically. Ginny and Vince are not into sports, nor are Marie-Ann, Dave and Kath. Marie-Ann is too large to entertain much activity, but she has a great personality.

Ben and his gang climb out of their truck. They're up for it. The remaining party is carted off, further up the track. Gerald shouts out to us that there's a shortcut through the garden to where lunch will be served. "See you in half an hour," he adds, in case we forget that this is just a temporary stop.

The young men are already thrashing about in the water on the opposite side, before Frank and I are ready. Looking at them, Frank wants to be part of their crowd; young and carefree. Perhaps he can impress them with one of his backward dives – something he excelled at, back in his schooldays. He stands on the edge, his back to the pool and executes a fairly nifty dive. The lads weren't even looking, so it's wasted really, except that I'm fairly impressed. Anyway, where is he? I'm in the water now, wondering where he's going to pop up and surprise me – as he does. I'm waiting to be grabbed somewhere!

Then his head appears. He swims slowly round until he spots me. What's that on his head? Oh my God, it's blood. He's making feeble strokes towards me with a pseudo-nonchalant look on his face. "He doesn't know he's bleeding," I think to myself. "Trying to pretend nothing's happened." But the blood is running down his face now. "No use pretending; you've hit the bottom, you chump. This pool isn't deep like your sports pools back home."

I help him out onto the paving stones. The rest of the gang are still unaware. "Don't tell them," Frank says, hoping he can keep this a secret between us. "Don't be daft, Frank," I snap, "you've got a great gash on the top of your head that needs looking at. You're lucky you didn't break your neck." I'm feeling compassionate really, but sometimes Frank pushes me too far. I've dunked my towel in the water and I'm dabbing his head gently. He's definitely suffering from shock now. I help him on with his shirt and jeans, over his wet trunks. Neither of us has brought dry underwear. That's what rushing around in the morning does for you! Still in this climate we're not going to get piles or rheumatism. However, Frank's shivering.

Ben has noticed us now. He comes round the pool. I can read his thoughts, "Oh no, not my Dad again." There always seems to be an incident of one sort or another where his Dad is concerned. He's concerned for his Dad, but he's not going to let this spoil his wedding week. When he sees that Frank is in my capable hands, he goes back to join his mates.

We follow the rest of the group as they cut through the gardens to the eatery. Word gets around quickly. 'Papa Shag' has cut his head open. Gerald comes over to look at Frank's wound. By now the heat of the sun has congealed the blood and there's really nothing else to be done except to keep Frank calm and quiet. Gerald leads us to the dining area, which is shaded by a vast thatched roof, and seats us at a table, away from the madding crowd. Their laughter and hilarity stops as soon as they see us. Now they're whispering and glancing round. We feel like lepers. Frank and I are not at all hungry now. There is so much lovely food to choose from – a feast fit for a king. But we can hardly get anything down us and Frank's head is thumping, he tells me.

When we return to the trucks, the guides are in deep discussion. Gerald thinks that Frank should sit in the front cab. The back of the truck will be far too bumpy. So one of our guides moves into another truck to make way for Frank. We bump off down the track, heading for the Rio Domajagua falls, whatever they are. I hope Frank is OK, down there in the front. What a shame he's going to miss out.

We have stopped in the middle of a forest now and must continue on foot. Frank climbs out of the cab looking pale but, in spite of his headache, he's determined to keep with us. He says that if Marie-Ann is capable, then so is he. About eight or nine young men have jumped out of the cabs and are fitting us out with rubber shoes (akin to 'Crocs'). Cor! They're gorgeous (not the shoes)! The men are lean and lithe and brown-skinned with lovely dark eyes and white teeth. Mmmm, never seen such a nice-looking bunch of youths in all my life!

We set off up a shallow river, following the young men, who might be finding this mundane, if they do it for a living. I just love it. Gerald splashes along beside us, keeping an eye on Frank but also keeping up his light-hearted humour. The sunlight filters through the trees; it's magical. Eventually we reach a shady lake with rocky cliffs on the far side. In the far corner, water is cascading over the edge of the cliff – bright water becoming dark as it reaches the sombre waters of the lake. Only the near edge of the pool is in sunlight. The rest looks cold and uninviting.

Gerald gives us our options – if we're not planning to swim, there are other things to do, mainly sitting on the seats around the front edge of the lake, walking in the woods or going to the snack bar. A little hut is just being opened up for that very purpose. If we only want to bathe in the lake, that's fine, otherwise we'll need to swim across to the waterfall, where the lads will be waiting to help us climb up the rocks. I can't wait. I turn to tell Frank that I'll see him later, but he's already taking off his jeans and shirt. This holiday is not going to be spoilt by a bit of concussion. I'm worried about him, thinking he might collapse if he does anything strenuous, but he's adamant;

probably worried I'll get off with one of these gorgeous guys. Dream on!

We swim across the lake. It's not cold at all; it just feels unfriendly. There's no rush. The lads are waiting in strategic positions on the cliffs, to help haul us up. This is quite strenuous, even when you're fit for fifty. I can't remember ever putting so much strain on my knees. But it's all so worthwhile when a warm, brown hand reaches out to help you, especially when it's that lad wearing the bandana. Those hipster shorts of his make his body look so long and slinky, rather like a warm brown snake, I suppose. Cor! He can squeeze me to death any day. "Come on woman," I say to myself, "get a grip of yourself." I turn to check if Frank is OK as I reach the top. He's getting there, but not with his usual gusto.

The water cascading over the top is coming through a wide channel of smooth rock, which curves right over our heads in a big arc. It's as clear as clear can be, with a turquoise hue. So unreal – like something out of Disneyland perhaps, except it's all so natural. We must now swim through this channel and round a corner to reach the next rock climb. We take our time, absorbing the beauty and strangeness of our surroundings. It's so amazing. When we round the bend, more smiling lads are waiting at the bottom of the next waterfall, which cascades down time-smoothed rocks. Onwards we go, up and up. Each channel twists a different way, but all of them are as smooth as the first.

After the seventh waterfall, we've reached the top. (We don't realise, until we read about it later, that there are still twenty more cascades above this). But this is adventure enough for us – out of this world. 'Bandana boy' has reappeared several times during our climb. I can't think how he gets ahead so quickly. We join the rest of our group, who are gathered at the top, waiting for the 'all clear' to descend. It seems that we will be 'chuting' back down, as in water chutes. The lads help each of us to get into a good starting position, then give us a shove. And off we go with shrieks of delight, whooshing down the smooth rock and falling off the end with a big plop, which briefly submerges us. We then swim along the beautiful channel to the top of the next waterfall. It's too exhilarating for words.

After these amazing descents, we reach the top of the cliff above the lake. The joy rides are over. We must now jump into that dark lake (or face a very tricky descent). It's higher than any high-dive we've ever encountered but hey ho!

I look at Frank. He's done really well so far and I'm glad he didn't miss out. But he looks nervous now – once bitten, twice shy – but I'm sure he's not going to hit the bottom here. The water's too deep. I go first, trying to keep as streamlined as possible, my toes pointed and my chin tucked in. What a drop! When I surface, Frank is still up there, looking worried. "Come on Frank," I whisper, "take a leap of faith." Then I add, "but keep your legs together. We don't want any more injuries." He jumps.

This trip has been truly stunning for me – doubly so for poor Frank. Our return from the falls is by a much quicker route, which helps Frank, who is still travelling in the front cab. On arrival at the hotel, we go straight in for dinner – we're quite hungry by now. We plan to have an early night and give that poorly head a long rest. "Got to be in good nick for your son's wedding tomorrow, Frank," I say.

* * *

Another beautiful day greets us – just perfect for Ben and Kerri's wedding. Frank has slept well and is feeling much better. I bathed his head last night, to tidy it up a bit. It's a nice neat split; could almost be mistaken for a parting and it doesn't seem to need Steri-strips to hold it together. With his dark, curly hair, it's quite well camouflaged. He'll do! We return from breakfast to change into our best attire, ready for the wedding ceremony at 11 o'clock.

Kerri has been really good at keeping down the costs. She has made not only her own wedding dress but waistcoats for the groom, the best man and her father. Helen and Lucy have made their own matching bridesmaid dresses. As all three have just graduated from a fashion design course, this has been a golden opportunity for them.

We're all now assembled in the garden, waiting for the bride to appear. It's scorching hot. Ah! We can hear sweet music. Here come the three minstrels up the garden path, playing a wedding march on their guitars. We can't see the bride. Oh, here she comes, on her proud father's arm, looking radiant in her cream brocade dress. Behind her come the two pretty bridesmaids in blue. Ben's waiting near the gazebo, where the ceremony will take place. He's looking nervous, chewing his lips.

The gazebo is only big enough for the immediate wedding group, so the rest of us guests gather round, roasting in the sun. We strain to hear the quiet voice of the wedding official. I wish he'd speak up to make this wedding meaningful. We only manage to hear the "I do's" and see the exchange of rings; other than that, we can't follow much at all. I feel a pang of sadness for Ben and Kerri, who have travelled all this way for their special day only to have it made insignificant by a whispering official.

Then the guitar trio strikes up as Ben and Kerri step down from the gazebo as man and wife. Playing songs like *Island in the Sun* and other Caribbean tunes, they walk ahead of the wedded couple, leading us all down a pretty avenue towards the more formal gardens, where the photographs will be taken.

Many youngsters put more store in their wedding photos than in the ceremony itself. So do the photographers! This one is certainly making a meal of it. We go through countless groupings and regroupings – seated on the grass, standing on the grass, kneeling on the grass, standing by the rose bushes, sitting by the rose bushes; the list goes on. The poor bride is even more radiant than before. We all are – we're glowing like electric fires and sweating like pigs! Frank seems to be holding out well today, but I wish the photographer would allow us to get on with the wedding celebrations, or at least get us a glass of water. However, it's not over yet. He now wants us all down on the beach for more photographs.

We spend almost as long being snapped by the sea as we did in the gardens. We're absolutely hanging now – parched, worn out and wet through with perspiration. The men have large dark patches of sweat down the backs of their shirts and under their arms, but thankfully the women's perspiration is a little more discreet.

At last, he's got enough photographs to well and truly milk the bride and groom. Now we can hobble back to the hotel, in shoes that were not intended for standing about in the tropics in the midday sun. As well as swollen feet, Kath and I have puffed ankles from the insect bites we received yesterday. Kath's look much worse than mine. She must really be suffering, because I could rip the skin off my ankles.

The reception is a bit of a blur. We have toasts; we have lovely food; we have speeches and the bride and groom cut their wedding cake, and eventually we all drag ourselves back to our apartments, exhausted. It has been a day to remember, but perhaps not for all the right reasons.

* * *

It's Tuesday – the coral reef day. Every day, it seems, we have to rush off for breakfast. Perhaps we shouldn't have booked all these excursions. Wouldn't it be just lovely to laze on our own beautiful beach? Yesterday evening, after a well-earned rest, we enjoyed a slow stroll along the shore, then paddled back through the gently lapping waves. It was so relaxing and did my feet the world of good. Today, no doubt, will be action-packed. A mini-bus is waiting outside the hotel and we pack ourselves in. From our group, only Lucy and Helen are coming with us today. Ben and Kerri have already done this trip.

After being driven through the manic traffic of Puerta Plata, we arrive at Sosua, a very touristy place with several hotels along the coast. We join the end of a long queue which straggles diagonally up the beach and wait for our boat to arrive, quietly anticipating the day ahead of us.

One of the several boats cruising around off shore pulls in to the jetty and our queue gradually moves downhill. At last, we are climbing aboard our boat, a large catamaran. This will be a new experience for us. It's good to be out of the sun, and as the boat gets under way, we find relief from a cool breeze blowing through the inside. Some passengers prefer to stay outside, roasting. I take an instant dislike to an obese couple who have commandeered a four-person seat outside. Sipping wine from their oversized glasses, they think they're the cat's whiskers. Don't they know how gross they look, spread out along that bench like lumps of blubber, rolls of fat concealing their swimwear? Like two red-roasting walruses. They'd look better on a spit!

I'm not feeling so good now. Serves me right for criticising other people. I think I'm going to be sick. I leave my seat, not knowing quite where to go. My head is spinning. I can't hold on much longer. But in the nick of time a tall lad takes my hand and directs me swiftly out along a pod at the back of the boat. Here he holds me steady as I retch and spew into the sea. What a charming young man, to gently hold me as I vomit. He hands me a tissue and leads me back to my seat. This is Hamlet, one of three good-looking Dominican boys attending to our needs. The Captain introduces them to us. Edward and Christopher are the other two. They look a little younger than Hamlet but are equally smart in their white shirts and khaki shorts. I'm feeling much better now, as the engine drones on, skimming the catamaran through the water.

The Captain is Canadian. He's very red in the face and I'm not sure if it's because of the sun or the rum he's drinking. He seems full of himself, making funny quips. But I don't think he should be in charge of a boatful of passengers.

The boys are bringing round trays to put on our knees, prior to our imminent lunch. Whatever kitchen facilities they have on board, they have certainly produced some delicious-looking meals. As the boys draw nearer, piling food onto each plate in turn, that old familiar feeling wells up in me again, and before I know it, I'm desperate to get outside before I'm sick. Edward sees me just as he's emptying the last contents of his bowl onto someone's plate. He grabs my hand and pulls me through the mayhem of servers and diners, but this time I'm too late to reach the pod at the back, so he proffers his stainless steel bowl, still steaming from the hot food it held, and I vomit into it with immense relief. Immediately, I feel disgusted with myself. I sincerely hope this bowl gets a good autoclaving before it's used for food again.

I stay outside until lunch is over. I can't cope with any food smells right now. Frank comes out to see if I'm OK but I just need to be quietly on my own for the time being. Our catamaran is towing a small wooden boat and I'm fascinated, watching it being swung from side to side by the turbulent water thrown out from the engines. For a while, it takes my mind off sickness. It won't hold many passengers in a crisis though, I think to myself.

If I had known what a long journey this was going to be, I doubt if I would have come on the cruise. Ignorance is bliss, they say, but I am certainly not finding this voyage very blissful. Before we reach our destination I'm sick for a third time, and it is dear handsome Hamlet who leads me out along the pod once more. Now I'm feeling rather like a wet dishcloth – all limp and washed out. When the boat finally drops anchor, I have no interest in snorkelling at all, so I sit on the sidelines and listen to the instructions being given to the rest of them. The snorkels and flippers are down on the lower deck, where steps lead down into the sea. The three boys will give instructions on how to use the snorkels and help fit everyone out with the correct sized flippers. The Captain gives a warning not to get too close to the reefs, then says that anyone who does not wish to snorkel can sunbathe on the deck if they wish to – "or you can swim to the shore if you like," he adds, rather flippantly. Everybody in sight is making for the exit to the lower deck – such an untidy rabble of folk, one of whom is Frank, all over-eager to get on with their snorkelling.

In the solitude of the empty vessel, I reflect on what a waste of Frank's money this will be, to come all this way just for me to mope about in the boat. I look over to the shore. Perhaps I *could* swim there. It doesn't look too far away and I'm quite a strong swimmer – or would be if I didn't feel so drained. I mull over this idea for a while, not feeling enthusiastic but thinking I must do something. I can take my time; there's no rush.

Eventually I muster up enough energy and make my way outside. On the top deck, a few young women are lying face down, gently cooking themselves in the midday sun. They don't see me as I quietly make for the stairway to the lower deck.

There's still a pile of flippers left near the exit. I find some that fit and realise I've never worn proper rubber flippers before. They seem really heavy, not like the little plastic ones I once wore as a child. With my flippers secure, I lunge into the water, thrusting myself off the bottom step and flapping my flippered feet to propel myself in the water. Ugh! It feels almost as if I've got balls and chains attached to my feet. But I fall into a gentle rhythm of breaststroke and keep going, knowing I can make it – no probs.

Feeling rather pleased with myself, I reach the shore at last. It's steeper than the beach back at our hotel and the waves are stronger, but I soon clamber out onto dry sand, glad that I have made something of today's trip. Then I look round at the catamaran – and panic. It's a long way away. It didn't look that far from the ship to the shore. Did I swim that far? What am I going to do now? I'm frightened. Then I see a young man in goggles and rubber cap swimming towards the beach. I shout, to ask him if he's from the catamaran. He's not and he's foreign, and no, he won't swim back to the boat with me – if indeed he has understood anything I asked him!

Lots of thoughts are going through my mind now. For a start, nobody from the boat knows I am here. The boat could leave before they discover I'm missing. There might be dangerous creatures lurking in the waters, just waiting to get me. This is not England. I can't take anything for granted here. I'm completely alone and I have to sort this out myself. I'm working myself up into a real panic – almost panting. I take off my flippers. I can't stand them. I'll just carry them in my arms. Then I realise how extremely stupid and irrational I am being. No flippers and no spare arms to swim with? You idiot. I put the flippers back on again. Now what? I can't set off while I'm breathing like this; I must calm down.

I decide I'll have to swim on my back with the gentlest of strokes and really concentrate on my breathing. I mustn't start gasping when I'm out there. I go for it, screwing my face up tightly as I crash through the surf. "Just keep calm," I tell myself as I turn over onto my back. I flap my flippers very, very gently; a hardly perceptible motion – if anyone was watching! With my arms waving gently at my sides, I'm making slow progress through the water. My main concern is not to gasp; nor to think of what might be swimming around me or beneath me. At least I'm making headway. But when I consider that I'm a good way from the shore, I look round and find I'm not heading towards the catamaran at all. I'm way off course, making the distance even further for myself.

Coming round in a huge arc I finally reach the boat and haul myself weakly up the steps, all faint and floppy. There's no one to welcome me back with open arms, to congratulate me or even make me a nice cup of tea. The coral reef swimmers are still snorkelling and the girls on the roof are probably fast asleep. Nobody will believe that I actually swam to the shore and was dead scared to swim back.

Now the snorkellers are returning noisily up the stairs, all dripping wet. Ah here's Frank. He's not looking happy. Oh no! He's been stung. His forearm is spattered with white dots and feels numb. He claims the current carried him too near to the reefs and while he was flapping to get away, something stung him – probably a sea urchin.

All concern seems to be on Frank now. Never mind *my* trauma. The fat couple, who have now re-commandeered the seat for four, are giving Frank their advice. He ought to see a doctor as soon as we get back. But the Captain chips in, "I shouldn't bother mate. They'll only take your arm off." And he sips his replenished glass of rum. Nobody really knows what to do and anyway, nobody can be certain what has stung him. He's sitting quietly by my side now. Is his bloodstream full of poison, or is it just confined to the skin of his forearm? We'll just have to wait and see.

When the next meal comes round, I disappear outside and again watch that boat at the back swinging to and fro. I wait until all smells of food have gone. Then Hamlet, at the request of the Captain, entertains us with a speech from – naturally – *Hamlet*. He's a confident and talented lad, as well as being so kind and courteous. I hope he makes something of his life.

The boat docks at Sosua and I, for one, disembark gladly. No more boat trips for me. All I have to do now is endure the minibus journey to our hotel. When all feelings of nausea have passed, I'll probably manage a huge meal tonight. But what of Frank's arm? It's still numb but as he feels no adverse effects anywhere else, he's loath to see anyone about it, assuming he'll be OK. I sincerely hope so. That's two eventful trips we've been on now.

* * *

It's hard to believe that this is our penultimate day. We have all day to do our own thing – no need to rush anywhere. We open the balcony doors and, for the first time this holiday, enjoy lying in bed, looking out over all the sunny trees and listening to the birds. It's good being on the first floor.

After breakfast we amble down to the beach, where we lie in the sea, letting the gentle waves lap up our legs and over our backs. It's so relaxing; cooler than lying on the beach and less strenuous than swimming. Frank's forearm is still tingling. I think he should have had it checked out. But Frank's philosophy seems to be that if his arm hasn't dropped off yet, he'll be fine.

Ginny and Vince arrive and stretch themselves out on some sun beds under a palm tree. After a while we go up and join them on adjacent beds. Then Ginny asks, "Have you seen those little black and white striped fish yet? They'll come and eat bread out of your hand." We're sceptical. "Here, we've got some bread. Go and try it." We trot back into the sea, wading out to look for these fish, although not convinced. At least Ginny and Vince have got rid of us, if that's what they wanted. But sure enough, after standing still in the water for a while, we are surrounded by a small shoal of stripey little fish and they are actually taking bread from our fingers. Amazing!

When the bread is all gone and we've tired of the sea, we take a little walk westwards to explore the coast. Ginny and Vince can have the sun-beds to themselves. We're not used to non-action holidays, anyway. Coming back along the beach we discover a new entrance to the hotel complex, which brings us into a street full of little shops. It's called Caribbean Street and it's not far from our holiday flats. We didn't even know about it. We stroll through, not much interested in shopping but heading for a quicker route to our apartment. I stop briefly to look at photos of holidaymakers, displayed in one of the shop windows. "Hey look Frank, that's us," I exclaim. And there, right in the middle of the display is a lovely picture of us, lying in the sea, looking straight at the camera. It could only have been taken a couple of hours ago. There's an expensive price tag attached to it, so we don't go in to buy it, which is so sad because it's one of the nicest photos of us ever. However, it makes us feel a little creepy to think that someone has been taking photos of us, secretly.

After lunch we're not sure what to do, already tired of idleness. "Let's go and have a look round Puerta Plata," suggests Frank. But it's not something you can do spontaneously, on this type of holiday. Outside the hotel foyer we find a really nice, softly-spoken taxi driver who agrees a price to take us to Puerta Plata and show us around.

We're not, however, very enamoured with the first place he takes us to. It's a two-storey, glass-fronted showroom, which he recommends we should see. No sooner are we inside than we are lured to a counter by a smartly suited, silky-tongued man, who tempts Frank to buy his lady some beautiful jewellery. Frank declines. The man shows us more pieces, some set with transparent amber and some with larimar, which is a precious stone unique to the Dominican Republic. I'm becoming a little interested now. To think that larimar is only found in this country. What a souvenir that would be to take home! The man perceives my interest and Frank's stubbornness and keeps knocking down the price, lower and lower. But Frank is not going to be conned by anyone. Almost three quarters of an hour later, he gives up on us and we come away with a tiny lump of larimar and a similar-sized piece of amber apiece, just for keepsakes.

I actually feel sorry for our taxi driver, who would, no doubt, have made some commission, had we purchased something. But Frank's not the type to be forced into things like that. He's more likely to dig his heels in. Anyway this is certainly not what we have come to see in Puerta Plata. We're more interested in the lives of the people who live here.

Our next port of call is a church, where I find that the most striking feature is the entrance doors, on which are carved, in low-relief, life-sized figures of Christ and his disciples – so bold and so memorable. The taxi driver continues on, stopping at various little parks and viewpoints, but there doesn't seem to be much here for visitors to see. Now he asks us if we mind if he stops to pick up a chicken for his wife. We don't.

He parks the car down a little back street and takes us into a long, dark and narrow place where at first, we can't see a thing. Although it has a shop-front, it isn't a building at all; it's more of a black canvas-roofed tent, where light shines in at the far end. We can now see trestle tables down both sides of the shop, laden with huge bunches of bananas – probably enough to supply the whole district. But we're here for a chicken, aren't we? The taxi driver acknowledges the shopkeeper, whom we can hardly see in the gloom, then leads us down towards the daylight at the end of the tunnel. Right across the bottom there's a chicken pen, where contented chickens are scratching about in the dust.

In his smart taxi-driver clothes, our driver snicks in through the wire gate and starts chasing chickens round and round the henhouse. This is a real spectator sport. Or even a comedy show. We could be watching Mr Bean! The chickens are taxing our poor man to the extreme. He's becoming so exasperated, running this way and that, trying to snatch hold of one – popping out from behind the henhouse on one side, then suddenly reappearing on the other side. The varmints keep evading him at the very last moment, with a flapping and clucking and a flurry of dust. But our man is not giving up. Finally he triumphs with a plump, squawking chicken in his hands. Ugh! I see him break its neck. In spite of witnessing a chicken being killed (and someone has to do it) this is the side of life we wanted to see; not a jewellery outlet.

So, with his forehead still glistening and his chicken safely in the boot, the taxi driver dusts himself down and takes us back to the hotel, where we pay him the agreed fare. We didn't really see much of Puerta Plata, but the final episode made up for that.

To round off our evening, we take a stroll along the shore, going in the opposite direction this time. At the far end of the bay, we follow a track up and round the back of a tall hedge. This is probably beyond the perimeter of the hotel's estate, but we love exploring out-of-bounds places and want to know where it leads. But we're in for a bit of a shock. We see makeshift tables set up behind the hedge, being laid out with ornaments and other objects, mainly of carved wood. What completely throws us though, is the tallness and blackness of the men manning these stalls. They seem very intimidating and we don't feel safe at all. Where are they from and why are they setting this up behind a hedge at sunset? We beat a hasty retreat.

* * *

Today is Thursday, the last full day of our holiday. Tomorrow we leave at noon for that long flight home. We have an action-packed day ahead of us – pony trekking. Frank has never been on a horse or pony in his life. I, on the other hand, wanted a pony all through my childhood and eventually, on my thirteenth birthday, I was given a little brown one. It was a china ornament! I still love horses, especially the smell of them, but am less confident about riding now.

Our packed minibus calls at Sosua en route, where we are joined by another packed minibus from a sister hotel. This must be a popular excursion. Let's hope we have a trouble-free day after the incidents of our last two trips. Third time lucky, eh?

The destination is quite far, heading eastwards. In the fields we see tall black Negroes cutting sugarcane. We've worked out by now that these men are Haitians. If most of the Dominicans are not well off, what must life be like for these poor migrant workers from Haiti? Perhaps we should have bought an ornament from them last night.

After a long drive we arrive at a ranch where rows of ponies are tied to a rail, waiting impatiently for the off. Frank's feeling a bit dubious now – these animals look quite frisky. This feeling is confirmed when a pair of them begin to get skittish. The one behind, on which a young man is mounted, rears up and is immediately kicked in the stomach by the horse in front, which has performed a handstand. What a good start this is, for the nervous ones amongst us.

The owner of the ranch comes over to greet us. She's a tall, blonde, blue-eyed Scandinavian – very attractive and well built. I perceive that Frank is keener to go trekking now! We are going to be divided into three groups: the competent riders, the moderate riders and the beginners. Well Frank doesn't want to be in the beginners' group, so we opt for the moderate one. The competent group sets off ahead of us and we follow a little way behind. These ponies are very strange to ride. They don't have the same gait as those we are used to back home. Where we would go up and down in the saddle when trotting, this is impossible on these horses. They seem to move their legs in a different sequence, which joggles you all over the place. When they gallop you have to sit low in the saddle as if you were cantering. It's weird.

The horses are descended from those brought over by Christopher Columbus. Their step is isochronous (I found this out from Wikipedia), which is 'a 1,2,3,4 ambling gait, slower than other breeds and very elegant. The breed is called Paso Higueyano, or high stepping'.

Each of our groups is looked after by two or three Dominican youths, who are extremely adept in the saddle, but their biggest fault is that they keep making kissing noises from behind, which encourages our mounts to speed up. Before long we have caught up with the competent group in front. Segregating us was a complete waste of time. We hope we're not going to be treated like the competent contingent. These horses, we are finding, appear to be trained only to follow each other. Apart from that, they just do what they want to do. Both my horse and Frank's seem keen to push past the other horses. This is impossible on a narrow pathway, although they keep trying to squeeze by. But as soon as we come to a river, our two horses rush down the steep stony riverbanks, skidding and slipping, then overtake in the water and rush up the opposite bank. All we can do is hang onto their manes for dear life. It's not doing much to build our confidence. Frank looks quite pale. Every time the lads pass round the hipflask of rum, he takes a good swig to steady his nerves. Most of us have a swig; that's the only refreshment available and it *is* a bit of a novelty – a sort of Holy Communion on the trot, instead of on our knees at the altar. We're sharing rum and germs with everyone.

It's time for our elevenses now. We dismount on the edge of a forest and tie our horses to the fence. 'Blondie' tells us, "This forest was used to film part of Jurassic Park." As we walk in under the tree canopy little wild pigs scatter amongst the undergrowth, while we're imagining huge dinosaurs crashing towards us through the trees. But no such thing happens. In fact it's uncannily quiet here.

We reach a clearing at the top of a steeply-wooded slope, where we are motioned to sit on conveniently-felled logs. "Where's the coffee then?" we wonder, but this isn't a conventional coffee break. Using machetes, the lads slash open coconuts and pour rum into the milk, handing round a neat half shell to each of us. Not what we expected, for sure!

After a short rest and feeling slightly fortified, we remount our horses and set off at a joggling trot. What next? Well nothing untoward happens until we approach the venue for our lunch stop. As we draw nearer, Frank, who has been lagging behind somewhat, comes racing past. His horse gallops towards a low hedge and as it jumps over, Frank shouts, "Yee ha!" and hangs on superbly. I marvel at his horsemanship and sudden rush of confidence.

Our lunch, however, is not so spectacular. In fact it's dire. I reflect on all the lovely meals that I missed on those last two trips. But now that I feel like eating, the choice is minimal. There are three metal trays on the table, rather like the ones used for school dinners. The first contains cheese slices, the second, slices of Spam, or something that looks very much like it, and the third is full of dry slices of bread. It all looks as if it was prepared earlier – far too early, in fact. For drinks we can choose from bottled beer, a different type of bottled beer, or some other bottled alcohol. There is no bottled water, no coffee, nothing. We can take it or leave it. Although we enjoy the coolness inside the building and the company of the younger members of our party, there is no enthusiasm for the food.

So, not feeling at all sated, we climb back into our saddles for the next leg of the trek. This time we don't have any rivers to cross, but we do trot alongside a gently-flowing river for a while, and being so hot and sticky by now, most of us can't resist the urge to jump in for a swim. Blondie and the youths are quite happy to hang about while we have some fun in the water. There aren't many amongst us who don't take the plunge. Fully clothed, including our shoes, we frolic in the water for a good half hour or more, diving from a ledge on the opposite bank, dive-bombing each other and dementedly depleting ourselves of the last vestiges of holiday euphoria.

Laughing, wet and dripping, we remount our horses for the last time. We're cooler now and worn out. Sitting on our saddles in wet trousers is not much fun though, and our seats will be the last to dry.

By teatime we are back at the ranch, gasping for a drink. Frank's feeling parched and dizzy, and goes to the bar for water. They don't have any. Unbelievable! It's been an enjoyable trip but they certainly haven't fed and watered us very well. We'll just have to hold out until we get back to our hotel. Frank seems in a bit of a daze now. He follows some folk down to the nearest minibus and plonks himself on the back seat. I'm behind him in the queue and by the time I get there, the first minibus is full. I'll have to go in the one behind. We're all mixed up now. I'm with the Sosua crowd.

From my seat, I can see Frank's head and shoulders at the back of the vehicle in front. However, by the time we pull out of the ranch, he has disappeared from view. Where's he gone? I'm worried about him, but I can't do anything until we get back. First, I must endure the long drive to the hotel. Now we're passing the fields of sugar cane to see that all the workers have gone home (if they have homes to go to!)

When we reach Sosua, my minibus peels off towards the coast while the front one continues straight on for our hotel. We go all round the hotel complexes, dropping people off; eating away my time and delaying me from getting back to Frank.

At last we pull up outside the Riu Merengue, where the first group are standing in a circle around the entrance steps. I'd have thought they'd be in the dining room by now, eating and drinking to make up for lost time. But when I look through a gap, I see Frank, slumped on a luggage trolley, unconscious. I push my way through. Why the hell are they just standing here gawping? I lift an eyelid and see that his eye has almost disappeared over the top. I'm no doctor, barely a nurse, but I'm sure I've seen this condition before. It looks like a hypoglycaemic coma. And there's Dave taking photos of him. They think it's a laugh. They think he's drunk. I know he's not. This is serious.

Then, like an angel, our taxi-driver appears and draws his car up close, forcing a gap in the circle. With some difficulty, I help him to drag Frank onto the back seat and we set off for help. We don't go far – just round to the clinic in Caribbean Street, where our man helps the doctor to lift Frank onto a bed, then leaves us in the doctor's care.

* * *

For almost three long hours I've been sitting next to Frank's bed waiting for him to regain consciousness. The doctor has inserted a drip into Frank's arm and for all this time I've been holding his elbow and forearm, in case he inadvertently flexes his arm when he comes to and re-jabs himself. I have no idea how well qualified the doctor is but he seems kind and caring, so I can only put my trust in him. But I'm worried sick about Frank. I'm also worn out and hungry, and my shoes still haven't dried out from swimming in that river.

Then Ben turns up at the clinic. He's so relieved to find us at last. Apparently the courier has been frantically phoning all the hospitals in the area to find out which one Frank was taken to. I perceive that she's not very happy with us and to think we were only just around the corner from the hotel. As I talk to Ben, Frank opens his eyes, rears up and vomits all over the wall. The doctor comes rushing in and checks his pulse and heartbeat. Now that his dad has come round and is seemingly OK, Ben leaves, to let the courier know where we are. I want to clean the sick off the wall for the doctor, but he's not concerned about it. However, he seems increasingly worried about Frank's condition. Frank is now trembling all over and his heart is racing. The doctor calls for an ambulance.

We are now tearing to Puerta Plata in an ambulance. A nurse sits in the back with us, constantly checking Frank's condition as we hurtle along. I feel as if I'm in the middle of a nightmare. But thank goodness all those motorcyclists are not around to get in our way.

Frank is rushed to a single room on the first floor, where nurses begin to wire him up to monitors. A doctor appears and starts asking me questions, while I'm struggling to remove Frank's damp blue suede trainers. I'm trying to give this man sensible answers, but I'm somewhat distracted by the state of Frank's feet. His toes are like blue cauliflowers and I chastise myself for not taking off his shoes hours ago in the clinic.

The ambulance lady comes to the door and advises me to leave Frank and return with them to the hotel, otherwise I will find myself stranded. I reluctantly take their advice, trusting that Frank is in capable hands. It's a wrench though and I feel like a traitor. I'm also exhausted.

It's after midnight when they drop me off at the hotel. I stand alone, shivering – not from cold, just fright. I'm frightened about what will happen to Frank, about whether we'll be on our flight home in less than twelve hours' time and most imminently, will I be able to find my way safely to the apartment without being attacked by some predator which is lurking in the bushes. I set off with trepidation, glancing nervously behind me, around me, ahead of me all the time, rushing past imaginary danger points, hovering at the slightest noise. I'm a nervous wreck, undoubtedly.

With great relief I enter the main door and creep upstairs. As I cross the landing, Ginny comes out of her apartment door and hands me something wrapped in paper. It's sandwiches that she has saved for me this evening. Oh bless you, Ginny, how thoughtful. I tell her as much as I know, then head for bed with my midnight feast.

* * *

I awake and realise that I actually slept, after all. I thought I would lie awake all night long. There's no time to hang about though. I must get up and phone the hospital to see what's happening. Will Frank be well enough to fly home today?

The answer is no. They think they need to keep him in hospital for the time being, to carry out further checks. Well, if Frank's not going home, neither am I. But I'll need to pack all our stuff up anyway, and vacate the room for the next set of guests. I work like an automaton, taking all the clothes out of the wardrobe first and laying them on the bed. I don't even have to remember which things are mine and which are his, as we brought one big case for both of us. Before I leave, I gather my senses enough to remember to check the safe. Good job I do. We'll need our money and passports!

I drag our hulking case all the way to the hotel and explain my situation to the man on the desk, leaving the case in his care behind the counter. Then I head for the dining room. The rest of our party are in there too, having their breakfasts *before* they pack their bags. As soon as we're finished, Ben and I are planning to take a taxi to the hospital to find out what is happening to Frank.

On arrival at the hospital, I lead Ben up to Frank's room, which seems more like a B&B than a hospital room. Frank is propped up in bed with wires coming out of everywhere, looking weak and forlorn. The doctor arrives and we ask why Frank can't leave the hospital. He's a bit vague with his answers, but mentions the bill that will need to be paid. Luckily Ben has his credit card with him. We go down to reception to find out what is owed so far - £1,350, for just one night of treatment! Tentatively, Ben pays up, trusting fervently that the insurance will cough up when we get back to England. On arrival back upstairs we find that Frank is being stripped of all his monitors, ready to be chucked out. He won't need to stay a moment longer now that the bill is paid. I help him dress while the doctor doles out some pills for him to take home. If we get a taxi straight to the airport, we still have time to catch our flight.

I phone the hotel to see if our luggage can be rushed to the airport, but I'm told that the courier has already taken it, just in case Frank was allowed out of hospital in time. As we walk down the hospital steps to hail a taxi, we see a young mother, newborn baby in her arms, climb onto a waiting motorbike to be driven home, side saddle and no-handed. I think I've seen it all now!

We reach the airport and are rushed through customs, where we find Kerri in floods of tears, thinking that her new husband will not be coming home with her. We're all so relieved to be on the flight, although little do we know that we'll be sitting in this tin can for an hour before we take off, with condensation dripping on us from the roof. The only special treatment given to Frank is to have a seat by the aisle. I hope he'll endure the flight. He's very subdued.

At last, our plane is speeding down the runway, flying away from all this paradise. Paradise? I'm not so sure about that! When we eventually reach home, Frank goes straight to bed while I call the emergency weekend doctor. She arrives at two o'clock in the morning. I've been hanging around since yesterday teatime, not daring to go to bed or even allow myself to fall asleep on the sofa. She throws away his tablets with disgust and prescribes some different ones, advising him to rest for a couple of days. Other than that he seems fine, except that his forearm will remain spattered with white dots for many years to come.

* * *

When I return to work the following week, the Curator asks with great interest what sort of holiday I have had. This time I am speechless. I just burst into tears.

CHAPTER NINE

Bad Friday

March 1987

Peter and I pushing the bikes up a steep hill in Exmoor

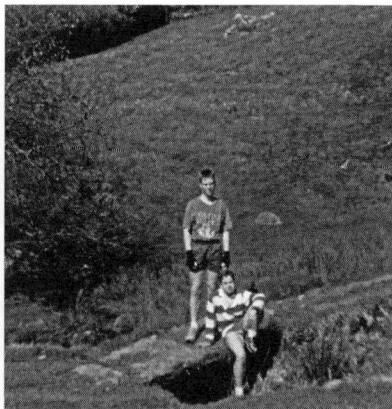

Malc and Peter (seated) having a rest near Simonsbath

In the crisp early morning sunshine we left our hillside home in Butterrow, on the side of Rodborough Common, and freewheeled down the steep descent into Stroud. Full of enthusiasm, we pedalled on towards the cycle track at the bottom of the valley.

It was Good Friday and we were heading south on an Easter weekend cycling trip.

This was to be a real challenge for two thirteen-year-olds, my son Malc and his school friend Peter. Just two weeks earlier, Peter's father had taken them both on a 73-mile bike ride, all the way across the Severn Bridge into the Forest of Dean. I'd been amazed at their ability to do such a distance without suffering any aches and pains afterwards. Now, on the strength of this achievement, we were attempting an ambitious trip from Gloucestershire to Exmoor to visit some close friends. They had recently moved to Bratton Fleming, on the other side of Exmoor, and I knew this trip would stretch us to our limits. But spring was in the air and summer just around the corner. We were optimistic.

I was a frustrated, would-be touring cyclist, waiting for the least excuse to spread my wings. This was my chance. The first day we would head for the Blackdown Hills beyond Taunton in Somerset. There, we had some farming friends in the little village of Staple Fitzpaine. They were always delighted to see us.

Beforehand, I had consulted a seasoned cyclist friend from the local cycling club to see if he thought we'd be capable of cycling this distance, especially with panniers on our bikes; over eighty miles on the first day. He'd been very encouraging. So here we were, leaving home at 7.30 am, knowing it would be a push. All we had to do was keep up a steady pace and not squander our time, but just yards onto the cycle track at Dudbridge, my back tyre punctured on glass. Off with the panniers and turn the bike upside down. What an inconvenience. We could do without delays.

Soon we were on our way again, happily climbing a hill out of Nailsworth and winding our way up to the village of Horsley, which sits on the edge of a high plateau. As the road levelled out and we regained our breath, we sped along towards Wotton-under-Edge, trying to make up the time we had lost in mending the puncture. Then we realised that large snowflakes were fluttering down from this apparently blue sky. We were delighted and tried to catch them in our mouths.

We continued – so did the snowflakes. They were coming down a bit faster now and it wasn't so sunny or so funny. Our clothes were getting quite damp, so belatedly, we put on anoraks, feeling ill equipped for this sudden change in the weather. At least we'd brought woolly gloves.

Togged up, we tried to keep the momentum going before swooping down yet another steep and winding hill over the Cotswold edge into Wotton. The only café open was halfway up the sloping main street. It was rather smart, so when we three soggy cyclists trooped in, dripping dirty droplets all over the newly washed floor, we didn't feel much of a welcome. The two women behind the counter gave us disapproving looks. One of them was still holding the wet mop in her hand. They scowled as we took our hot drinks to a table by the open fire and spread our gloves around the hearth. The gloves didn't even steam; there was hardly any heat from this newly-lit fire. But we huddled close by, trying to warm our wet feet. We were not at all keen to be back in the saddle.

Bracing ourselves at last, we put on our warm wet gloves and ventured out into the wet snow. We dried the saddles with paper serviettes we'd saved from the café, then made our way southwards, towards Chipping Sodbury. This town, in clement weather, is a charming old market town on a gentle slope, built of very mellow stone and with the widest market place imaginable. But today it was just a refuge that we had to reach as quickly as possible.

We arrived at lunchtime, sodden. There were many pubs to choose from but we dived into the first one we saw. Luckily, in the far corner of the main bar, we found a little snug with its own roaring fire. We claimed it for ourselves, stripping off our outer clothing, so cold and wet that we felt no sense at all of being on holiday. I reasoned (realising how unreasonable this whole ambitious plan of mine had been) that it was pointless trying to cycle to Taunton now. We were seriously behind time. The snow showed no signs of stopping, in fact it had become a wet blizzard.

No other customers were near this cosy corner. We savoured the roasting fire, with our clothes steaming like kettles, dreamily feeling as if we were in a sauna. Wallowing in this warm fug of familiar vapours from our own wet and sweaty clothes, we wished we could have stayed there and be warm forever. But eventually I came to my senses and thought up a new plan of action – to change to a westerly direction and head for Temple Meads station in Bristol. From there we could catch a train to Taunton. With this plan in place, we stayed in the pub for about two hours, becoming half dry and much warmer.

The ten or so miles to reach the centre of Bristol seemed daunting but an achievable distance. The route would be flatter now, since we'd left the Cotswolds behind us. However, it would be main road all the way and when we looked out of the window, we couldn't see much at all. We forced ourselves out onto the bikes with just the invisible carrot of a train journey dangling somewhere in front of us. The conditions were terrible but at least the traffic was only crawling along.

After barely fifteen minutes Malc complained, "Mum, I can't go any further, my calf muscles are all cramped up." Peter then admitted that he had cramp in his hands.

"Great," I thought. "One can't pedal, the other can't hold his handlebars." What should we do? I was rather hard on them. "What are you going to do then, stand here all night?" (It seemed like night by now). We stopped for a while, being sprayed by every passing vehicle and blinded by snow. We had to keep going; we couldn't just hang about getting colder and colder. "We'll ride a few yards then walk a few yards," I said, "but we must keep moving. At every single café or pub, we'll stop and go in. OK?" So on we crawled.

But no pub or café materialised until we reached Downend on the edge of the city. At last, we could take shelter. The pub looked quite seedy, but we couldn't wait to get inside. Our entrance caused rather a stir; three white, wet apparitions accompanied by a cold draught and a flurry of snow. We felt somewhat embarrassed by the attention we were receiving, so we found a table as far as possible from the main bar. Here we sipped our mediocre coffee from dubious mugs while puddles of water formed beneath us on the tiled floor. There was no conversation between us. The boys probably wished they'd never set out on this expedition and I could think of no chirpy words of encouragement. The only consolation was that we'd reached the big city at last.

From now on, the route was all built up. The snow in our eyes made it really difficult to see ahead. Suddenly, a zebra crossing loomed into view with three women coming across. Jamming on the brakes in the nick of time, I skidded to a halt and missed them. The boys were totally unprepared. Malc came piling into me, then spun to a stop in the middle of the crossing, facing the way he'd come. Peter, right behind him, careered past me on the other side and also slithered to a halt in the middle of the crossing. The women were trapped between them. They went mad. "She managed to bloody well stop, so why the bloody 'ell couldn't you?" they yelled, waving their umbrellas threateningly at the boys. I felt dreadful. I hadn't had time to warn them. The boys were visibly shocked by this outburst of abuse, but at least none of us was hurt – the panniers had probably protected us.

It was just after this episode that Peter realised his purse was missing with all his holiday money in it. Oh boy! He must have left it in that pub at Downend. There was no way we would turn round and cycle back, so we carried on towards Temple Meads, looking for a police station. The police would surely help, especially when they saw the state we were in.

With great relief, we found one near to the railway station, locked the bikes outside and entered. Everyone behind the counter was very busy; rows of men and women banging away on typewriters. So we stood and waited – and waited, shaking uncontrollably from cold. The boys were now in a terrible state, with cramp in their legs. They sat down, lay down, stood up, lay down, sat up and didn't know what to do with their poor bodies. I was convinced that the police would take pity on us and run us out to that pub. How wrong I was.

When my turn came at last, I couldn't even tell them the name of the pub. The front line, on reception, consulted each other then turned to ask their colleagues behind. None of them had a clue what this pub might be called. Eventually they decided to ring directory enquiries. No luck there, either. Directory enquiries were so busy, even the police couldn't get through. I had a feeling they thought it was all rather trivial. There was one solution – I would have to cycle back myself. I felt so guilty anyway, for allowing the boys to get into such a state, that I was prepared to do anything to make amends.

So I left the boys in the police station to wait for me. At least they were out of the snow and would surely be given a nice hot cup of tea – if anyone behind that counter had an ounce of compassion. It was now rush hour. I had five miles to cycle out into the blizzard and five miles back. I gritted my teeth and went for it. At least I could remember the route in reverse.

At long last I reached the pub, but it was all locked up. I walked around it, looking for another way in. Then, peering closely into the dirty window I could see right through to another indoor window where a man was washing up.

I banged on the door and rapped on the glass and eventually attracted his attention. But it was not good news. He hadn't found any purse left on the table or indeed, anywhere. Had anybody else found it, perhaps? I'd never know. All I knew was that I couldn't afford to subsidise Peter, especially with the added cost of the train fares. I felt very depressed.

As I left the pub and rolled off the kerb, my front wheel rode over what looked like a shoe-sole flattened onto the tarmac. Or was it? "Hang on a minute," I thought, and between the traffic,

I went back to inspect it. I peeled the leather off the road and found, to my jubilation, that this was indeed Peter's purse. Inside were twenty-seven very compressed pound notes. A miracle, it seemed. I rode back with renewed energy – even the snow was easing now.

So as night fell, the nightmare came to an end. We caught a train to Taunton and then, in the dark, negotiated eight miles of country lanes to find Ruttersleigh Farm. I knew it was somewhere at the bottom of a long track, hidden by hills. Even in daylight it was not visible from the road, so we hoped our lamplight would pick up the farm sign.

At last! We cycled through the open gateway and bumped all the way to the bottom. As we turned the corner, the cheery lights from the farm windows lit up the yard. The dog barked and the back door was flung open. What a warm welcome! What a cosy farmhouse and hot food awaited us! What utter relief all round!

* * *

The following morning, after a humungous fried breakfast and fond farewells, we set off on the next leg of our journey. The clouds were ominously low and heavy as we progressed westwards towards South Molton. But mercifully it didn't rain or snow. Exmoor National Park in Somerset was somewhere nearby on our right, while we were in Devon, following the lower contours of the park.

From South Molton we turned north towards our destination, having found the day's cycling quite boring. Now, as the road inclined past some huge quarries, we perked up and pressed harder on the pedals. We were nearly there. Our friends were looking out for us as we arrived in the unexpectedly modern village of Bratton Fleming. Malc reacquainted himself with their two teenage sons, who were well impressed with the boys' achievements.

The next morning, while the four boys were contentedly chilling out, I was whisked away on an Easter Sunday tour of the surrounding area, including the fascinating Braunton Burrows and Bideford. Our holiday had improved each day, both pleasure-wise and weather-wise. By the time we returned on Easter Monday, climbing and plunging through Challacombe and on across Exmoor, we were wearing sleeveless T-shirts and carrying a little more wisdom in our heads.

Spanish Hat Trick

March 1997

They both look pleased with themselves

At last! Frank and I are finally leaving the comfort of Finca la Mota, the hotel in southern Spain where we've been staying. Waving 'Cheerio' to the owner, Arun, we pedal off down the track towards the main road. We're beginning our unplanned cycle tour in Andalucia.

At the junction we turn right; westwards. 'Go West Young Man' is a phrase that comes to mind, and although being neither male nor young, I feel like a pioneer. Anyway, to cycle eastwards would only bring us back to

Malaga and mayhem. Although this is a main route through the mountains, there's not much traffic at all.

Arun has been our host and chef at this lovely inn since we arrived four days ago, tempting us with his succulent dishes. Now we must face the music and let the fates take care of us. We are heading into uncharted waters – or in our case, mountains – and it's only our ignorance and inexperience that has been holding us back. The Spanish people we have encountered so far have been friendly and helpful, and in Spain, cyclists are revered on the highways, the drivers always giving them plenty of space. Not that we plan to cycle through volumes of traffic. No! The only plan we have is to avoid big cities and find quiet mountain routes.

Although it's early March, the temperatures have reached 36 degrees most afternoons. We haven't yet acclimatised to all this heat. If we could get our act together and set off early in the morning, as we do on planned cycle club tours, the temperature would be just perfect. But left to our own devices, we don't have that sort of discipline. After all, we *are* on holiday. So we don't set an alarm clock to get us up at the crack of dawn, and we don't rush down to breakfast; just the opposite, in fact. We amble down, eat a leisurely breakfast and chat to anyone who can understand us. Then, inevitably, Frank will look at his watch and say, "Blimey, do you know what time it is?" and we start to rush around.

Today, I'm wearing a long-sleeved cotton top to protect my arms from the sun. My cycle helmet is probably doing the same thing for my head, although, conversely, back in England I usually find it far too hot, especially after cycling up hills. Frank doesn't wear a helmet. He hates hats and likes to feel the wind in his hair. But as we pedal along, he admits that his head is beginning to burn.

"You really ought to wear a hat, Frank," I nag. "You might end up with sunstroke. You'll probably collapse somewhere up a mountain," I add, just to make him feel guilty, "then I'll have to go searching for help."

"Oh I suppose I'd better buy one then," he grumbles, "Else I'll never hear the last of it."

"You could get one like mine, with a peak to shade your eyes," I suggest. I am wearing a red Perspex peak attached to an elasticated band under my helmet. It's a sort of seasidey 'kiss-me-quick' type of thing but it helps a bit.

"I wouldn't be seen dead in a daft thing like that," he sneers.

"Well, whatever!" I think to myself, and we pedal on.

Soon we are swooping downhill to a town called Coin, pronounced Coe-in. "Better go and have a look for a hat then," he says. "Mustn't be long though, or we'll never get anywhere." At the bottom of the hill we turn left for the town centre, not even noticing the surrounding buildings as we cruise in, only interested in buying a hat.

We arrive in a nondescript shopping street and walk up and down, looking for the right kind of shop. Seeing our perplexed faces, an elderly man comes across the road, his eyebrows raised and hands upturned, to enquire what it is we are searching for. Frank pats himself on the head, indicating that it's a hat he's after. "Ah!" smiles the man and motions us to follow. In single file, we squeeze down narrow alleyways, trying to avoid people and obstacles with our laden bikes. Soon he brings us triumphantly to the place we are looking for – a back-street barber's shop!

"No," chuckles Frank, as I burst out laughing. The poor man looks puzzled. Frank makes a better job of mimicking a hat and the old man says, "Ah!" nodding his head vigorously. We follow him all the way through the alleyways back to the shops.

Soon we are outside a sports shop with a huge glass window almost to the ground, the likes of which, in England, would probably get kicked in on a Friday night. Frank enters to buy his hat, the one he doesn't really want to wear, while I stay outside with the bikes and the elderly man hovers. Frank is in there for ages but eventually reappears, wearing his new purchase; a white-as-white, high-crowned cap with a big wide peak. It looks awful – the sort of cap that Americans wear to play golf. I don't tell him how stupid it looks on him, though. At least he's got a hat to protect his head. The elderly man grins broadly and nods at Frank, admiring this lovely hat. He motions me to take a photo of them both. They look really happy together – the one because he has done the right thing and bought a hat, and the other because he has successfully led us to the right place.

But Frank is hovering now. He's picked up my vibes and is now regarding his reflection in the shop window. His smile fades to a frown. "It doesn't look right, does it? Do you think they'll take it back?"

The elderly man has now picked up on Frank's vibes, and seems deep in thought. "Un momento," he says and with that, turns and toddles off down the street towards the alleyways. We dither outside the shop, wondering what he's up to and if he'll be coming back any time soon. We're itching to get going. Ah!

Here he comes, looking slightly sheepish. What's he got in his hand?

He steps onto the pavement and proffers a rather worn-looking navy blue cap. Frank tries it on. It suits him perfectly. It's made from a lightweight mesh material and has a small navy blue peak. Frank admires his reflection in the shop window. That's more like it!

Well, what now? He turns round and offers his new white cap to the helpful old man, who is thrilled to bits. Everyone's a winner! But the man is gone before Frank changes his mind, so I don't get to take another photo of them in their 'swapped-hat' jubilation.

A Trip to Jerusalem

July 2013

Frank hands me up the folding bikes, one at a time, then shuts the heavy hatch cover on the deck of the boat. On his narrowboat tug we have cruised up the River Soar to its junction with the River Trent and have just moored against the opposite wall at Trent Lock. Across the vast expanse of river, where the Trent flows in a huge curve from the west, there's a sailing club. In the light breeze, yachts are skimming to and fro, through the sparkling water. Beyond them, back down the River Soar, we can see the prominent chimneys of Ratcliffe Power Station smoking out their vapour.

I have promised to take Frank to the oldest pub in England, Ye Olde Trip to Jerusalem in Nottingham. This is the city where I spent four years at art college in the 60s and I want to show him around. It's early afternoon and a warm sunny day, so what better time than now to make this short trip. The whole 10 miles distance can be cycled on riverside and canal-side tracks. Perfect! No great exertion but a nice bit of gentle exercise.

It takes a little while to unfold the bikes and pump up the tyres. Then, with my purse, mobile phone, spare inner tube and tissues squashed into my little handlebar bag, our water bottles filled from the nearby water tap, our lightweight cycling jackets pinned under the straps of our pannier racks and Frank's toolkit strapped to his seat post, I think we're ready for all eventualities. Frank locks up the boat and I have to lean down to take the keys from him, because this boat sits low in the water. We're not very tall, so it's hard for us to climb out onto the wall. I've had to clamber up on my knees.

At last we're ready, and looking forward to our first cycling jaunt for over a week. The path is wide and smooth and with our eight gears we're soon whizzing along with ease. Although I'm taking Frank to this old pub, I'm leading from the back – rather like a dog-owner taking its dog for a walk.

As the river turns south, we carry straight on, alongside a cutting of about a mile in length. This is called the Cranfleet Canal, and it conveniently cuts out a bend in the river. As we approach the final lock, which takes the canal out into the river again, a huge lake comes into view on our left. At this point we stop, as we've just spotted a café next to the lock.

Sitting outside on wooden decking, we lick our ice creams and marvel at the huge width of the mighty Trent. There's a map on a board nearby, showing that the lake behind us is part of the

Attenborough Nature Park, a huge expanse of lakes probably formed from gravel extraction, just like the Cotswold Water Park, not far from my home.

I'm wearing sunglasses and have my red peaked cap pulled well down over my eyes, but not to shade them – no. I am self-consciously trying to conceal a huge black eye, the result of a nasty boating accident. I'm feeling extremely lucky to be out here cycling, today. Things might have been very different. This is what happened...

* * *

Last Saturday we had set off really early from our mooring, just below the famous Foxton Locks, to cruise up the Leicester line of the Grand Union Canal. After some miles, we'd come to our first lock of the day. As I was the crew member that preferred opening the locks rather than driving the boat into them, I was put down on the bank to carry out my duties – to open up the top gate-paddles to fill the lock with water. Frank drove the boat back out into the middle of the canal, in preference to tying up at the bank, because the boat frequently goes aground near the banks, especially after a period of dry weather, when the water levels are low.

I was about to try out the new long-handled windlass that Frank had recently acquired for me. It should give me more leverage with its extra length, making my job easier. I attached the lever, which is rather like the starting handle of an old car, and wound up the paddle with my right hand. I couldn't be sure if this long handle had made my job any easier, as all paddle mechanisms vary so much. But as the lock slowly filled with water I was firmly hanging onto the handle, for the simple reason that I couldn't remember if I'd put the safety catch onto the cog, or not. Unusually, the paddle gear on this lock was hidden from view behind the stout post of the lock gate, instead of being in the front. I would have to reach behind, to find out.

Then SMACK! In that moment of changing hands, the handle whipped back and whacked the side of my face. Stunned is the only word to describe how I felt. It was not pain, just a stunning numbness, and as my hand went up to cover the wound, all I could think was, 'Blimey – you could die in a split second.'

Frank was looking towards me when he saw my hand shoot up to my face. Blood was pouring off my elbow and he felt frightened for me, thinking I might keel over and fall into the lock and drown. As he was contemplating jumping off the boat to save me from this awful fate, I began heaving the gate open. He was dumbfounded, but all the same, he drove the boat in and tied it quickly to the side before helping me climb aboard. We'd need some padding quickly, to stop the bleeding which was now finding its way warmly down my neck. What a quandary we were in! And we seemed to be miles from anywhere.

(Paradoxically, only a week before this, while attending a boat rally at Stoke Bruerne on the Grand Union Canal, we'd been to a first-aid class for boaters, where the instructor's opening words were: "You've just moored up for the night in a lovely secluded spot when your partner has a sudden heart attack. Where are you?")

Well, where were WE, and what were WE going to do? There wasn't a house in sight. One thing was certain; we couldn't leave the boat in the lock.

While I pressed a wad of dressing onto my cheekbone, Frank climbed out to close the top lock gate. The paddle had already spun itself shut. He then began winding up the paddles on the bottom gate to empty the lock. He'd need to jump back on board before the boat sank too low and I would need to get out to perform one more task before we could seek help – which was to open the bottom gate as soon as the water level was low enough.

In my dazed state, I managed to heave the gate open, hoping the thick pad on my cheek would stay stuck while I let go of it. I felt rather light-headed now, so I sat on the verge while Frank tied up the boat and shut the bottom gate. Still all I could feel was numbness and not pain.

Frank had a quick look at the map. If we were to walk a little further down the canal, there was a road beyond the next lock, with a house on the other side of the bridge. We could try to get help there. "Are you going to be able to do that?" asked Frank apprehensively. But I was determined that I would. So taking his arm, we walked gently down to the next lock and crossed the bridge. A wide driveway led down to what seemed like a farmhouse, where a wide front door stood wide open. In the hallway a frantic mother was trying to rally her children together, calling to them up the stairs to hurry up or they'd be too late. I'm sure the last thing she needed was to see an injured person on her doorstep, seeking help. In a fluster, she scribbled down a taxi number for us on a scrap of paper, slammed the door shut and rushed her kids to the car. Well! No room at that inn! What now?

The only option we could decide on was to get back to Foxton locks and civilisation. That would mean turning the boat around.

But to do that, we would have to go through several more locks to reach a turning point. It was not on the cards. Perhaps then, if we walked back up the towpath, we would reach a house, somewhere. Leaning on Frank's arm, we retraced our steps. When the boat came into view, we could see it was listing at an angle. The water level must have dropped. We couldn't possibly leave it like that; things would start falling off the shelves and then who knows what other damage might happen?

Frank sat me down gently against the hedge. All this activity was becoming too much for me. His plan was to open all the paddles on both gates to let some water through. Then when the boat refloated, he could push it further from the bank, into deeper water. Until this was done we couldn't think of leaving it, for we had no idea when we'd get back. It was one delay after another.

As the water began gushing through the bottom gate, a narrowboat came chugging up towards us. The couple on board looked really annoyed. What did this bloke on the locks think he was doing, letting all this water out? Then they saw me, and the blood. They pulled into the bank to see what had happened. And what angels they turned out to be; a couple from America, taking their holidays on our canals. They were heading for Foxton and offered to take us there, where we could summon a taxi. I was helped down into the saloon and seated comfortably on a settee while Frank stayed out, chatting to the skipper, periodically peeping in to see how I was doing. I think he expected me to collapse at some stage.

During the hour it took us to reach our destination, which included going through a tunnel, I sat numbly while the lady spoke in quiet tones as she made us all a cup of coffee. In her soft, gentle and soothing accent she told me about where she lived in America and what the countryside was like. She had a very calming effect on me but I can't remember a thing she told me, nor even her name. All I know is that a nicer couple couldn't have come to our rescue. We were extremely lucky.

Alighting at Foxton junction, we thanked them both profusely as we waved farewell. Frank phoned the taxi and was told it would be there in 25 minutes, so there was no option but to sit in the comfort of the Foxton Locks Inn, where Frank had time for a swift half while keeping an eye out for our taxi. I didn't want anything except confirmation that I was compos mentis. At least my wound had stopped bleeding.

At last the taxi arrived and conveyed us to a hospital on the outskirts of Market Harborough. We gave the driver a tip; we were so relieved to have finally reached medical help. But as he drove off, we realised this was not a normal hospital at all; it could only be accessed by pressing numbers on a keypad. What a stupid taxi driver. He didn't even know where his own hospital was. Frank pressed the numbers for Reception several times but nobody would let us in. Then Frank tried to trick them by ringing one of the wards instead, and a sister came down and opened the door to us. However, all we could do was sit ourselves in the sumptuous armchairs in Reception while Frank summoned another taxi. I reflected that it was a jolly good job I hadn't been an emergency!

The same taxi driver arrived, not seeming to be the slightest bit abashed for making such a grave mistake. Now, a fairly short ride into town brought us to the 'Cottage Hospital' and another taxi fare. But at least we had arrived.

We were greeted by a warm and friendly receptionist and asked to wait in a small room, which looked a bit like an old school cloakroom with its coat hooks removed. In fact the whole building seemed like an old Victorian school. The two other people waiting before me were soon dealt with and in no time at all I was summoned through to a treatment room.

Two middle-aged nurses greeted me. They were kindness itself – so gentle but so thorough, having only basic equipment at their disposal. In my misfortune, they thought, I had been very lucky not to have been blinded in one eye or killed with a blow to the temple – just a little over half an inch either way could have been disastrous.

There was no X-ray machine here. They could only press my cheekbone to decide that it wasn't broken. Next they checked my eyesight, which they considered to be unaffected. Now what to do with my gash? They were not qualified or able to do cosmetic stitching, they told me. For that, I would have to go to Leicester infirmary. But as it was a straight slit, they offered to glue it. I could choose. So I chose glue because I trusted them. Even though they hadn't done it before, I knew they'd give it their best and I could see that they worked well as a team. They read the instructions carefully, then, while one held the split together, the other applied the glue. We all kept perfectly still to allow it to set. Then, bingo, I was fixed. I was so chuffed and so grateful to them.

After that saga we summoned a taxi to take us to the bridge next to the farmhouse we'd first called at. From there, we would only have a short distance to walk up the towpath. Frank was amazed at my resilience and my offer to 'do' the remaining four locks in the flight, so that we could moor up safely for the night and relax. Then I could properly rest and recover.

* * *

So that is why I'm very happy to be here today. We crunch the last of our ice cream cones, then set off for Nottingham once more. Now we're cycling on finely gritted tracks, passing lakes and hedgerows, and copses of young trees. To me, this development looks fairly recent but seems well used. On one lake we see windsurfers tacking up and down, some overbalancing and crashing into the water. In the next lake, there's a party of excited young canoeists laughing and splashing about, while further on, almost hidden in the reeds, is a line of solemn fisherman staring silently at their floats. Their silence is interrupted by the buzz of a motorboat at full speed, pulling a water-skier up the river. It's like the 'Riviera of Nottingham' here!

At every information board we stop to check where we are, because the track keeps veering away from the riverside. Then after several miles of the nature park we reach habitation, where the track becomes a street and we draw alongside a canal once more. We are in the Beeston suburb of Nottingham now, famous for Boots, the chemist chain. My cousin used to work here in the laboratories, when we were in our late teens. We would travel together on the train from Grantham, she to work and me to college.

Now we cross over a little humpback bridge and for the

remainder of our journey, the canal is on our left, with all views of the mighty river lost from sight. Every now and then, a road bridge passes overhead. We're not quite sure where to exit the canal path, but we want to make sure we're well into the city.

A busy road looms ahead; we must be in the city proper by now. So we cycle up a ramp to confront the traffic at the top. Oh, this is Carrington Street! Not that I came here often, but as I was born a Carrington I always felt a little tinge of importance when walking along it, in spite of not knowing who it was named after.

We don't relish cycling in strange cities, so we push the bikes over a crossing, passing Bunneys' Bike shop on the other side. It looks like a really good shop. We'll have a look round it while we're here. Cyclists can always sniff out a proper cycle shop, which usually has at least one seasoned mechanic to hand who knows the workings of genuine, hand-built touring bikes, like the ones we have locked away back home. If we had the room to store them on the boat, we would be riding them now in preference to folders. Anyway, we nose around for a while, admiring this and that, but all we come out with is a pair of brake-blocks for my folder.

There are signposts to help us find the city centre and that's where I'm taking Frank first, to show him the magnificent Council House, remembering it as being a huge and impressive building, facing a large square. Although it was very familiar to me then, I am impressed all over again, seeing this lovely neo-classical building, standing prominently in the city centre with its dome rising high to dominate the skyline. Still recumbent, on either side of the entrance, are the two mean-faced stone lions that frightened me as a child. But this building could almost be mistaken for a cathedral looking out over a continental piazza, for the whole area has a different buzz about it now. We sit on one of the many benches, watching children splashing about in the modern-looking water feature at the far end of the square. There was never this recreational feel about the place before.

Time is getting on. Frank wants to find a Millets or Blacks store to look for a bag with a strap, to carry his camera across his shoulders, so we head up the streets on the other side of the square – and surprise, surprise; they've all been pedestrianised. No more queues of vehicles waiting at traffic lights, chucking out exhaust fumes. Gone is all that grime. I can't believe the wonderful transformation. Nottingham has done itself proud.

Well, it's about time we looked for that pub. We're getting a bit thirsty now and the main reason we came here was to find Ye Olde Trip to Jerusalem. We head back the other way, in the direction of Nottingham Castle. I know it's somewhere near there. We cross a couple of minor roads, mount a flight of steps and then negotiate ourselves over a dual carriageway called Maid Marian Way. Now we just need to go down Castle Road, past the bronze, life-sized statue of Robin Hood and we should be there.

As the road heads downhill, so the cliffs on which the castle stands get higher. We're near the bottom of the hill now. I know it's somewhere nearby. Ah, here it is! We've rounded the corner to see it tucked in against the pink cliff-face below the castle, as it has stood since the 12th Century, when crusaders frequented it, allegedly. Frank is impressed, I can tell. We take a few photos, then get someone to take a photo of us in front of it – me with my sunglasses on and my peaked cap pulled well down!

The place is buzzing. Apart from all the tourists, I expect many of these folk have dropped by after finishing work early on this Friday afternoon. And it's a glorious afternoon, after all. But I don't remember ever seeing these tables and chairs outside before. I remember the pub as being almost on the street. It all looks quite unfamiliar to me now. The council must have purchased buildings on the opposite side to create this fabulous space. But isn't it time we went in for a drink? We've waited long enough.

No wonder so many people are sitting outside, because there's not a lot of room in here. We make our way round to the room with the bar and find it's heaving. The three bartenders are rushing round to keep up with demand like they haven't a moment to breathe. They have little space to manoeuvre, so have to keep their elbows well in, to avoid knocking drinks out of each other's hands. We don't recognise any of these beers; we'll have to sample some before we make a choice. 'That'll hold up the queue a bit', I think to myself – 'but hey, so what? We're on holiday aren't we?'

Eventually we get served, and as we've just noticed a staircase, we take our drinks upstairs, hoping to find some spare seats. And, unbelievably, there's hardly a soul up here. We can have the place almost to ourselves. We settle at a table in the first room but don't stay seated for long. There's so much to look at, so much to read about – a veritable museum.

Some rooms of this inn, we learn, are cut into the soft rock of the cliff against which it is built, and on which stands the castle. We read about a secret passageway leading from here to the castle, where rumour has it that Queen Isabella, wife of

Edward II, used to meet her lover, Roger Mortimer. We can't see any secret door. They must have concealed the entrance behind some furniture. Then we learn that there's a network of caves beneath the inn, while in the rocky roof of the room next door is a large hole going right up into the castle. We rush to have a look – it's a great funnel-shaped hole, big enough for two Santas to descend together. There are also stories about the ghosts that supposedly haunt this place. I don't think I'd dare sleep here, even if you paid me. It has such a palpable creepy presence of its past.

We've finished our drinks already and there's still more to look at. While Frank goes down to get us another drink, I read about Daniel Lambert, the fattest man in England. I don't know why his picture is here, mounted on the wall, because he was a Leicester man. At the time of his death he weighed over 52 stones. I wonder if this record has been surpassed in these days of overeating.

Well, I think we've read about everything there is to read up here. It's time we headed back to the boat. I've bought some nice Lincolnshire sausages to cook for supper. We drink up and go downstairs. I think this trip has been well worth it. We've had a lovely afternoon.

It's slightly cooler outside now but still OK for cycling in T-shirts. We're soon whizzing along the canalside towards Beeston, thinking more about sausage and mash I think than anything. I'm trying to keep up with Frank. I don't want him to think I'm not as fit as he is. We reach the humpback bridge and he's up and over it in no time, and has turned left into the canalside street. I'm not far behind, just coming over this cobbled bridge, ready to swoop round behind him.

Then it happens – as I turn left, the front wheel spins right round on gravel and jams, throwing me over the handlebars. CRUMP! I land on my face and the backs of my hands. I lie still for a moment or two, not wanting to move. Frank has come back and a car has stopped right by me. I see legs getting out of the car and a lady comes over to me. Apparently she's a trainee doctor. That's lucky. But I still lie there for a while, wondering if my teeth are OK. There's a lot of skin in my mouth. I really don't feel like getting up – I'm sort of in denial and don't want to know. But the rest of my body seems all right. I'm just so cross with myself for having another accident.

But I've got to move aside, there are more cars wanting to come over this bridge. Goodness knows why there's this sudden rush of traffic. I sit on the grass at the side of the narrow road – a sorry sight, I suppose, with my face and hands embedded in grit and the back of my right hand now black and swollen – and the shiner of a black eye as an added extra. The doctor calls for an ambulance, then tells us about the rugby tournament that is about to take place this weekend at Beeston Rugby Club, just half a mile back up the track. She returns to her car as she's blocking the way, leaving me in Frank's tender care. She needs to put up her tent; presumably she arrived early to get a good pitch.

We wait and wait, but no ambulance arrives, even though we keep hearing one getting louder then fading into the distance again. Then a nice young man called Chris comes down from the club and suggests we go back to the clubhouse to wait for the ambulance there. He gets me a lift in one of the cars while he and Frank follow on behind, bringing the bikes. He takes us inside the building and sits us at the back of a dining area. The weekend action hasn't started here yet, but all the caterers are rushing about. One of them, feeling sorry me, offers to make a nice cup of tea. The thought sounds lovely, but there's no way I can drink it – my mouth is raw; apart from all the grit, I've put my bottom teeth through my top lip. She puts a pint-sized plastic mug of steaming hot tea in front of me, but even if I had been able to drink it, I couldn't have lifted it off the table. But her intentions are good.

Frank arranges with Chris to keep the bikes locked there safely overnight, and Chris has offered to bring them to our boat in his car tomorrow. Strangers can be so kind. Now I need the loo. I have to go and ask for a key first. Through the door is a row of sinks with mirrors all along the wall. I determinedly avoid looking into them. I don't want to see myself like this. Later I'll wish I'd cleaned myself up, but how am I to know that it would have been a wise thing to do?

We've been here too long. Chris is now offering to take us to the hospital in his car. But as we leave the building, we see two ambulance men coming up the track with packs on their backs. We intercept them. They are trying to find me. They turn and make their way back to the ambulance, which they've parked on the other side of the bridge, while Chris drives Frank and me down to them. Another drawn-out saga this is proving to be and I reflect, once more, that it's a good job I'm not an emergency, although, I have to say, I'm feeling really sorry for myself.

These two ambulance men take us on board. They are in no hurry to dash me to the hospital – what's the point after all this time? They are a lovely pair of chaps though, and one of them does all the necessary observations. They tell us why they've had such difficulty in finding us – they are a crew from Northampton and don't know their way around these parts. Well, if I *had* been an emergency, I reflect yet again, I'd probably be dead by now.

When all checks have been thoroughly done to me, we set off for the hospital. The poor driver even has difficulty finding this! On arrival, I'm wheeled inside on a trolley and left in a corridor, next to a drunk who has possibly broken his wrist in a fall. I try to ignore him, because he hasn't got anything coherent to say, and reeks of alcohol.

The wait is probably not as long as it seems, although it seems interminable with this bloke trying to engage with me. I don't know where Frank has been told to wait, but I haven't seen him since I left the ambulance. Now I'm wheeled into a curtained cubicle; about the second down in the long row, on one side of a large room. A nurse comes in and makes all the observations again that the ambulance man did so thoroughly only a while ago. Her name is Lorraine. I don't like her manner. She takes my blood pressure like she's trying to make my arm drop off and my poor hand feels as if it will burst open. Why couldn't she have done it on the less injured side?

In the cubicle next door, a woman screams. She's in agony. I listen to the conversation, in between answering questions for Lorraine. This woman has severed her Achilles tendon, poor thing. Now Lorraine wants me to get up and follow her down to the waiting room. Hang on, Lorraine, I'm thinking. I can't jump off just like that; I'm nearly sixty-nine. I've got to do it gently. In fact I'd quite like to lie here until the doctor sees me. It's much more comfortable than sitting in a chair. She waits impatiently but as soon as both my feet are on the floor, she's off, marching past all the cubicles and down into the busy waiting area. I just can't keep up with her. I've gone all wobbly.

Frank is waiting for me by the desk at the back of the waiting room. He's not in a good mood now and is talking of putting me on a train home. I'm too much of an accident risk. He doesn't know what I'll do next. I've witnessed people in casualty reacting crossly in the face of injury, through worry, but I suspect he must also be hungry. I know that I am – ravenous, in fact. We find somewhere to sit; somewhere near the back row, away from a rowdy family of about eight who are accompanying one patient. The kids are noisy, the women coarse. We are fed up with them already, and with these hard plastic chairs we must sit on.

The lady with the severed tendon arrives on a trolley and is helped onto the chair directly in front of me, at the end of a row. I feel furious that they are sitting her on a chair. She's in a terrible state and keeps being sick into a cardboard bowl. At least she's got her husband by her side to keep an eye on her.

What with the rowdy family, the groaning woman, me supporting my black and swollen hand and suffering my sore grit-embedded mouth and chin, plus Frank moaning away next to me, I've just about had enough. How long are we going to be stuck here? Then I see a café sign pointing upstairs and suggest that Frank goes and gets himself a meal before they close at 9 pm. That will take him away for a while, so that he doesn't have to keep looking at the state I'm in, and I don't have to keep listening to his complaints. I won't be cooking sausages tonight, anyway!

We all wait and wait. I count ten doors to ten doctors' rooms and although the staff keep coming and going in and out of them, there doesn't seem to be much processing of patients. It's hard to work out the ranks of the staff. When I started my brief nursing career, after leaving school, you could tell the status of the staff by their uniforms. Now it's a mish-mash of clothing and I can't tell who's who. But every time any one of them comes out of a door and walks past, I look pleadingly up into their eyes. However, not one of them makes eye contact. It must be a rule. I just want someone to take pity on me.

The husband of the lady in front has now gone off somewhere and she's left to fend for herself. As I observe her, she starts collapsing in her chair. She'll be on the floor any minute, I think. Just in time, I jump up and push my body against hers, to stop her from falling sideways onto the ground. I stand there for as long as it takes. Her husband returns, then runs to get help and soon a trolley is brought down for her to lie on. And not one of them – neither the husband nor any of the staff, notices what I have done to help her. I'm invisible.

At long last I am summoned to see a doctor on the other side of the room. There are more questions to answer and more observations to be made. He's also concerned about the blow to my cheek. He fills in X-ray forms and sends me on my way. The lady on the desk puts me in the direction of the X-ray department. It's through a labyrinth of empty corridors. What if I were to collapse on my way to X-ray? How long might it be before someone noticed me?

Anyway, I make it there in one piece although I feel very lonely. At least they are friendly in here. As well as the X-rays to my face and hands, the doctor has authorised for me to have a whole head scan, just to make sure things are OK from my last accident. I appreciate that.

When I arrive back at the waiting room, Frank has returned in a slightly better mood. All we can do now is wait, wait, wait. Time ticks by – ten o'clock, eleven o'clock – well it *is* Friday night in a big city, I couldn't have timed this better. Then Lorraine summons me into a room at the side. She's going to clean me up. A bit late for that, I'm thinking, it's all caked dry. In her usual very brisk manner, she opens up a pack with a single sterile gauze square in it and attacks my face. I'd like to scream at her as she roughly rubs backwards and forwards over the grit and raw skin on my lips. With the same piece of now dirty gauze she does my nose and chin and then the backs of my hands. She might as well have used a floor cloth, I think; there wasn't much point in using anything sterile. I'm feeling quite faint now. I'm so drained and hungry.

Back I go to my seat, where Frank is chomping at the bit with all this not knowing what the hold-up is. He keeps going to the desk to ask if they can estimate how much longer we will need to wait. Then Lorraine rushes by and drops a pack of sandwiches onto my lap as she passes. I must have told her how hungry I was. Oh, bless you Lorraine. All is forgiven. You must be having an awful night as well. But I don't know yet how I'm going to eat them.

It's after midnight when the doctor sees me again. It's good news. Nothing is broken. We can go. Where though? We are directed to a door at the front of the waiting room, which leads into a draughty covered area where we are left to stand and shiver in the dark. We didn't bring our little cycle jackets with us and it's pretty cool out here. But I see that Frank is carrying my handlebar bag. I hadn't noticed until now. 'Good on yer Frank,' I think. 'The boat keys are in that bag.'

There are 'taxi' posters all over the walls and Frank rings one of the numbers. Taxis keep pulling into the kerb to pick up waiting ex-casualties – some of them drunk. How will we know which is our taxi? I suppose we just have to work out whose turn is next. Well, after trembling in the draught for far too long, it's seemingly our turn now, and we climb into the most recently arrived taxi.

"Where you wan go?" asks the Chinese taxi driver. Blimey, where DO we want to go? We came here along bike tracks, now we're going back by roads. But still, the taxi driver is sure to know. "To Trent Lock. It's not far from Long Eaton." "Tren Loh? Where tha?" Oh God! Doesn't he know? Well he knows the direction of Long Eaton, so he heads out that way.

After a few miles he pulls into a petrol station to ask. But it's gone 1 am and the place is all shut up. There's a car parked suspiciously in the dark on the forecourt, with four Indians inside. He asks them if they know Trent Lock but, no, they don't. We carry on to Long Eaton where he drives round and round the streets until he finds someone to ask. Luckily, they have a vague idea – you just have to look for a sign to the Trent Lock Inn, which is down a long lane off the main road. Hopefully our boat will be moored somewhere down there, although we don't know anything about the area, except that we are moored by the side of the river.

Well, we go back to the main road and eventually find the sign to the inn. Now we're bumping down a long track in the dark for a mile or so but at last we reach the Trent Lock Inn, which stands in eerie silence in the dark. The taxi stops here, as the road ends. We don't know in which direction our boat might be and there is very little light to see the way. We can make out a walkway over a lock and a bit further on there's a bridge. Will our boat be this side of that bridge or the other? How on earth are we supposed to know?

Now the taxi driver shows his true colours. He may not be able to speak the language very well, and he might not know all the obscure places surrounding Nottingham, but he has a big heart. He says he will wait here while we go to look for our boat and when we find it, we can come back and pay him. How trusting is that? So we set off, deciding to cross the bridge first, to look on the left of the inn. And it's the right choice. Just a hundred yards along the wall sits our boat, patiently waiting for us, not very far at all from the inn. We go back and pay the £20 fare and thank him warmly. At least he's got another destination to his repertoire. We walk back and clamber clumsily aboard, trying hard not to wake our neighbours. The water level has dropped a bit and the boat is even further down the wall. At long last we're home.

* * *

After this second protracted episode, it's not all doom and gloom. The following morning, as promised, Chris kindly brings our bikes from Beeston Rugby Club to Trent Lock and we look out for him. Frank offers him money for his troubles but he won't take a penny.

Apart from a damaged mudguard my bike seems unharmed. Meanwhile I have remembered that my cousin Jan lives not far from here, at Wollaton. So after ringing around to find her number, I give her a call and invite her and husband Rob over, to visit us. After all, we'll be staying here for longer than the statutory two days, so it will be good to socialise a bit. I'm glad I haven't been sent home on the train!

Jan and Rob and their little dog arrive the next morning for coffee. I have forewarned them that I am not a pretty sight. Then they take us back to their house, together with a load of laundry. During the following two days, Jan repeats this laundry service for me and we also lunch with them in the Trent Lock Inn. I'm feeling better already.

Now, in spite of looking a sorry sight, I'm ready to resume my boating duties. So on the fifth day we set of westwards along the river. There's no rush to get home. This is still 'holiday' time.

A few days later, while working our way through Rocky Lock on the Staffs and Worcester Canal, who should pull up in the boat behind but the first-aid instructor from Stoke Bruerne! I feel quite embarrassed that he's seeing me like this and only briefly explain away my injuries. Luckily he is in the process of teaching new boaters how to work the locks, so we get through the lock with efficient speed and make our quick getaway.

This holiday has been extremely eventful. Not at all what Frank and I had bargained for. Every day I see the legacy of my windlass accident in the mirror, which reminds me that I must take more care. And I doubt I'll be making any more trips to Jerusalem in a hurry.

CHAPTER TWELVE

Off at a Tangent

March 1997

Carratraca welcome

Frank and I are still finding our feet, so to speak. We've been hanging around this hotel in Spain for two days now, not quite ready to strike out on our intended cycle tour.

Last autumn we answered an advert in a cycling magazine;

someone called Barry was offering accommodation for cyclists at a hotel called Finca la Mota in Andalucia, the southernmost region of Spain, mentioned earlier. Over the phone, Barry has told me about the hotel. It was built in the 17th century as a farmhouse and was later converted to an inn. Each spring teams of racing cyclists are invited there, to do their training. Now Barry was extending this welcome to touring cyclists. The offer included transportation between Malaga airport and the inn, which was located on an undulating plain west of Malaga.

We jumped at the idea. Fancy being collected from the airport and then taken back again! If we were to stay at the finca for just the first and last nights, we wouldn't have to negotiate ourselves in and out of Malaga. That would be a great relief. But it seemed a bit of a cheeky thing to do. Surely they'd want to make some money out of us.

A friend has lent us her Lonely Planet book and a map of Andalucia. Wherever we end up each day, we hope to refer to the book and find accommodation. With our Spanish phrase book at hand, we think we'll get by. Already we can count to ten, ask for a beer and also a coffee with milk. But now we're dithering. We've got cold feet. And because we're enjoying the hospitality of Finca la Mota so much, we're not ready to leave in a hurry.

Our early morning flight over the Pyrenees was superb; not a cloud in the sky. But when our bikes were brought through from the plane, mine was damaged – the front lamp bracket was bent right over. Frank was cross. He said it must have taken an almighty blow to bend such a thick piece of metal. We examined both bikes thoroughly for other signs of damage and luckily there were none. So while I held my bike, Frank tried to straighten the bracket with his adjustable spanner, cursing because it wasn't man enough for the job. After a lot of swearing and spanner slipping, he had to concede defeat.

When we finally pushed our bikes through to 'Arrivals', we saw our names on a placard that was being waved in the air. The tall man holding it looked thoroughly exasperated. As we approached, he lowered the placard, greatly relieved. He was middle-aged, good-looking and, we discovered, English. He introduced himself as Richard, shaking our hands warmly. He admitted that he'd been on the verge of giving up on us, thinking we must have missed our flight. Poor chap, I thought, his arms must be ready to drop off. After putting our bikes into the back of his ample car, he drove us to a cycle shop on the outskirts of Malaga. And while the bike was being fixed, Richard treated us to coffee in the café next door. Now we could relax and get acquainted.

We were delighted with the inn. It reminded us of a hacienda in a cowboy film but was devoid of visitors on that beautiful sunny morning. Arun, the owner, with time on his hands, tempted us with his cooking – a huge plate of spicy spare ribs with chips. We ate this, washed down with San Miguel, under the shade of a veranda at the back of the building. Arun was a jolly, rotund Spanish man whose wife was English, he told us. But we didn't get to meet her, for she was in England at the time. And we didn't see Richard again until the end of our holiday.

The sky was a deep clear blue and the temperature rising by the minute, even though it was only the beginning of March. Wonderful! What an amazing panorama; all around us we could see mountains on the horizon. Then from the front of the inn, looking southwards, there was a less distant, forested mountain, where a swathe of trees had been felled right through the middle to prevent the spread of forest fires. It left a wide stripe down the mountainside, which we used as a landmark on several occasions to get our bearings. We knew that just the other side of this mountain were all those touristy places on the coast: Marbella, Fuengirola, Torremolinos and Estepona, to name but a few. Living near Slad in Gloucestershire, where Laurie Lee grew up, I knew that these were the places he had walked through, as he described in his book *As I Walked Out One Midsummer Morning*. But back then, in the 30s, these had been small villages. Now they are built-up coastal resorts to which millions of people flock every year. We were determined to avoid them at all costs. All we wanted to see were the 'white' Andalucian villages and to cycle on quiet roads through the mountains.

Later, on that first afternoon, we took the bikes out for a trial run, to test the state of the roads, pedalling westwards along a main road. Seeing a signpost to Tolox and rather liking the sound of that name, we turned southwards towards it. From a distance, it seemed that the town had been formed by pouring masses of white blocks down the mountainside to settle in the crevices. But as we came nearer, these blocks transmuted into dazzling white buildings, forming tall narrow streets to keep out the sun.

We noticed that our cycle chains were dry, and having forgotten to bring oil with us, thought we'd try our luck with our language skills to buy some. 'Aceite' was not the easiest of words to say, for the natives to understand us. And in Andalucia, we had to remember that the 'Cs' are pronounced like S's and not

'Th's, as they are in most of the rest of Spain. 'Tolox' however, became a frequently spoken word when things went wrong.

Arun was surprised when we told him we'd been to Tolox. He didn't think we could have gone that far in the time it had taken us. What rubbish! Hadn't we stopped to buy cycle oil and then taken photos next to a giant cactus on the way back? He probably thought touring cyclists rode like snails. The surface of the roads was superb and we'd bowled along.

After showering, we went down for our evening meal. The wine was free, we read, so we poured over the wine list and chose a really good one. There were less than a dozen other people staying that night and not one of them a cyclist to whom we might have chatted. We were served by Juan, a tall and extremely charming young man, who always seemed to be at our table when we needed him, patiently explaining all the dishes on the menu. After dinner, we found our way to the back staircase leading to our bedroom, glancing in through the open bar door as we passed, attracted by the noise. It was full of local men standing at the bar, shouting excitedly to each other. We'd probably have felt quite uncomfortable amongst them. But our room was quiet and pleasantly cool. We slept like logs. Next morning, on our way down to breakfast, we were disgusted to see the state of the bar floor. It was inches deep in monkey nut shells. What a mess! Those men must have been munching all night long.

Without wasting time, as we so often did, we set off for a spin in a different direction this time – roughly north-eastwards. On the way, I accosted an old man on an ancient tractor to ask if we were on the correct road to Càrtama. It was difficult to make myself understood. The cycling, however, was very easy and the roads smooth and traffic free. We passed through Càrtema without lingering then turned northwards, towards the town of Alora. This town looked impressive from afar. It sprawls across three hills which rise up from the plain. There are the ruins of an ancient castle sitting on the top of one of them. I'd read that this castle, initially, had most likely been built by trading Phoenicians. Later, after their conquest, the Romans had restored it to their own liking. Then came the Visigoths, who further altered it, followed by the Moors, who extended it in their traditional ways. Such is the history of Andalucia.

When we'd puffed all the way up the winding road to the top, the town didn't seem quite so special, although there were marvellous views all around us. The only shop we could see was on the top corner of an incredibly steep, long street that petered out into the hillside below us. It occurred to me what a terrific sledge run this would make, if it ever snowed here in winter. But inside, the shop was disappointingly ordinary, so we just bought a bag of crisps each. We didn't feel like exploring the town. We were hot and tired and it was so spread out we wouldn't know where to begin. So we headed back downhill, diverting to Àlhaurin el Grande, through which Richard had driven us the previous morning. Here we stopped for a beer. Arun had taught us to ask for a 'caña' instead of a 'cerveza'. It was easier to say but was still a glass of beer. We sat out in the street in the heat of the afternoon, watching all the hustle and bustle of people and traffic, and the heat haze coming off the roads.

For the rest the afternoon, we chilled out at the inn. Arun cooked us a plate of chips each and we sat, sweating, under a canopy at the front of the inn, studying our map. We still didn't feel ready to let go of the safety net of Finca la Mota.

"How about a circular tour tomorrow?" Frank suggested. I thought that was a very good idea. We could be a bit more adventurous and still come back to a good meal and another free bottle of wine. The perfect ending to a sweltering day of cycling! We scrutinised the map. We knew our way to Alora now, and it wasn't hilly – until you reached the hills. So we looked for a route going through there. It was quite a detailed map, although not as good as the OS ones we used back home. Frank found a tiny road, west of Alora, which circled back almost to Càrtama. That would be just about the right distance for us, in this heat wave they seemed to be having.

At dinner that night, the omnipresent Juan brought us another good wine to try. What luxury this was. Free wine, eh? Everything else was on tab and we'd square up on the last day. On our way to bed, we passed that noisy bar again then enjoyed another cool night's sleep.

* * *

Now it's our third morning at Finca la Mota, and we're about to set off on our circular tour. We clean the dust and grit off the chains before re-oiling them. And with our map, indispensable Lonely Planet book and fresh water in our bottles, we say "Cheerio" to Arun. "See you later."

It's déjà-vu to Alora. We spin along the gently undulating road in the warm morning air. But by the time we've climbed that hill into the town we're stinking hot. It's hard to believe it's early

March. English temperatures won't reach this high in the height of summer. On the western outskirts of Alora, we stop for a break, eating the Kit-Kats we've just bought before they melt in our hands, enjoying the views on the other side of the three hills.

We slog onwards. The road is fairly flat and we amble at a steady pace, looking at the outlines of unknown mountains looming ever nearer. It is early afternoon now. So hot! When we come upon a roadside bar, we stop for a lager and sit in the shade. It can't be many more miles to that little road going back towards Càrtama. No rush! We sit for ages, discussing our future plans and having another lager. Lovely. So refreshing but probably not doing us any good. Eventually, we drag ourselves back to the bikes and set off, keeping a sharp look out for the return route. Where the devil is that road we're looking for?

Now small trees, vibrant with fresh new leaves, are growing up the banks on either side of the road. They're very pretty. The terrain is changing gradually; so is the gradient – it's definitely uphill now. I'm baking hot. Pushing harder on the pedals is making the palms of my hands so sweaty. They're sliding about on my handlebars. I wish I'd worn my cycle gloves. Sweat is pouring off my forehead. It's burning my eyes like crazy. I'm struggling to keep up with Frank, who stops to wait for me. He's suffering anyway, although he might be pretending he's not. The heat is unbearable. But we press onwards, believing that perhaps our map is inaccurate and we'll soon find that little road.

After ages of grinding uphill, we come to a very sharp bend where we can see right into the mountains. What a wonderful viewpoint. But where are we? We sling the bikes down and flop gratefully onto a flat grassy bank. Frank gets out the map and spreads it in front of us. "Now where exactly are we?" I ask. Tracing our route on the map, we estimate where it was that we stopped for a drink. According to the map, our little road should be not far from that bar. "Do you think the map is accurate, Frank? What are we going to do if we don't find that road?" We hadn't, until now, anticipated the possibility of not finding it at all.

Frank looks at his watch. "You know what, we can't go back now. There wouldn't be enough daylight left. I think we'd probably get lost, cycling after dark. And even if we made it, the inn might be all locked up by then". We give each other apprehensive glances and in spite of the heat, I shiver. There's a sinking feeling in my stomach. What are we going to do? There's nothing but the mountains and us.

We return to the map to see where this road will take us, if we are to carry on. It's a very squiggly line and hard to follow. But it's leading to a place called Carratraca, in the middle of nowhere. As the crow flies, it doesn't look many miles away, but with all the twists and turns it could be four times further, and uphill at that. When we look across a steep narrow valley to our right, we can see the road coming back towards us, higher up the mountainside. That's just one squiggle.

We get out the guidebook to read about Carratraca. "Well, it's a town," says Frank, "and there's a hostel on the main street. We should be OK. We'll just have to keep going. Are you up for it? Not that we've got any choice."

Off we go again – not eagerly; just doggedly, pushing, pushing on the pedals, to get to the next bend, then the next. We have barely a gulp of water left in our water bottles. But hey! The scenery is fantastically beautiful. We begin to feel privileged to be here; for the honour of having these mountains all to ourselves. It's still a grind but a grand experience, all the same.

Later, as the shadows get longer, we put on our cycle jackets. They are bright red with a broad yellow stripe down each sleeve, with red and yellow striped collar, cuffs and bottom band. These are the Stroud Cycling Club jackets. Now we must look like a couple of red blobs amongst the green scenery.

It's not uphill all the way, we find. Several times we descend into a valley to cross a mountain stream, then have to begin climbing all over again. Sometimes the sun is in our eyes, next it's on our backs and we're following our shadows, looping backwards and forwards up the mountainside. Already the sun is sinking and still there's no sign of the town. Will we get there before dark?

As visibility is fast diminishing, we see buildings ahead and are soon freewheeling into Carratraca. We've made it. We're laughing now. But there's a horrible stink about the place as we pass a cascade of white water, which churns down a gully towards the road then disappears somewhere underneath us. "That's sulphur," says Frank. "Poo! Stinks like rotten eggs."

Well, never mind that. Now we must find the street where this hotel is supposed to be. It's not a big town, so we soon find the road we are seeking. We can't find the hostel though. After pushing the bikes the whole length of the street to the other end of town then all the way back again, we realise it's this dilapidated building that we've passed twice; all boarded up. We can't believe our eyes and let out loads of expletives to release our frustration. All that struggling to get here and now this! Whatever are we going to do now?

Further down the street we spot some neon lights, so we head towards them, hoping it might be a café. Apart from our immense thirst, now that we've stopped we're feeling hungry. Hopefully we'll get a meal here. As we enter in our bright red jackets, all conversation ceases and all eyes are upon us. It's so embarrassing. Maybe it's because I'm a woman. You never see women in bars here. Or perhaps it's just the surprise factor of seeing these two brightly-jacketed strangers appearing through the door at dusk. I'm reminded of the night Laurie Lee wrote about, when he walked into a bar in Andorra after climbing over the Pyrenees in the snow. He caused the same reaction. But his achievement had been unbelievable.

There is no food to be had here. It's just a drinking bar. Frank orders two lagers and we stand awkwardly at the bar, trying to replenish our great thirst. I'm surprised Frank didn't order *agua* instead. It would have been much better for us. Perhaps he's too tired to remember that word. He surprises me again though, by suddenly asking the barman, "habitación?" When did he look up *that* word?

There is no reaction from the barman, just a blank face. But we can hear murmuring in the background. There's a bit of stirring amongst the locals. Now a man in a flat cap appears from behind us and tries to tell us something. We can't understand a thing. Oh, it's such a struggle, trying to converse. Eventually, we get the message. Somewhere in the town, there's a place called 'Casa Pepa' where we will be able to stay for the night. I believe the man in the cap is related to the owners. He takes us outside and points in the direction we need to go.

A little way along the street we pass a telephone box. I

suddenly remember that Arun will be looking out for us by now. He'll be worried. We don't want him sending out a search party. "I must try to phone Arun, Frank." "How are you going to do that, then?" he asks. I hold the phrase book under the streetlight, trying to learn what to say but it's a struggle to make out the words. Then, with plenty of small change at hand, I step inside the unfamiliar booth to try my luck. When the high-pitched voice of an operator erupts in my ear, I'm thoroughly unprepared. But I must try, for Arun's sake. "No entiendo," I say, having just looked that up in the book. She reels off another string of gobbledegook and at that moment, a youth comes roaring up the street on a motorbike, drowning out everything. I put down the phone. I'm not going to get anywhere, I can tell.

We push the bikes to the end of the street where, hopefully, somewhere along this adjacent street, we'll find a bed for the night. It can't be far now. Oh! Here it is, 'Casa Pepa' – our sanctuary. It's a very plain-looking building, barely discernible from the rest of the street of whitewashed flat facades, except for the little balconies on the upper windows. There's the obligatory tangle of electric wires, running underneath them.

We ring the bell. A plump woman opens the door, looking rather surprised. But her face breaks into a warm smile as we ask "habitación?" and she realises from our anxious faces and our accent that we are two lost souls with no grasp of the language. She invites us into the hallway. From the inside, the place somehow seems much bigger. A slim little man appears from nowhere and offers to wheel our bikes through to somewhere in the depths of the building. This is her husband. They are both very welcoming and we begin to relax.

But we still have the dilemma of what to do about Arun. We show the lady our Finca la Mota card and somehow convey to her that we should be staying there tonight. She's as sharp as a needle and soon comprehends. In no time at all she's phoned up the finca to explain. We are very relieved. Now we're taken up to our room. I think it's in the attic. It seems we have to negotiate a labyrinth of dark little staircases to reach it. It's a very large, dimly-lit room with a roof light. There's a double bed in the middle and two single beds on adjacent walls. She leads us to the bathroom, which is a few steps down from the bedroom. It's a little box room with no windows, just a vent. Apart from the toilet and sink, there's a bath crammed in as well, looking more like a short box with a seat in it. We smirk at each other. It'll be fun having a bath in that. She leaves us and disappears downstairs.

I let Frank have the first bath. I'm quite happy to stretch out on the bed for a while. But as he turns on the taps, that same old stink wafts through. Rotten eggs! I creep in to watch Frank's reactions. He can't stand offensive smells. Having been both a nurse and a mother, I can just about cope. So what we thought would be a bit of a laugh has turned into a smelly joke. But a bath is a must, we being so hot and sticky. I stay to help him rinse his back. There's no lying down in *this* bath. Not that he would have wanted to, anyway.

Then it's my turn. I don't hang about. I want to be nice and clean in the quickest time possible. But we've forgotten something. We haven't got a single fresh garment to put on, have we? Through all the worry then relief of getting somewhere to stay, we have forgotten that all our clothes are back at the inn.

With disdain, we drag up our stinky, salt stained Lycra shorts, pull our moist, smelly cycle tops over our heads, roll on our soggy socks and lace up our sweaty cycling shoes. Oh well. Beggars can't be choosers.

There's a tap, tap on the door. Our landlady has come to fetch us. Where's she taking us? We follow her down the dark staircases to the hallway, then through a heavy door into an old fashioned-looking room with pictures of Jesus on the wall. Her husband and two young adults are seated round a large table. They nod and smile as we enter, and motion us to be seated. Blimey! They're giving us an evening meal as well. We thought this was just a B&B. We'd been preparing ourselves to go out on the town to find a restaurant – not that we'd have been allowed into one, in our whiffy Lycra.

The silence is not awkward, especially as Señora soon re-appears with a large cauldron of steaming stew. "What do you think it is, Frank?" I whisper. But before he has time to reply, the lady has put down the stew and with a big grin, holds her hands to the sides of her head, wiggles her fingers like ears and says "Baa, baa!" She's quite comical. We settle down to eat, feeling honoured to be sharing the family's meal.

It's amazing how much can be communicated without speaking. Using just arms and expressions, we learn all about this big iron table we are seated around. Underneath it, there's a heavy metal bowl, about 18 inches in diameter and about 12 inches off the floor. This bowl is surrounded by a footrest. When it's cold (Señor and Señora play-act the scenario; he rubbing his hands together and drawing in his cheeks, she wrapping her arms around herself and shivering) this bowl will be filled with glowing embers of some sort. They mime the act of filling the bowl with something, then hold their open hands down towards the bowl, drawing in breaths of relief, rubbing their hands together and saying "Aaah!" with smiling faces. The young man and woman grin but seem a little too shy to participate. We're laughing. Our hosts are so entertaining.

With the fire now installed, a heavy cloth will then be laid over the table. Señora spreads her arms wide to depict the size of this cloth, puffing her cheeks out to indicate its vastness, her eyes popping. Then, with her arms bent at the elbows and palms uppermost, she portrays its great weight, rocking her forearms gently up and down, frowning and breathing in, in little gasps. Now Señor pretends to lay the cloth over the table, sweeping his hand right down the side of the table and onto the tiles, to show how far it would drape along the floor. We have understood perfectly, so far. Now for the finale; they show us how the cloth will be tucked around each person's thighs, to keep in the heat. What a marvellous idea. We are offered another helping of "baa." It's delicious. Now it's time for bed. Feeling thoroughly sated, both physically and mentally, we thank our patrons and wish them *buenos noches*.

That night, I seem to have the Goldilocks syndrome. First I try sleeping in the double bed, but as we both keep rolling into the middle, I can't drop off to sleep. So without switching on the light – it being on the far wall – I grope my way to the nearest single bed. But I soon realise that this is too hard for me. I toss and turn, trying to relieve one hip, then the other. It's no good. I'll have to try the other bed. I creep round to the far side of the room, feeling my way around the bottom of the double bed. Will it be third time lucky? No! Anyway, I'm past sleeping now. I shall probably be awake all night. My body can have a rest, at least. I listen to Frank snoring gently. Oh, envy, envy!

* * *

The sun is shining through the roof light when Frank wakes up. I don't tell him what an awful night I've had. What's the point? After freshening up with 'rotten egg' water, we curiously open a door adjacent to the bathroom to see what's in the cupboard. But rays of sunshine hit us in the face. How amazing. There's a roof garden out here. An abundance of potted plants grow all around, some climbing up the trelliswork at the far end. It's wonderful. We walk towards the edge – well almost; there are railings to prevent us from falling into the garden down below. A secret garden! A big square garden around which Casa Pepa is built. No wonder the building seems so deceptively large on the inside. A tall and pretty tree grows up from the centre. We can look straight into its new, sun-dappled leaves. And around the walls, there are yet more luxuriant potted plants. It's a revelation to see all this greenery behind the whitewashed street of flat façades.

We collect our meagre belongings, then head downstairs, where Señora directs us, in a motherly sort of fashion, to a different room. We are feeling like relatives now. This room is much longer than the one we dined in last night. It's more akin to a café with round tables along both sides. She seats us at the top end, facing the kitchen door. Oddly enough, there's no smell of sulphur coming from the kitchen. Perhaps they have a different source of water for cooking.

With smiling faces, she and her husband bring out our breakfast, beginning with two boiled eggs apiece; not something you normally get offered for a continental breakfast. The two of them watch us fondly, standing smilingly, side by side in the doorway. As soon as we've devoured our last mouthfuls of boiled eggs, they are at our side with toasted baguettes, butter and marmalade. Just a simple breakfast, but they're making us feel so special. Our large coffee pot is refilled and we are encouraged to have more, and more toasted baguettes. I think they want to build us up for our journey back to Finca la Mota.

Now it's time to leave and we must pay our dues. But Señora asks us for such a small amount of money – not even the price we'd have paid for one evening meal. We won't hear of it. The two of them could not have been nicer to us. So we give her four times as much. She doesn't want to take it. We insist. She's over the moon – almost crying. Señor fetches our bikes, which were probably out in the garden, and we wave goodbye with a tinge of sadness. We love them to bits.

We'd like to see more of Carratraca before we head off down the mountains. It seems to be a bit of a spa, with its abundance of smelly, sulphurous water. We push our bikes along the streets, passing a small, round, beautifully-tiled swimming pool with steps down from the pavement. There's no water in it now but, apparently, Queen Victoria bathed here, according to the brass plaque on the wall. I could hardly believe that Queen Victoria came all this way to a little town in the mountains to immerse herself in the milky, stinky waters. Years later I discovered that it was not our queen but her granddaughter, another Victoria, wife of King Alfonso 13th of Spain.

On the outskirts of town, we noticed a few new houses on the mountainside with private spa pools in their gardens. The owners had obviously made the most of any sulphurous streams running through their grounds. I don't think I'd consider it to be an advantage. It reminded me of a farmhouse I had seen in my youth, in the fens of Lincolnshire; a newly-built, posh-looking place, right in the middle of a field, which was full of stinking, rotting cauliflowers. I didn't envy them.

We look for the *Oficina de Turismo* to learn more about Carratraca, but are even more intrigued by the building itself. It's an eight-sided tower, perched on the side of a mountain, with stunning vistas. It is painted yellow ochre with terracotta-coloured mouldings. There are rectangular windows all round on both floors, with a cupola on the top for viewing. It wouldn't look out of place on a mountainside in Tibet, I think to myself.

We lock the bikes and go eagerly inside. But it seems we've arrived at an inconvenient time. Excited schoolchildren are swarming everywhere. We squeeze by them, up the wooden flights of stairs to the viewing point, cursing them under our breath. They all seem to be in a rush to descend. But it's well worth the effort when we reach the top. We are facing another whole range of mountains, looking southwards. It's awesome.

By the time we come back down, the children have all but disappeared. Then as we step outside, a chorus of cheers greets us. The school kids have seen our bikes and are waiting for us. They seem more interested in us two cyclists than in their school trip and insist on having a photo taken with us. We're thrilled by their enthusiasm. But as I'm the one with the camera, I don't feature in the photograph, although they proudly hold my bike centre stage.

We've been made to feel very welcome in Carratraca, but now it's time to leave. Cycling back is wonderful. It's absolutely plain sailing, apart from the few valleys that we have to climb out of. Eventually we're down on the flat again, stopping for a celebratory drink at the same bar we stopped at yesterday. Only yesterday? It seems much longer ago than that. While we sip our drinks outside, we spread the map on the table and scrutinize it. We're determined to find that little road, even though we could go back via the long route, through Alora.

"I know it's somewhere quite near here," says Frank. We gaze up and down the road, then back up again to look more closely at a wide gateway with no gate. It's just a few yards further up, on the other side. "I reckon that must be it, you know," he says.

"But it's a dirt track, Frank, not a road."

"I don't care. I'm sure that must be it. There's nothing else," he insists.

We sip up and go for it, quite eager now to see if this is indeed the planned route. The surface is not difficult to ride on. It's baked hard. How lucky we are. In wet weather it would be a quagmire. Apart from the dust we're making, it doesn't feel much different from a tarmac road. We spin along nicely for a few miles, across a flat, featureless landscape, until we are brought up short by a large tree growing next to a wide, almost dry, riverbed. "Might as well stop and eat our snack here," Frank suggests. We bought some biscuits in Carratraca. "No one would make such a long track as this if it didn't lead to somewhere. It probably continues over on the other side," he adds.

There's an astonishing sight, further up river. It's half of a bridge, poised in mid-air, going halfway across the river. The other half must have been washed away in a flood. What immense force of water would it have taken to wash away such a large stone bridge? It seems unbelievable that this riverbed could have been a raging torrent, just a couple of months ago, in the winter barely past. Or maybe it happened many winters ago and nobody has bothered to repair it. We must count ourselves fortunate to be having this heat wave. Better than storms and floods, any day.

We walk across the riverbed and luckily, pick up another track in a similar direction. Whether or not it's the correct one we're not certain, but it does eventually bring us to another river. This one is equally wide and also wet! But the water is shallow, bubbling over pebbles. There's nothing for it but to take off our shoes and socks and carry the bikes carefully over. We wade across, wobbling to keep our balance in the icy cold water. Better to endure the pain underfoot than to topple over. This is probably more invigorating than a dip in sulphurous water.

On the other side there is a continuation of the track, but it's a narrow footpath now, between bushes. We have to push the bikes through. At last we reach a proper road and soon get our bearings – there is that wooded mountain with the stripe down the middle. We'll just head in that direction.

By teatime we are safely back at Finca la Mota. Arun is really pleased to see us. Oh it's lovely to have a shower and put on clean clothes before venturing down for dinner and a free bottle of wine. That little cock-up yesterday, going off at a tangent from our planned circular route, has given us all the confidence we need. And the Spanish people have proved so warm and welcoming to us cyclists. Tomorrow, we will set off on a proper tour. Definitely.

CHAPTER THIRTEEN

Bungling Through Brittany

Easter 1993

Dave, Frank and Rob – Dave has noticed something in the water

The whirring of a helicopter made everyone look up. Was it going to land on the beach? We'd all been anxiously awaiting the arrival of an ambulance. Rachael, who had been leading us on a cycle tour in Cornwall, was lying unconscious on the roadside

197

– knocked off her bike by two boisterous Labradors that had raced straight across the road and slammed into her. The owner had let them off the lead for a run along the beach, not anticipating that a line of cyclists might be pedalling up this quiet little coastal road. However, seeing the result of his actions, he'd been quick to summon help.

The helicopter landed swiftly and the rescue team were soon in attendance, having appeared through bushes on the edge of the beach. By now Rachael had begun to stir. Such a relief! Her split helmet was carefully removed and soon she was being whisked away to Truro Hospital. The remaining twelve of us watched until the helicopter was out of sight. We were still in a state of shock, wondering what to do next. Then with the help of the dog owner, we found a local housekeeper who was willing to take in Rachael's bike. After that, there was no point in us hanging around; we needed to reach Golant Youth Hostel on the south coast, where we were booked in for the next two nights. Once there, we could get in touch with the hospital and find out Rachael's condition.

In spite of being privileged to cycle round Cornwall for the Easter break, five of us, with holiday time in hand, had chosen to cross the channel into Brittany for ten more days of cycling. Rachael would have been one of us. She was always good fun to be with and although she had not been planning to lead us this time, with her schoolma'amish qualities and the fact that she was a little older than we were, she would probably have had a levelling influence on us.

That evening we received news from the hospital that there were no broken bones but Rachael was badly bruised and shaken, and would be kept in hospital for a couple of days. So on our final day, before leaving Treyarnon Youth Hostel, to where we'd returned for our cars, her friend, who would be taking her home, drove her first to the hostel, so we could say 'Cheerio' and witness that she was on the mend. Heartened by her smiling cheerfulness, I stupidly went up to give her a big hug, making her yelp with pain because she hurt all over. What an idiot!

* * *

So today, on this bright sunny morning, only four of us are on the ferry to Roscoff, having spent last night at Plymouth YHA. We are Frank, Rob, Dave and myself. Rob and Dave are both in their 30s, while Frank and I are in our late 40s. But we're all young at heart, or might I say, rather immature at times.

We dock in Roscoff at 3pm in warm sunshine. This looks promising. "Well," we're all wondering, "where shall we start?" Then I remember a lovely road to Morlaix, which runs alongside the river all the way from the estuary to the town. The others have never been on this route and agree to give it a try. We set off southwards towards St. Pol de Léon, stopping there for a while to eat the fruit we've bought from a market stall. Sitting ourselves down next to the cathedral with its twin towers soaring above us, we soak up the pleasant sunshine, savouring the ambience of our surroundings. It's great to be back in Brittany again. I love it.

Now heading west, we cross a bridge over the estuary of La Penzé. Looking south, we see that the river runs slowly through gentle green countryside, while to the north, the terrain is all harsh and jagged. The town of Carantec shines in the sun, built on a rocky outcrop, facing St. Pol across the estuary. But on this road, it's nice easy pedalling – just right to loosen our limbs, after six hours on the ferry.

We reach the Rade de Morlaix, where the road curves southwards along the riverside. The others will enjoy it, I'm sure. I'm remembering when I rode down here with my two teenage sons five years ago, loaded with camping gear. It was great. How I wish they still came cycling with me. But they do their own thing now. It's hard to let go! Anyway, I mustn't get sentimental, even though I'm hoping to revisit some of the places we went together.

As we progress, the estuary narrows and now the road is tucked in against the low cliffs, following the contours of this beautiful river. I can imagine that these cliffs shelter the river craft from westerly gales. However, I haven't seen a single boat sailing by yet. Perhaps the tide is too low. In the distance the great viaduct of Morlaix comes into view. It looks magnificent from this direction; a great feat of engineering.

We have now reached the massive marina of Morlaix where, as we cycle past, the noisy jingling from moored yachts rings in our ears. We're heading towards the towering viaduct and into the bustle of traffic that we've managed to avoid thus far. From here, it seems, we are confronted by hills in every other direction. Our first port of call must be the Auberge de Jeunesse to make sure they have vacancies. But we walk slowly through the old town, marvelling at the dwellings that have been built right up against the huge, sloping uprights of the viaduct, as if it were a city wall. There are grand buildings on both sides of the wide street, many of them tall, centuries-old, timber-built houses. Hopefully we'll have a better look at them in the morning.

Feeling less energetic now, we push our bikes up to the hostel. We have stayed here before, on a 'Rachael' tour, and remember what a steep climb it was. That time we'd been booked into one big room, all fourteen of us together. This time I am to be segregated, as the others will be sharing their room with 'strangers'!

After showering, we search the locality for somewhere to eat. This part of Morlaix is not very appealing. We could be in the scruffy back streets of any city and there are no decent cafés in sight. So we buy a take-away and eat it in the street, then find a bar.

* * *

In the morning, we meet in the kitchen. The other hostellers seem to have left. Did they depart at the crack of dawn? We've packed our panniers ready for the off but we're in no great hurry to leave, as we haven't yet decided where to go. And anyway, we want this holiday to be laid back. We're not planning to break any records. We're just happy that the weather is so pleasant.

A bare oval table stands in the middle of the kitchen. It looks dirty and the wood is cracked and dried out – quite unsavoury for eating from but we may as well have our breakfast, now that we're here; that is, the bread and cheese slices we bought last night. Rob is curious about a carafe of wine that's been left in the middle of the table. Is it a carafe? Is it wine? It looks suspiciously like a hospital pee bottle and the wine is rather an orangey colour. We have a bit of a snigger about it but don't even sniff it. Someone must have left it here for a joke, surely?

Over breakfast, I suggest that we carry on in a southerly direction to Huelgoat, less than 20 miles from here. I cycled there with my boys and am aware that it's uphill all the way. But I don't tell them that, or about the huge boulders in the forest. Let that be a surprise.

Rob and Dave have pedalled off before Frank and I are out of the gate. Which way did they go? We feel cross. If we lose each other, there's the chance that we may not meet up for the rest of the holiday, although that's being a bit dramatic, as we all know we're heading for Huelgoat today. But we still feel annoyed. As we struggle to the top of the hill, to where we suppose the main road to be, Frank says "Sod them then. We'll just have to do our own thing." At that very moment they cycle past us on the top road. "Hey," we shout, "wait for us." And we race to pull in behind them. Would they really have cleared off without us? For the next few miles we pedal along in silence, simmering.

It's been uphill ever since we left Morlaix. But as the road levels out for a while, we stop at a roadside shop for some snacks. By now we're all mates again and the rest of the journey is pleasant on this designated scenic route, although it's still uphill. By midday we are cycling into Huelgoat. We sail straight past the sign to the 'Grotto' without them even noticing. I'll save that for later. Firstly, we want to buy food for a picnic lunch and then find somewhere nice to eat it. I know just the place.

With our crusty baguettes sticking out of our panniers and all the other goodies we've bought tucked inside them, I now take the lads to a good picnic spot I know. I can see the surprise on their faces as we enter. To think that this amazing valley of boulders is just yards from the roadside – some are as big as houses and most look as if they've been rolled down a huge mountainside to settle in this little valley. Clear water rushes down through the gaps and on under the bridge to the lake beyond.

We lock up the bikes and explore for a while, until greed and hunger force us to find a good picnic spot. We choose a huge boulder next to a little stone mill, from where we have a good view of the town beyond the bridge. The river twists and gurgles below us – beautiful crystal-clear water. As we sit munching and surveying our surroundings, Dave is observing an obstruction sticking out of the water, making the flow even choppier. He's becoming obsessed by it. "'Ere," he asks, in his lovely laid-back Gloucestershire accent, "what d'ye think thaa' is down there?"

We all strain to look. We haven't a clue.

"Looks like a wooden cray' to me," he says, "'sgot somethin' in it but I don't know whaa'."

Eventually, he can contain himself no longer and climbs down to investigate. We follow on behind. "Ey, it's full o' bo'ulls. Someone must'ave stored them 'ere for a jolly."

Rob and Frank are really interested now. "More fool them," says one. "Come on; finders keepers," adds the other and all three begin to take off their shoes and socks. "It's not going to be easy, lads," I think to myself, although I'm not putting myself out to help them.

They find the water freezing and the riverbed littered with stones, but that won't deter them now. They wade in, cringing as they acclimatise. Dave reaches the crate first. It's absolutely wedged in; they won't be able to shift that. So it will have to be emptied, a few bottles at a time. We form a chain and the bottles are handed to me on dry land, two by two. I hope nobody is watching us taking this booty. I conceal the bottles carefully in a gap between the boulders, making the lads impatient as they wait for me to take the next ones. "Come on, hurry up," says Frank, "my feet are going dead."

At last, we've landed 24 bottles of lager. Whatever are we going to do with them all? But that's a question soon answered, because Rob has already found his bottle opener and we climb back up to our perch, each with a bottle of lager in hand and the lads still in their wet bare feet. Oh, it's such a refreshing drink – more so because we found it. I'm glad we came here and I'm feeling quite popular right now. I might be feeling a bit heady soon but that won't matter. We've finished cycling for today.

A little later, after the chaps have had another one and I've made mine last, it's time we found accommodation for the night. We climb down and pick up a few bottles each – two in each hand, with Dave taking the extra one; a bonus for making the discovery. It's going to be quite a squeeze to fit them into our panniers but I'm sure we will.

It doesn't take us long to find somewhere to stay; a family room in a modest hotel. All we need now is to shower then we'll be out on the town for a nice meal. That will be enough for today.

* * *

Frank unpacked both his panniers last night and hung his clothes in the wardrobe. Consequently, he is the last to be ready this morning. Laid-back Dave, on the other hand is the last to get up and the first to be ready, which annoys Frank. I was woken up really early by a noisy dustcart. I jumped out of bed and slammed the window shut in annoyance, then hoped I hadn't woken the others.

As I have already suggested two interesting destinations so far, the lads are quite happy when I come up with a third – that is, to cycle to Châtaulin, which I know to be a very pretty town with a river running through the centre. It's southwest from here. But we're not rushing off yet. There's a lively market in town this morning so we saunter through, seeing what wares are for sale. Then I see some lovely, fluffy ducklings squashed into crates, with no headroom to stand up. The poor little things look so distressed that the sight of them puts me off looking at anything else.

On the outskirts of town Frank notices a large, rather nice but dilapidated building for sale. He'd like to buy it, he says. We go back into town to find the selling agents for details. I am to learn in years to come that everywhere Frank goes on holiday, he wants to live.

Well, we'd better set off for Châtaulin, hadn't we? Time is getting on. We'll be following another scenic route today – they are everywhere in these parts. That's why cycling in Brittany is so great – a network of scenic routes on quiet roads.

Today is lovely and warm. We've been really blessed with this summer-like weather so early in the year. As we approach Brasparts, Rob has an overwhelming desire to sunbathe. It's infectious. We all want to stop and sunbathe. There's a wide flight of steps leading to a churchyard, which faces due south. Perfect. The three of them choose a spot each and lay up the steps to absorb the warmth – like three old men having a midday nap, I think to myself as I snap them on my camera. Then I find a space to join them.

After about half an hour, one of them remembers the lager that's bursting our panniers. So we sit on the steps with a bottle each and spend another half-hour drinking it. Gosh, this holiday is so laid back we're hardly going to get anywhere. But coming to our senses we muster up enough energy to carry on. We've barely cycled ten miles so far.

I've never entered Châtaulin from this direction. I liked it more when I came here first with my son Pete. We had hitchhiked on a boiling hot day from further up the west coast, hoping to buy a new wheel for his bike. It was a market day and the stalls blotted out the view of the shops. Now, all we see are the bog-standard shops lining both sides of the river. It's still a beautiful town though, with the River Aulne running through the centre and baskets of flowers adorning the lovely stone bridge. And behind, forming a pleasant backdrop, are the wooded hills that we've just cycled through. But first impressions are often the best.

Halfway down the main street on the other side of the river, we find a hotel and book another family room for the night. It's quite a dark and dowdy-looking room, but not expensive when we're sharing the cost. It has the ubiquitous, weak-flowing shower in an unventilated box, but we take it in turns to wash off today's light layer of sweat and change into our best clothes for an evening on the town – Ha ha!

* * *

Today we are going to cycle to Quimper, the capital of Finistère. It's another short hop of 20 miles but who wants to be rushing around, this weather? We're taking little back roads, which are hillier and twistier than the main ones, but we've got all day to do it. The ride itself is not very eventful, but as we cycle along, we're singing at the tops of our voices, bawling out old favourites. Dave knows all the rock 'n' roll numbers that Frank and I learnt in our youth, because he plays his parents' old records at home. But apart from the pop songs we know, we manage to get Dave singing Billy Cotton's signature song, *Somebody Stole My Girl*, which he will sing incessantly for the remainder of the holiday; a great hoot. Near Quimper, we cut across to visit a huge hypermarket on the outskirts of the city, where we buy provisions for tonight. Frank and Rob have volunteered to cook spaghetti Bolognese!

We wander around the city for a while. This time I'm determined to have a good look at the cathedral, having given it a miss on two earlier occasions. This was because I'd read that the two towers had been added at a much later date, and that put me off. Then I'd read somewhere later that it is the finest example of Gothic architecture in Brittany. So now I'm going in to see for myself. And yes, it is truly magnificent, both inside and out. We all spend quite some time admiring it before eventually seeking out the Auberge de Jeunesse.

The hostel is quite spacious but fairly outdated. A handful of people are staying and we attempt to converse with them, as much as we can with our limited language skills. We also chat to the warden, who calls herself Madame Léylène. She seems to like us – well the three chaps, that is. When we're all freshened up, we look for the kitchen, where Dave and I hang around reading magazines, occasionally being called on for advice in this complicated task of cooking Bolognese!

At long last it's ready, and with our remaining bottles of lager as an accompaniment, we eat our delicious Bolognese in the large, frosted-glassed, dining area. It's the best meal we've had this holiday.

* * *

We've decided to stay another night in the city, partly to catch up on our laundry; we're running out of smalls, and anyway, we'd like to spend more time looking around Quimper. It's late morning by the time we've finished the washing. Dave and I plan to cook dinner tonight, so we'll buy something nice to eat while we're out and about.

Out on the city streets, we spend as much time sitting outside cafés as we do sightseeing. Well in actual fact, you can do a lot of sightseeing from an outdoor cafe, watching the world go by. We've become rather lazy lately.

Dave and I have bought some nice lamb chops for dinner and two bottles of red wine. We haven't told the others what we'll be cooking. It should be a nice surprise. There'll be carrots, greens and potatoes to go with them – rather an English meal. We hope that won't disappoint them. But as we enter the kitchen, we realise we've got nothing to make a decent gravy. Rob and Frank quickly offer to go out and find us something, which means we can now get on with our surprise meal unimpeded, while they can evade any other chores.

We prepare all the vegetables first; we're planning to have a variety of greens to make up for the lack of them over the last few days. Then we start to grill the chops – all eight of them. They are thick and succulent and cost us a lot of money. But we can't wait to get our teeth into them. We've got the spuds boiling nicely. Perhaps it's time we put the greens on. We wish they'd hurry up with that gravy salt. They have been gone a long time.

Well, apart from the gravy, it's all ready to dish up now. We've got the plates warming under the grill – all we need now is for Rob and Frank to return with the gravy granules. I've mashed the potatoes. Now I've got to keep them warm without drying them out and we can't keep the chops cooking much longer; they're done enough.

Gosh, we're getting quite cross now. Everything's got to be kept warm or it will be ruined. I pile the various greens together onto a large plate, then find a big saucepan lid to cover them. They'll just have to stand over a pan of boiling water to keep them warm - Bah humbug! Still no sign of the other two. I've never seen Dave get more than slightly annoyed before, but I can see he's pretty cross now. I suggest we open a bottle of wine. Why wait for those two sods?

We've completely finished the first bottle of wine before Rob and Frank show up. Inside, we're seething, but we try to remain civil. They are full of mirth and dying to tell us what happened, but our ears are closed. We don't wish to know. I just need to make some gravy then we can eat our warm, spoilt dinner off boiling hot plates.

The dinner is actually not too bad. Dave and I have made a good job of keeping it warm. We open the second bottle of wine and pour ourselves very generous glasses full, while keeping theirs moderate. They've obviously had enough lager to keep them going – the traitors. But in the end we've got to hear the whole story, they can't contain themselves any longer. They keep chuckling and raising their glasses to each other, saying "Yeerd mat," whatever that means, so they'd better tell us what it's all about...

On the way back from the shop, they called into a bar for a very swift lager but were challenged to a game of table football by a man called Michel. The two of them beat Michel and his mate hands down and were rewarded with a drink. But Michel, the revered champion of the establishment, challenged them again. Once again our two were the winners. Another drink! I imagine that Frank and Rob must have been feeling quite mellow by now. Michel was teaching them how to say "Cheers" in Breton – "Yec'had mat!" which sounded to them like a guttural "Yeerd mat." By this time, all the locals were involved, encouraging them both to have one more match – third time lucky, and all that. Again our two were victorious and *they* were now the revered champions. This time it was the locals who bought them drinks. I imagine Rob and Frank must have almost forgotten what they went out for by now, but luckily, not quite.

Eventually, Dave and I soften towards them, but we're damned if we're going to do any washing up - *they* can jolly well get on with it. Just as they begin their task, Madame Léylène comes into the kitchen to speak to us. "Would we like to go to a disco?" she asks. She will take us in her car. Of course, it's Saturday night. The city will be heaving tonight. We've never been clubbing in France before.

The washers-up speed up and soon we're all excitedly getting changed into clothes more suitable for disco dancing, although there's nothing very smart in our panniers. Madame Léylène is waiting near the entrance door and her car is just outside, she says. We file out and squeeze into her little Renault. Blimey, what a crush after all that food and drink.

We take off up the hill. It feels like an aircraft taking off and her driving is atrocious. We can't hang on to anything, but we're packed in so tightly we can't go anywhere. We're scared stiff, all the same. When we get to the designated place, we find her parking skills to be even more terrible. We'll be glad to be prised out.

Where's this disco then? That's what we're all thinking. We can't hear much noise. She leads us through a doorway into a room where, in one corner a mediocre, four-piece band is playing downbeat music, while the corner opposite serves as the dance floor. Dance floor? It's no bigger than my little kitchen. The floor is slightly raised, with a low rail down one side, to stop dancers from falling onto adjacent tables. And it's certainly not heaving in here. Gosh, we're really going to party tonight!

However, not wanting to disappoint our hostess, we spend the rest of the night pretending we're enjoying ourselves. Madame gets to dance with each of the lads in turn – two people at a time on the dance floor is the very limit. But I'm sure that's all she really wanted – a bit of male company. She must be a lonely old bird, I'm thinking, even though she's amongst hostellers morning and evening. And she's not old; early 50s I'd say. By the end of the night we feel as if we've taken her out for a good time, except that she still has to drive us home.

* * *

Sunday morning and we're feeling slightly jaded after last night. That was a night to remember, I don't think! We're in no hurry to leave the hostel and I'm sure Madame Léylène won't be chivvying us out by a certain time. Today we're going to mosey on down to Concarneau on the south coast. It's another easy ride, but we'll have loads of time to look round the old walled town, which we didn't get to do last time, when we came here with Rachael, nor the time before, when I was with my boys.

First, we have to negotiate our way out of Quimper's traffic. Then it's a fairly easy ride to Concarneau – so laid back, we're in danger of losing momentum. The lads take off their T-shirts and Dave can't stop singing *Somebody Stole My Girl*. The rest of us wish we'd never encouraged him.

We arrive in the early afternoon – so early we haven't even stopped for a snack yet. That can soon be remedied. We find a café making crêpes, which we haven't tried so far, this holiday. Sitting under a striped awning, which shades the customers and the outdoor chef from rain or shine, we watch them being cooked. We've all chosen the egg and bacon version. When they arrive, I'm dismayed to see that the egg yolks are almost raw, something I hate. Still, the coffee is very nice. I'll have to wash mine down with that. I don't think I'll be bothering with crêpes any more.

It's too early to book into the youth hostel so we cross the bridge to the old walled city, locking the bikes in a prominent position, where any meddler will be in full view of the public. We never lock them on 'out-of-sight' bike racks.

It's good to have this time to meander around. A few years ago, I camped on the other side of Concarneau with my sons. We arrived at dusk and left early in the morning, so all my hopes of sightseeing here had been quashed. For years I'd had rosy preconceived notions about this town, after reading a schoolgirl book in my early teens – false notions, I guess; for it was set in the 40s and the girls, I recollect, were at a posh boarding school here. Now I'm hoping to make up for my long-awaited ambition to explore old Concarneau. We amble round the crenellated ramparts, observing beached fishing boats below us as they gradually refloat on the incoming tide. It's quite soporific. And although this historic fortified island seems idyllic, it doesn't live up to my long-held expectations, in spite of its picturesque location and ancient walls. We wander slowly back through the centuries-old streets at ground level, perusing the shops and market stalls, as we go to reclaim the bikes.

The hostel is only around the corner. We book in, take a shower, then eat a modest evening meal in a café. After that, with nothing better to do, we walk round the illuminated ramparts in the dark, which personally, I find much more magical.

* * *

We've decided to head east from here, in the direction of Lorient, hoping to put a bit more vim and vigour into our cycling before we end up like couch potatoes. It's good to be spinning along at a good pace again. The truth be known, we've probably got a westerly wind helping us. It's an exhilarating ride, racing each other on swooping roads. Around the halfway mark we cycle into Quimperlé, where we stop briefly to share a packet of biscuits. Rob drops half of his on the pavement but picks them up with a grin. "They haven't had time to get contaminated," he assures us. We're standing on a bridge with a river rushing under us and nearby, in the middle of the street, there's a circular church, looking out of place. Perhaps it's the street that is out of place, because I believe the church would have been here first. The town looks interesting. I wish I could spend more time here but we're not in the mood for lingering. We're on a roll now and want to keep going.

In order to miss out the environs of Lorient, we head further north towards a place with the fascinating name of Inzinzac Lochrist, where there's a hostel. That will be enough distance for today.

It doesn't take long to find the hostel. Inzinzac is either a large village or a small town. However the hostel is closed. Nobody is answering the doorbell. Then we translate a notice that's pinned to the door, telling us to fetch the key from a certain address. Off we go round the streets again, asking locals for their help in finding this place.

A pretty young woman with long blonde hair answers the door. Yes, she is the warden but operates the hostel from her home, she says. I can see through the door that she has young children, so working from home seems the obvious answer. We pay her for two nights and she hands over the keys, trusting us to treat the hostel with respect. That's great, we're all thinking. Like having our own gîte at hostel prices.

We stop at a row of shops and stock up on food. We'll be

eating in tonight. The hostel is a lovely modern building, but with pleasing traditional architecture. Inside it's spick and span, with a smart kitchen-diner looking out onto the stone-paved garden. A modern-looking picnic table and benches, made from a pale wood, have been placed at an angle outside and there are potted geraniums along the wall of the hostel. It's very pleasant. Upstairs there are four small bunk-bedded rooms, built into the roof, with dormer windows. As we are the only people staying here, we choose a bedroom each and spread our clothes out. We didn't anticipate such luxury.

I've offered to cook us a meal tonight. Meanwhile, the three lads are going to catch up on their washing. Frank offers to do mine for me. Blimey! No man has ever done my washing for me in my life. It's a bit embarrassing but, why not? By the time I have cooked the stir-fry, all the washing is hanging outside on the clothesline.

We spend the evening perusing the map, planning where to go tomorrow. The consensus is to cycle to Carnac, then on down the Quiberon Peninsula. That will be an 80-mile round trip. No problem. We've got loads of miles stored in our legs after ambling about for days and there will be barely a hill in sight.

* * *

Before we all set off for Quiberon, Frank has offered to cycle to Hennebont with me, along a riverside cycle track that we noticed on the map last night. It's not many miles from here and we leave quietly, before Rob and Dave have even stirred. Hennebont is another walled town and I'd like to take some photos. I visited it briefly with my boys but we didn't have a chance to look round it properly.

Cycling along this path in the fresh early morning air is enchanting, with mist rising from the river as the sun warms up. But once through the gated wall at Hennebont I'm rather disappointed. There are so many parked cars everywhere. It may have proved to be an interesting place, if we had more time to spend here, but as the shops and cafés are still closed, there's no point in hanging about. For a second time therefore, I have given Hennebont short shrift and now it's time we returned to Inzinzac for breakfast.

We're ready to leave for Quiberon by 9.30 am. Rob will carry the map and a tool kit. The rest of us are travelling light with only our water bottles and a spare inner tube apiece, plus a few snacks to share on the way. It will be great cycling without panniers today.

We race along, with a westerly wind behind us again, going through places I vaguely recognise, especially the long flat bridge over the wide Rivière d'Étel. Soon the prehistoric menhirs of Carnac come into view – acres of them, everywhere we look. There are so many ancient standing stones here that as you wander amongst them, you tend to become rather blasé. I've been here before and am even more blasé. (Nowadays, they are fenced off, like Stonehenge, which tends to give them more reverence, I suppose.)

We've cycled past the turning to the Quiberon peninsula, so we must backtrack a little way to find it. Ah yes, this is it. I remember cycling down here before with my boys, when we swam on the west coast of the peninsula. It proved to be a hairy experience, especially when we realised we were swimming near a whirlpool. That's probably why it's called La Côte Sauvage (The Wild Coast).

The sea air fills our nostrils now, as we pedal straight down the middle. We can't see the sea from here because the landmass has widened out, but we feel the wind blowing in off the Atlantic. It's very refreshing and thankfully, pleasantly warm.

The town of Quiberon sits right at the bottom of the peninsula, like a secret resort, for the enlightened few only. But before we head for the beach, we trawl the town centre for a bank. Rob needs more money. Then, with the irresistible smell of pasties emanating from a nearby shop, we buy one apiece, eating them outside in the street. Now it's high time we went on the beach. We haven't put a foot on any sand since we arrived in Brittany. We pedal off in the direction of the shore, only to be pulled up short by Rob, who has just spied a signboard giving prices of ferry fares to the three offshore islands. They are Belle Ile en Mer, Houat and Hoëdic. Wouldn't it be great to take a trip to one of them? But when we look up, Frank is nowhere to be seen. He obviously doesn't know we've stopped. We cycle to the end of the road and look round the corner. No sign of him. We're just expecting him to cycle back, any minute. But he doesn't. So now what can we do? We pedal round and round the town hoping to intercept him, somewhere. It's unbelievable that we don't bump into him.

Time is getting on. We've spent ages searching, to no avail. We really don't know what to do. We certainly can't hang on forever. We'll have to start back soon. I've got a sick feeling in the pit of my stomach. It will be like a grand abandonment if we just leave without him. However, in the end, that's what we do. We haven't even been on the beach.

I hate every minute of the journey back. For a start it's harder pedalling in this direction – into wind. Also Rob and Dave are cycling relentlessly, unaware of how I'm struggling to keep up with them. I suppose my heart is not in it, riding away like this. We now seem to be returning via a different route and have to keep checking the map. What will poor Frank do without one? I'm riddled with guilt.

We arrive back and sit at the garden table, waiting, waiting and waiting; not feeling in the mood to get on with any of the chores that could be done. When *is* Frank going to turn up? I go in to make coffee, then we sit and sit, making it last as long as possible. With the tension and apprehension, hardly a word is spoken between us; we're just hoping Frank finds his way back.

Suddenly, we hear the sound of tyres, and in a cloud of dust, Frank comes careering in through the gateway like a bat out of hell, chucking his bike against the wall in show of anger. His face is red; he looks furious. He seems to think we left him on purpose. Why on earth would we have done such a thing? I go in to make him a coffee, while Rob and Dave try to defuse him and assure him that we spent ages searching for him. He's calming down now. I'm sure it was worry, not anger that was getting to him – that if anything went wrong with the bike, he had no tools; that if he got lost, he had no map. And other concerns, like the sun going down on him.

The sun has gone down now and I offer to make supper again, partly because I want to keep it simple. I can't face a pile of washing up. It will only be pasta and a jar of sauce, anyway. No big deal. There are still a few treats in the cupboard, for afters. I reckon we'll need those. By the time we get round to showering, it's late. I hate showering after hanging around for a long time. But needs must. Meanwhile, the lads work out a return route northwards, which will bring us back towards Roscoff.

* * *

It's perfect weather for cycling, with warm sunshine and barely a breath of wind. We're planning to cycle to a hostel in a village called Maël Pestivien – a little over 80 miles to the north, we estimate. We have no intention of rushing. We'll just take it as it comes. We're taking a lovely route through small villages and one town, called Rostrenen. But first we must take back the keys.

We're a homogenous group today, happy with each other and the world around us: the spring air, the blossom on the trees and the birds singing sweetly as we cycle along sun-dappled roads in gentle countryside. We're not talking, just listening. Rob is trying to help us identify birdsong, as he knows his stuff. Outside a place called Bubry, we stop next to a lake for a rest. Sitting on a verge of fresh grass dotted with clumps of primroses, we eat our biscuits and watch ducks in the throes of the mating season. With a quacking, a squabbling and splashing, they chase each other across the water. A blackbird sings from somewhere above, and in the trees across the lake, a green woodpecker is laughing at us. It's magical.

On we go, steadily knocking off the miles. Later on, we stop at a small roadside supermarket for refreshments – meat pasties, fruit and fresh pastries for afters. We'd better make the most of our favourite French pastries, for in a couple of days time, they'll be off the menu. At another shop, which now can't be far from Maël Pestivien, we stop once more, to buy provisions for tonight. We have no idea if there'll be any food on offer when we get there.

We arrive at Maël Pestivien, not feeling particularly tired in spite of the distance we've covered, because we've been pedalling gently all day. We can see an old stone farmhouse where we thought the hostel ought to be. Wow! It is the hostel! It can't be, this sad-looking building with a saggy roof? But yes it is. We can hardly believe it.

We push our bikes across the wide, dusty yard, prop them against the wall and open the creaking, heavy wooden door. In the gloomy corridor that we've now entered, we come face to face with a well-built, ruddy-faced man, wearing dusty working clothes. He's the warden; quite a pleasant fellow, who is keen to tell us about his project, of renovating this property all by himself. As well as being the warden, he's the builder, the cleaner and possibly the farmer as well. How does he do it all? We negotiate our overnight charge and hand him the monies due. There are no receipts or anything official. We don't mind. We only want a bed for the night.

Now to find the dormitories. He points us in the right direction, up a very wide staircase. The banister rail is about four inches wide with a grooved, wavy pattern all over – it looks like woodworm damage, made by very fat woodworms. Each staircase step has a plank nailed on top for extra strength, because the treads are so riddled with woodworm. There is a wide half-landing where we turn to ascend to the first floor. From here we turn up another wide flight of stairs. On the next half-landing is a boxed-off cubicle. This is a toilet! I shall hate using it.

Lugging our panniers all the way to the top is almost as strenuous as today's cycling has been, although maybe our legs are beginning to ache slightly by now. At the summit, another shock awaits us. There are no dormitories, just one big open space of an attic with wooden posts all over the place, supporting the roof. Old dusty mattresses are laid side by side around the edge. We choose four of them, beneath an open dormer window, but have to remove dead flies before we can lie anything down on them. More dead flies litter the floor between them. This really is a comedown after Inzinzac Lochrist. It's a good job we're so versatile.

Leaving our belongings on our chosen mattresses and taking with us any valuables, we make our way back downstairs to look for the kitchen and dining room. Yet another shocking discovery awaits us. There isn't a proper kitchen or dining room. We're in a large, high-ceilinged room with a couple of mismatched dusty tables in front of us, surrounded by a meagre selection of old chairs, which are also in need of a good clean. In spite of the huge window, it's quite dark in here. The glass is covered in grit and grime and besides, the sun has moved round to the other side of the building. The papered walls are a dingy dark green, with a high stone fireplace on the facing wall. When our eyes have adjusted, we're aware of an animal staring at us intently, but this morphs into a stag's head, on the wall above the fireplace, which surveys us with its glassy eyes. It's uncanny, making us shiver slightly.

On the opposite side of the room is a long, curved bar, just like the bar of a pub, but without the beer pumps. Behind, the shelves beneath the bar are crammed with all we could possibly need – saucepans, plates, cutlery etc etc. Everything is either chipped or bent and nothing matches – just a gathering of any old jumble.

Rob is the first to spot the flypaper hanging from the ceiling. It's absolutely covered with dead flies and sickens us. It must have hung here for weeks. It's directly over the bar, where people are supposed to prepare their food. We're glad to be having something simple tonight – beans on toast. But because everywhere is so unsavoury, we don't even want to use their stuff. So we'll divide the two tins of beans into four small saucepans – the most wholesome ones we can possibly find, which we'll wash first. Then we'll each eat our own heated-up portion straight from the pan. And instead of making toast, we'll just take slices of bread directly from the bag and eat them dry. That will leave us one saucepan apiece to clean afterwards, in that dirty tin sink on the wall behind the bar. Sorted!

We're debating what to do about sleeping. There are blankets lying around in the attic but when were they last washed? We're not prepared to use them. Instead we'll sleep in our clothes, inside our own sheet sleeping bags (which we always bring to use in hostels).

On the middle floor is an unfinished bathroom; well, not so much unfinished as hardly started. There's a huge bath standing on a bare wooden floor with a basin next to it. The crude plumbing is bare, as are the walls and ceiling, which have been stripped back to bare wood. But this is what we must use.

* * *

The sound of Frank choking wakes us up. "I just dreamt I was drowning in a cess-pit," he gasps, but we soon realise why. We all feel like gagging, for pungent farmyard smells are rising up through the open window – cow manure, sheep pee, diesel from a tractor starting up and many other stinks. Then a cockerel crows to herald the arrival of the new day, although it's barely light. Below us, cows are mooing gently, while not far away sheep baa at their bleating lambs. Somewhere dogs are whining, yapping, barking; one's howling. Dave hears the first cuckoo call of the year and we all listen intently to catch it the next time it calls. And, in spite of all these extraneous noises and smells, songbirds are singing sweetly outside our window. We think that if ever we wanted to describe this place, it would have to be by recordings of the sounds and smells; more so than the condition of the building.

I get up to be the first in the bathroom. I'm going to try out the bath. There was hot water for the basin last night, so I'm hoping there'll be more today. It's a huge bath and I enjoy a good soak before having to put my sticky cycling clothes back on. When I return to the attic, Rob and Frank are smirking, sharing some sort of private joke. I'm intrigued. Eventually they let on. Rob has discovered that the bathroom is directly below here, and he and Frank have been peeping through the floorboards, the swines.

Before we leave the hostel, we're eager to take a good photo for a keepsake. With our cameras at the ready, we walk along past the great kitchen-diner window to the far end of the farmhouse. From there, we should be able to take in the whole façade. But what we discover makes us gasp with incredulity. The gable end is falling away. We are actually standing on stones that have fallen from the top. They are now covered in grass and weeds. Nothing is supporting the roof on the near side, so thank goodness we slept on the other side of the attic last night. Our movements on the floorboards might have dislodged those 'pit-props'. This hostel is beyond the pale.

Well, we can't dilly-dally any longer. We must now begin pedalling towards Roscoff, for in two days' time we plan to catch the 4.30 pm ferry for Plymouth. Today, Lannion will be our destination. It's north of here and somewhere east of Roscoff, and it's not far from Brittany's convoluted coastline. We've worked out the route; it's only half as far as we cycled yesterday but as we have less enthusiasm, it will feel more of a chore.

We begin by cycling westwards on a scenic route out of Maël Pestivien until we intercept the D11 at a place called Callac. This road will take us all the way to Lannion. It's a small, fairly twisty road, heading through mixed farmland, sometimes following the course of a river and occasionally passing through small forests. We plod onwards, turning the pedals mindlessly, with no great aim or anticipation ahead of us. The scenery is pleasing enough and the weather still warm but after yesterday's 'walnut shell day' (as we fondly refer to exceptional days out), this is merely mediocre. There's that sinking feeling that the party is almost over and soon we'll all be buckled down to our routines again.

Then out of the blue, Dave breaks into his mantra, *Somebody Stole My Girl*, but stops almost immediately, realising how irritating it has become. Rob takes over by singing the Hollies' song *All I Need is the Air that I Breathe* and we all join in with gusto. And so we continue with our repertoire of 'oldies', all the way to Lannion, buoying our spirits in the process.

We have stayed in Lannoin hostel before, on another of Rachael's trips – a five-day tour of the Pink Granite Coast at Whitsuntide in 1990. It was an action-packed holiday where we kept moving on, in order to complete the circuit in the allotted time. Consequently, we have never actually walked through the centre of this town. It looks charming – full of tall, half-timbered buildings, which overhang the streets and the square.

Feeling quite tired from all our exuberant singing, we're now in a more sober and sentimental mood. We go into a large church nearby to light a candle in memory of one of our club members, who died a few weeks ago from a heart attack while out on a club ride. He was only 49 years old but looked much older, on account of his fluffy white beard. It made him look like a lovable garden gnome. 'Fluffy,' as we called him, had recently gained his 'Randonneur' badge, which entailed doing a 200k, 400k and a 600k cycle ride within the year. He had completed the 600k, from Chepstow to Anglesey and back, just a fortnight before he died. Whether his death was a result of all this strenuous activity or not, we'll never know.

That evening, in the hostel kitchen, we open a tin of minced meat to eat with a load of spaghetti. Then I remember that last time I was here I cooking spaghetti in this kitchen with Fluffy.

(Later in the year, I will buy his hand-built Mercian bike – the one he died on. I was a friend of his, living close by, and as I am of a similar height, his sister will give me first refusal to buy the bike.)

*   *   *

There's no loitering around this morning, we'll head off for Roscoff straight after breakfast. It will be better to arrive early and hang about than to be too late for the ferry. There's a market in the old square today and if we had more time we'd love to have tried the Thai food. It's filling the air with such tempting aromas. But we haven't. We set off, purposefully spinning the pedals in a nice rhythm and accepting the fact that this holiday is almost over. As we cycle past the vast and beautiful beach at St. Michel-en-Grève, we remember the races and long-jump competitions we held here once, during our coffee break. No chance of anything so frivolous now.

I begin to sing *The Carnival is Over* as we spin along. It conveys my feelings well. I remember singing it with the same feelings the last time we returned to Roscoff this way. I'm a silly old so-and-so, wallowing in sentiments, almost in tears.

Now we're turning north towards St. Pol and Roscoff. As we've made good time, we stop for a celebratory lager in a bar at St. Pol. "Yec'had mat" we say to each other and any one else in the bar who might be impressed by our salutation. This holiday, bungling through Brittany with no plan at all, has truly been the most laid-back cycle tour ever. We've thoroughly enjoyed it.

CHAPTER FOURTEEN

End of the Line

August 1989

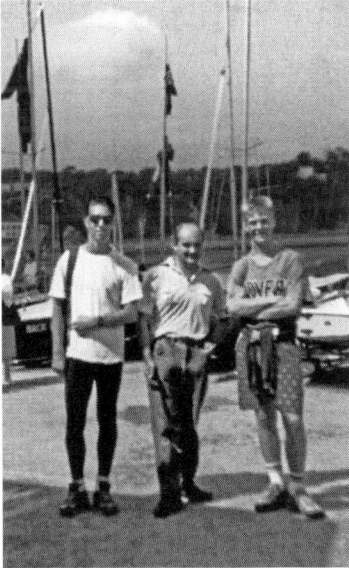

In Tenby harbour we bumped into a friend

"Why don't you cycle round the coast of Wales instead?" someone in the Stroud Cycle Club said as we were riding through the Gloucestershire countryside one Saturday afternoon. I mulled over this suggestion for a mile or two, then realised it was a pretty good idea.

I had already fulfilled my dream of taking my two sons abroad on a cycling/camping holiday, something that had taken several years to come to fruition, as we were so strapped for cash. But we'd managed it, after scraping together enough gear for a basic holiday. In fact we had gone abroad twice, both years to Brittany. That was as far abroad as we could afford. Now my boys, Pete just turned 17 and Malc 15, had reached the age where both would be eligible to pay adult fares on the ferry. That would take a huge chunk of money out of what we'd saved. However, if we stayed this side of the Channel, we could have all that ferry fare to spend. I would put this idea to my boys.

Luckily for me, Pete and Malc soon came on board with this new proposal. But they made one stipulation; on the way round, they wanted to visit the funfairs at both Barry Island and Porthcawl. I couldn't argue with that. Now they were older, they would be having much more input into steering this holiday. I was just lucky that they enjoyed cycling and camping as much I did. They also insisted that we should buy a new tent. The two cheap little tents we'd used before had had their day.

There was no defined plan for this holiday, except that we would spend three weeks away, as we had before. We also arranged to meet up with three young friends from the cycle club for the August Bank holiday, wherever we happened to be by then. I thought it would give the boys a break from being stuck with just Mum for company.

The first day we crossed the Severn Bridge, only reaching Chepstow in the early evening, having dithered about far too long and left Stroud much later than intended. The weather was fair, with a slight breeze and light cloud cover. We stopped to admire Chepstow Castle from the bridge over the River Wye, and the very pretty hanging baskets across the bridge itself. The nearest campsite was at the small hamlet of Beachley, which we'd already ridden over on the Severn Bridge. But to reach it, we had to slog up a big hill beyond Chepstow, turn right at the top, then return all the way down the other side, until we were back in front of Chepstow. It was worth the toil, I suppose, as the overnight charge was only £2. The campsite was very basic, with one dirty toilet and a water tap. The field was adjacent to the bank of the Wye, where it joins the Severn Estuary. That beautiful river, as I knew it to be, was reduced to a muddy-banked outlet by the ebbing tide.

We pitched our tent close to a huge pylon that dominated the field. That was the flattest place available. Our new dome tent gave us a more optimistic outlook on camping, as it was easier to erect than the previous ones. With one of the boys carrying the tent itself and the other the poles and pegs, their loads were fairly equal in weight. Their sleeping bags and camping mats were wrapped around these tent parts, in a roll across the top of their panniers. I carried all the cooking stuff in my panniers and my clothes in a roll-on top. The tent was plenty big enough for the three of us, it being a four-person tent. I remember sleeping like a log that first night.

* * *

The next morning, in similar weather, we slogged back to the top of the hill and carried straight on through Caldicot, Caerleon and Newport, on minor roads wherever possible, sometimes not far from the coast. However, through the busy centre of Cardiff we found no alternatives but main roads. Here we encountered more hassle from mindless pedestrians who stepped off the kerb in front of us than from the traffic itself. From bustling Cardiff we soon reached sedate Penarth on a 'B' road, heading for a campsite at Lavernock Point.

You could imagine this point as being the bottom corner of Wales, almost opposite Weston-super-Mare on the other side of the Severn Estuary. Unlike Weston though, we saw no sand or mud here, just layered rocks, like an uneven pavement – a real novelty for Pete and Malc. We walked a long way along the southern edge that evening, absorbed in flinging flat stones as far as possible, but oblivious, for a while, of the speed of the incoming tide. In the nick of time, we raced back and escaped up a steep little dirt track to our campsite.

* * *

The third day brought us to Barry Island where, as planned by the boys, we spent loads of time and money on rides at the funfair. Even I enjoyed the experience – they were good old-fashioned rides, not like the freaky ones you get nowadays. Afterwards, we still had time to reach Ogmore-by-Sea, where the basic campsite was in a small field, next to a farm. We had bacon and eggs – fresh from the farm, with fried bread for our evening meal, cooked in our little frying pan. I thought it would be a quick option but in actual fact it took ages. We had to eat one at a time, and being Mum, I cooked mine last. Meanwhile, the boys entertained themselves in the evening sunshine, daring the incoming waves to catch them as they stood on a low rocky ledge around a small inlet. As I ate my supper alone then washed up,

I noticed that some waves were unpredictably high. I shudder now, knowing how many people are swept off rocks by rogue waves and how many are dragged into the sea by rip tides – something I knew nothing about then. They say ignorance is bliss; but only if you get away with it.

* * *

Porthcawl was only round the next bay from where we were camped. But the next morning we realised we'd have to cycle to Bridgend in a big arc first, then back down to the coast again. That was the only way. As it was relatively near, we arrived before the funfair had even opened, so we bought a large portion of chips to share while we waited for the midday opening.

Being full of chips wasn't the best approach to fairground rides but luckily for me, and less so for Pete and Malc, there wasn't anything too gut-wrenching at this place. The best ride was on the old figure of eight, a type I remembered from Butlins in Skegness, back in the 50s, except that here, for the grand finale, the cars came whooshing spectacularly down a chute and through a trough of water, wetting the spectators more that the riders. We had several rides on this before resorting to the Ghost Train. It had been a bit of an anti-climax for the boys but at least they'd been there and 'got the T-shirt'.

Mildly satisfied with the day so far, we set off westwards, heading towards Swansea and the Gower peninsula, which I'd heard was a good place for seaside holidays. This stretch of our trip was not so enjoyable – often on main roads and adjacent to the M4. Nor was it very scenic, apart from the towering and often tree-clad hills on our right, which seemed menacingly near. The topography of this part of South Wales allowed for only a fairly narrow margin of flat ground between the mountains and the coast, along which ran the railway, the motorway and all subsidiary roads, which every now and then, swapped sides with the motorway.

With the sea in view again we could see many tall chimneys ahead, puthering smoke into the atmosphere. We were approaching Port Talbot. I knew nothing then about its famous steelworks but I thought it the direst town I had ever seen and felt sorry for the inhabitants who had to live there. To get through the terraced streets of grimy brick houses as fast as we could, we pedalled like mad. Then hearing buzzing noises behind us, we looked round to find we were being chased by about a dozen youths on scooters. We tried to pedal even faster, unsure of their intentions and feeling quite frightened. But we soon realised that had they wished, they could have caught us up quite easily. They were just intimidating us for a pastime, something to do in this uninspiring environment.

We negotiated our way into Swansea, stopping first for photos on a bridge spanning another muddy estuary, before tackling the town itself. But once we'd turned the corner of the bay, we found ourselves in lovely warm sunshine, heading south on a coastal road to Mumbles. Things were looking promising. Along the sea front we enjoyed a well-earned ice cream before taking out the map to choose a campsite on the Gower Peninsula. This stretches westwards behind the hills of Mumbles. We chose Oxwich Bay, because we could see it had a long stretch of sand. There was a campsite just half a mile up from the beach. So now, with not a cloud in the sky and renewed enthusiasm, we pedalled off to find it.

For several miles we cycled west, along a main road with splendid views of the sparkling sea to our left. Then turning seawards on the appropriate road, we careered down steep descents to reach Oxwich Bay. Of course, we couldn't possibly cycle past the beach without sampling it first, so we spent a good half hour on the shore before we even looked for the campsite.

The site was fairly full but with enough space to pitch our tent and allow us enough room to lounge about in the sunshine, at the front. We were really pleased with the place. It had good facilities, including a shop. We booked in for three nights.

* * *

The weather was glorious and the next two days were spent almost entirely on the beach, swimming, exploring or, in the boys' case, generally messing about on the rocks. They were happy, so I was happy. And I was happy anyway. The last thing I wanted was for them to get bored and lose interest.

Now that Bank Holiday was drawing nearer, we had to decide on a convenient place to meet our friends. On the map, Tenby seemed like an easily accessible place for them to find us. We couldn't contact them, as they were currently cycling and camping in France. This was before mobile phones. The plan was that when we reached our designated place of rendezvous, I would phone the mother of one of them.

* * *

So after our third night at Oxwich Bay, we were, rather reluctantly, compelled to up sticks and move on to Tenby, a long haul of about 83 miles. We felt fairly chuffed to be ready to leave by 9.30 am. but unfortunately Malc realised he'd left his watch on the windowsill in the washroom, so we rushed back down the long hill we'd just climbed to retrieve it. It wasn't there. We checked at the camp office to see if it had been handed in. It hadn't. So the only consolation I could offer Malc was that as we went through Reynoldston, which was the nearest village, we would report it missing at the police station, if there was one. I knew we'd be wasting our time, but Malc would feel less upset if he thought it might be found.

All this messing about cost us a lot of time and, although we searched, we didn't find a police station in Reynoldston. Then we spent even more time taking photos of wild ponies before we left. We were sorry to be leaving, I guess.

That day proved to be a long slog. We cycled along the top of the Gower peninsular to Gorseinon, then on to Llanelli where, on 'B' roads, we cut northwest to Carmarthen. Here we stopped at a café for sustenance. We were hot and tired. These smaller roads were quite hilly and often I had to push my bike up them. But we had to keep going. After a short break we set off south westwards on another small road, from which, although near to the coast on the map, there was no sea in sight. We pedalled through the outskirts of Pendine Sands and on to Amroth. Here the road took us inland, so that we had to find another route back towards the coast. The steep hills were even more frequent here, but at long last we passed through Saundersfoot and arrived in Tenby, tired out.

It was evening now and we needed to find a campsite quickly. But the one we found was fairly disappointing, with no views. It was surrounded by a wire fence and seemed to be next to an MOD rifle range. In the gathering gloom, I had to look for a telephone box to call my friend's mother and let her know exactly where we were, when all I really wanted to do was flop down on my sleeping mat to recover. However, I was nicely surprised to find that the boys had put up the tent in my absence. All we needed to do now was prepare a meal.

* * *

After Oxwich Bay, this campsite was a real comedown. But the day dawned bright and sunny, so we weren't downhearted. We had most of the day to explore Tenby then look forward to the arrival of our friends.

Tenby was fascinating, with its medieval walls and old harbour. There are three beaches – one facing north with the harbour, one facing south and then a really long stretch facing southeast. We walked the cobbled streets, marvelled at the medieval walls and admired the gardens on the hilltop before going down to the old harbour in the midday sun. As we wandered around it, we met a neighbour from Stroud who was on a day trip with his elderly mother. As well as living at the end of our lane, we also knew him from the local canoe club we were in. He was chuffed to bits to bump into us – almost literally, because he was semi-blind.

At teatime our three young friends arrived with their bikes on the roof rack, having driven directly from the ferry port to meet up with us. They were Andy and Liz, a fairly newly-aligned couple, and their friend Dan, who was providing the transport. All three were in their early twenties and were fun to be with.

They quickly pitched their tents adjacent to ours and afterwards, we snacked on any food we had available between us. It was a nice surprise to find we could all sit snugly inside our new tent, where Liz produced a game of 'Piggie'. This is a light-hearted game where you throw two little pigs, rather like throwing dice, and the score depends on which way up they land. Together with the wine we were drinking, we had quite a laugh.

* * *

The whole of the next morning we spent showing our friends around Tenby, like seasoned guides. Then we boarded the ferry to nearby Caldey Island and explored the old monastic buildings, enjoying the tranquillity. As it was yet another hot, sunny day, we sunbathed for ages on a gorgeous grassy bank overlooking the sea towards Tenby before returning on the ferry. There was still time to move on to a nicer campsite, so we packed up the tents and relocated to Manorbier, which was about ten miles further along the coast. Dan drove his car, carrying our luggage, while the rest of us cycled there.

This was a superb campsite, next to an old castle and in view of the sea. In the evening we strolled along the coastal path in the glow of a beautiful sunset. As the light was fading, we turned in for the night.

* * *

It was Bank Holiday Sunday and Andy's 21st birthday. To make it special, we held his head down a toilet and pulled the flush. Poor Andy took it in good heart, being of such an easy-going nature. However, after breakfast, he made a dreadful discovery; Liz and Dan had secretly formed an allegiance. She had changed her choosing. Andy was devastated. The next couple of hours were spent awkwardly as we busied ourselves quietly around our tents and bikes, feigning busyness but performing unnecessary tasks. All the while, Andy sat smarting outside his tent.

But being such a gorgeous day weather-wise, we couldn't possibly waste it. A couple of us went in the car with Dan to look for a cake shop. At the very least, we could buy a cake to celebrate Andy's 21st birthday. Dan, who had contributed the most, presented Andy with the lovely cream-filled gateau, like a peace offering in a way. That seemed to ease the tension and Andy brightened up somewhat. After all, Liz had been his very first girlfriend; there was plenty of time for others.

It didn't take long to polish off this cake and then, in brighter mood, we trotted off to the beach for a game of Frisbee. Later, to round off the day, we took Andy for a meal and a few drinks in a nearby pub. By night time he seemed fairly happy, although the alcohol must have played a part.

* * *

Our friends would have to return home later in the day but we made the most of the morning by cycling over to Pembroke. We ought to have gone into the museum. It looked extremely interesting from the blurb we read on the door, and from observing the gypsy wagon parked in the grounds outside. But being tight cyclists, we didn't want to fork out for the entrance fee, especially as we wouldn't have been able to spend much time in there. We didn't even get to see the castle.

So after a brisk return on the bikes, where I was only just keeping up with the rest of them, it was time for the trio to pack up and drive home. We were sad to see them go but also vaguely relieved. Now we could get on with our touring again. To pass the remainder of the day, we walked a few miles along the coast in the opposite direction, towards Tenby. It was a most scenic walk, spoilt though, by Pete and Malc, who kept pretending to overbalance on the edge of cliffs. And the more I reacted, the more they did it. I was really strung up by the time we got back.

As we lay in our sleeping bags that night, ready to drop off, we were disturbed by the return of our neighbours to their adjacent tent – a foursome of teachers. They must have been in the pub, listening to a person with a broad Midland accent, because for ages they kept emulating his voice. "Weyur gowin' 'ome t'marraow", one would say, then they'd all split their sides laughing.

It was such a relief when at long last, everything went quiet. Now we could get to sleep. But out of the silence, one of them suddenly uttered the phrase again and once again they all erupted into laughter. This went on and on sporadically, until we would gladly have strangled them.

* * *

We were packed and ready to go by ten o'clock in spite of our disturbed night's sleep. There was less enthusiasm about us than before the Bank Holiday – perhaps it was because we were back down to just the three of us, or maybe because the weather wasn't so promising; or were we just tired? Anyway, we were gone before the teachers showed their ugly faces – well they would have been ugly if we'd had anything to do with it!

As we followed the coast westwards, we came across St Govan's Head and went to explore. Halfway down the steep rocky path, we were fascinated to discover the tiny St Govan's Chapel, tucked in against the rocks. We gave it the once over, then emerged on the lower side to find the waves exploding on the rocks below, sending plumes of water high into the air. Pete and Malc were mesmerised and I had a job to drag them away.

From the map, this coastal road seemed to be leading to a dead end, so we back-tracked to Pembroke and continued across the estuary of the river (the Cleddau, but we couldn't pronounce it) north to Haverfordwest. The sky was overcast and it was drizzling slightly. We hadn't taken much interest in our surroundings that day, which was a shame because there must have been plenty to see on the way. When we arrived in the town, we wandered up a nondescript street until we found somewhere to eat – a nondescript pub. Maybe we were at the wrong end of town, but it didn't inspire us much.

After our fish and chips we studied the map more closely. We'd been a bit hasty in taking this route north to Haverfordwest, cutting out a lot of the western coast of Pembrokeshire. But we weren't prepared to detour back now, nor even consider going west from here, to St. David's or Fishguard. Already half of our allotted holiday time was used up and there was a lot more coastline for us to see further north. But in doing what we had done, it's possible we'd missed some of the best parts of the Welsh coast.

If we now carried on north-westwards we would cross the Preseli Mountains. I had been told how pretty they were and what wonderful views we would see from the top. We came out of the grotty pub and found the right road, riding gently for the first few miles to get acclimatised. As the road began to rise we started putting more effort into the pedals. It would be uphill all the way now and hard work. The higher we cycled, the mistier it became, until soon we were enveloped in dense cloud. Now it was raining – relentless, dismal, wet, wet creeping rain that gradually soaked through our clothes until it was literally running down our skin. We couldn't tell the difference between sweat and wet, but we ploughed onwards and upwards, miserable as sin. Forget the views – we could hardly see the road ahead of us. We must have been at the top now because the pedalling was easier, although all we could see was the three of us, moving in convoy through a gap in the gloom.

Before we began the descent, we stopped to check our brakes, feeling drenched and wretched.

"Mum," said Pete, "when we get to Cardigan can we catch the train home?"

My heart missed a beat. What! We were only halfway through the holiday.

"Don't worry, Pete. I know it's horrible now but it's only because we're high up. It'll be OK when we get down the other side, I'm sure."

"But I'd like to go clubbing next week," said Pete, and that comment cut me to the quick. He'd rather go clubbing than be on a cycling holiday. Malc was siding with Pete. He wanted to catch the train home as well.

My heart was heavy as we made our cautious descent down the other side and into Cardigan. We had indeed come out of the cloud but were still in dreary drizzle. In our soaking shoes we slopped around looking for a station sign or a TIC where we could enquire about the train times. We found the Information Office first, and dripping drops everywhere, pushed through the door. "Can you tell us where the railway station is?" I asked.

"Oh sorry dear," replied the lady, "the station closed ten years ago." That was a real smack in the face for the boys and even for me, I suppose. It would have been an easy option right then to escape from that soaking situation. But who could tell? By tomorrow the sun might come out again and the boys might change their minds and want to carry on. The lady behind the desk told us we would have to cycle a few miles up the coast to find a campsite. All I remembered was that the campsite began with a 'T'.

It was a real drag, pedalling uphill up the coast, feeling depleted of both energy and spirit. But we pushed on. That was the only option. At last we found this campsite at a place called Tresaith, where all we could see from the stony entrance track were long caravans. They were pitched in rows, almost set out like streets, on a vast grassy slope which ended in an abrupt drop into the sea. Each caravan had its front corners propped up by a tower of breezeblocks, to render it level and safe for habitation. We were fascinated by them and distracted for a moment or two from our own feelings of wretchedness.

Further round the track was an area for pitching tents. Where were we going to start? The prospect was daunting. Foolishly, when we should have known better, we had bought a new tent in a sale, where the inside had to be erected first – just like the two little ridge tents we had discarded. Consequently, the inside would get wet before we had the top on.

Moving clumsily in our uncomfortable wetness, we took the rolls off the boys' bikes and carefully extracted the tent parts from the inside, without exposing their sleeping bags to the elements. They wouldn't want to be sleeping in wet beds as well. In the drizzle, the boys pitched the inner tent onto the soaking grass as quickly as was feasible, while I attempted to hold the outer tent overhead, to prevent everything from getting too wet. But I realised I was hampering more than helping, although my intentions were good. The boys could do it quicker by themselves. So I left them to it and took my panniers off the bike. I was glad we'd had the foresight to buy a couple of tins of beans and some bread rolls in Cardigan.

With the tent pitched, what next? There was a small porch area on the front of the tent where we would each have to crouch in turn to take off our wet clothes, putting them into a carrier bag. The boys allowed me to go first. Sitting on a spare bag, I stripped off and put on dry clothes. Then I placed my carrier bag of wet clothes at the side of the porch. Next, I removed everything else from my panniers into the tent. I placed my wet panniers out in the porch with my clothes. Then Pete handed in the bed rolls.

Malc took his turn next, following the same procedure as me.

It wasn't easy in such a cramped space, especially for the boys, who had grown so tall. Pete was gracious enough to wait until last. Now it was my turn to contribute by cooking supper. I was just setting up the little stove inside the porch opening when a man appeared at the entrance carrying three mugs of steaming hot tea for us. What a wonderful and welcoming gesture from a fellow camper. We were overcome with gratitude. Another camper appeared and offered us a packet of biscuits. How kind people were. Our misery must have been palpable. Now we felt human again.

I lit the stove and heated up the beans and buttered the rolls, and we ate like royals (or so it felt). I would wash up in the morning. It was getting dark now, so we climbed into our sleeping bags, snug at last. For a while, we listened to our miniature radio, bought in France last year. Then we switched off and fell into luxurious, deep slumber.

* * *

The next morning, the sun came out to greet us, just as I had hoped. Would the boys carry on camping, I wondered? By the time we had eaten breakfast and I'd done a double washing-up, the tent was almost dry and ready for packing. If it stayed like this, we could dry our wet clothes on the bikes as we rode along. Today we were going to cycle up the main coastal road to Aberystwyth. Then who knows what would happen. But first we went to thank our kindly neighbours for the tea and biscuits.

Cycling was very straightforward. We only looked at the map once, to see how far Aberaeron was from the main road – no distance at all. We sat on the beach there for a while, eating the baguettes we'd just bought from a nearby shop; then went back for coffee.

Considering that we'd been cycling on a main road, there had been little traffic. Well it was midweek – Wednesday in fact. But with this lovely coastline, you would expect visitors to be flocking there. Perhaps the Welsh kids were already back in school. The beach was uncannily quiet. I had no idea what the boys were thinking. I didn't dare ask them if they wanted to continue with the holiday. I would just play it by ear.

By 4.30 we had reached Aberystwyth, with a view to looking round it. Then Pete suggested it might be best to check the train times first before we went into town. Now I knew for sure what their intentions were. As the railway station was quite easy to find from there, we soon arrived on a platform, where the wide double-door of a carriage was open to welcome us. The floor of the carriage and the platform were on a level with each other – a tempting step away and the train was due to leave for Birmingham in five minutes. It seemed to be waiting for us. Was it the hand of fate making the decision? The temptation was too great. We stepped aboard.

The journey was an enjoyable scenic and sunny one. I sat next to a Welsh lady who pointed out to me all the places of interest. Then after she'd left the train, some distance later, I began to wonder what we were going to do that night. We couldn't pitch our tents in the middle of Birmingham, for goodness sake. Would we ride to the outskirts? We wouldn't have a clue where to go though, or how far. I was beginning to feel quite concerned by the time we arrived in Birmingham at eight o'clock. It would be pitch dark in an hour. Perhaps we should catch another train going south from here, where we could put up the tent. I really didn't know the answer; nor did I know if the boys were expecting me to make a decision.

We looked at the timetables on a board and found there was a train going to Worcester – much later. That was in the direction of home, but we would have to look for a campsite when we got there. At that moment though, we were feeling very hungry. All the station cafés had closed, so we had to go out onto the streets to find something. It was not nice, being on those strange city streets in the dark. We stuck close together. Once again we chose fish and chips and brought them back onto the station, where we soon devoured them.

We duly caught the Worcester train, which I was horrified to find arrived at five minutes to midnight. Everything was getting horribly out of hand. How on earth could we find a campsite from there? Not to worry – the boys had no intention of camping. No! They were going to cycle home down the A38. But first we had to get ourselves onto that road.

Pete found the correct direction to take and one behind the other, Pete in the front and me bringing up the rear, we set off southwards, in the direction of Gloucestershire, while still in the lamp-lights of Worcester. Barely fifteen minutes later we heard a thud and Pete's bike dragged to a halt. Malc and I braked hard to miss him. Whatever had happened? Then we saw his panniers lying on the floor. The bolts holding the pannier rack to the seat post had broken, and the whole lot had crashed to the ground in a 90-degree arc. How maddening to have to get tools out and look for bolts at this time of night, when our prospects were so daunting anyway. But Pete was soon on the case. This was what he was good at. Malc and I just stood watching while he fixed it.

We soon reached the A38 and set off, resigned to our fate. All we had to do was keep pedalling for thirty-odd miles. But Pete's rear light was dazzling Malc and Malc's was dazzling me. So they switched theirs off. It was hard to see the verge and because so few vehicles were about, we rode down the white line in the middle of the road. We even switched off our front lights, unless a vehicle was approaching, because our eyes had adjusted to the darkness and we were able to see.

Mile after mile we pedalled, on and on, mesmerised by the white line down the middle of the road; almost in a trance. It felt surreal. At last, we were passing through Gloucester – nearly there. Soon we'd need to turn off the A38, through Stonehouse, to Stroud.

As we reached the outskirts of Stroud, the milkmen were out delivering. Dawn was breaking. So was my heart. "What are the birds singing for?" I wondered. "This is not a celebration." We had come to the end of the line and my cycling and camping holidays with the boys were, I felt sure, sadly over.

DAY of RECKONING

March 1997

Arriving at El Chorro

As we whiz past an unexpected opening in the roadside greenery, I hear a woman shout "Wheer's the shoovul Doock?" Hearing this sudden English voice in the middle of nowhere, in the middle of Andalucia, we pull up sharply. We're very curious to see who's talking – not only talking English but in the Lincolnshire dialect that I grew up with.

We gaze through the sturdy wire fence to see a maturing grey-haired woman walking across the large grassy plot, which is dotted with lemon and orange trees. She looks up, surprised. "'Ello, wheer uv you two coom frum?" Soon we're in lively conversation through the wire fence. We learn that they are Dory and Stan, from Lincolnshire of course, who are in the process of building a little 'finca' on this plot. What is surprising is that they look so very ordinary and talk as if they come from a rural background – not the sort of couple you would expect to up sticks and set up a new life in a foreign country; more the sort you might see at a whist drive in the village hall, or going to town on a Friday night to play bingo.

Stan shows us the footings and drainage trenches that have already been dug and meanwhile, they are living in a caravan. He points to a corner and now we see it, tucked in behind the trees. It looks as if they have established the garden first and the finca will be an added extra. But this is not their only property, we find; they also have a flat in Fuengirola, down on the Costa del Sol, where they go when there's a good football match on the telly. Flippin' heck, we think to ourselves, fancy having a flat on the Costa del Sol, just to watch a flippin' football match. But we haven't heard it all yet. They also own a little chalet at Chapel St. Leonards, which is (or was) a tiny village a few miles north of Skegness, in Lincolnshire. So in the two hottest months of the year, they return to good old England, where they can shiver to their hearts content in the bracing breezes on the east coast. What a varied lifestyle! What an inspiring couple!

We enjoy talking to them and they in turn seem glad to talk to us. They look to be in their early seventies, that is, unless the sun has aged them prematurely. This seems a bit old to be starting out on such a project, but we hope they'll have time to enjoy it.

This chance meeting has done us good; after the trauma of yesterday, it's good to talk about bricks and mortar and football matches. We'd just spent the last three nights at a climbers' hostel north of here, at El Chorro, where we'd learnt about the 'Camino del Rey' (the King's Walk). It wasn't as if the previous week of cycling in Andalucia had been unexciting – no. But to walk the walk would be the epitome of adventures.

We are on the last lap of a circular tour in the mountains of southern Spain, heading back to the inn from which we started nine days ago. This inn, called Finca la Mota, is situated in the plains of the Guadalhorce River, west of Malaga. Just over a week ago, we set off westwards from the comforts of the finca, feeling quite apprehensive about how we would fare with just a Lonely Planet book to guide us.

The first night we stayed at a hostel in the village of Yunquera, tucked up in a fantastic range of mountains called the Sierra de la Nieves. It was cool up there and we had to put on our fleece-lined winter 'longs' and jackets. Between villages, we encountered not a soul. Sometimes we felt so isolated that we imagined it possible that bandits might attack us. We'd heard rumours.

The first thing we did on arrival in Yunquera was to find a bar for a much-needed drink. When we turned round after being served, a crowd of children was gawping at us through the large shop-like window, their noses pressed against the glass. Well we did look quite colourful, I suppose, in our red cycling jackets with bright yellow stripes down the arms, but apart from that, they must be wondering what on earth a woman was doing in a 'men only' bar. I stood uncomfortably amongst disapproving glances, watching a gory bull fight on the TV, which was up on a high shelf.

* * *

In the early chill next morning, we walked down a steep lane through Yunquera to the fields beyond to view the village from a different perspective. This village seemed to be stuck in a time warp of bygone days, as many small villages were still, at that time. We saw mules being brought out of their cave-like hovels to be harnessed and loaded up for their day's labour. I have seen recent photos of Yunquera and it's changed a lot since then.

We continued on towards Ronda, where halfway up a mountain we sat in a pine forest to escape the heat. We had already passed amazing viewpoints on the way. We'd been blown away by the fantastic vistas. But the heat was exhausting when we came down from the heights and it was great to sit amongst these trees to cool down, inhaling the lovely pine aroma as we prepared for the remainder of our climb.

Almost in sight of Ronda, we had to take another rest. We huddled together under the shade of the only bush we could find, looking out over a massive valley, where Frank pointed out to me an 'inversion', he being a weather buff.

Once in Ronda we soon found ourselves a cheap hotel room, but it wasn't very nice, as it had no windows at all. The bathroom had a bath but there was no plug, so I had to put a sock in it! We both had a quick bath then went out on the town. But we'd barely left the hotel before being accosted by a man who generously offered to show us around, introducing himself as Francisco Caballeros. He was a tall good-looking fellow in dark sunglasses, whose black wavy hair was reminiscent of the Teddy Boy styles of the 50s, but without the sideburns. He told us he had nine 'cheeldren' – showing a mouthful of lovely white teeth as he made this statement. But we were hungry, so Francisco agreed to wait for us, loitering nearby, as we ate a meal on the veranda of a hotel, which overlooked a square. We couldn't seem to shake him off.

Afterwards, we allowed him to show us the sights of Ronda, a town perched on the edge of a huge and dramatic gorge. It was a stunning sight. In what Francisco said was a palace, I had a sudden impulse to play the piano I had spotted and surprised them with my rendition of Beethoven's *Pathétique*, which resonated well in the large room. Frank didn't know I had that hidden talent. He also didn't know that it was the only piece of music I could remember all the way through!

Luckily, we had the evening to ourselves, as Francisco had gone home to his nine 'cheeldren'. We strolled along a beautiful, wide promenade-like terrace with iron railings along the edge and gazed down into the vast depths of the gorge, where the evening sun lit up pretty irises that were growing out of the rocks. Across the gorge, we enjoyed a wonderful sunset as the red-glowing sun sank slowly behind distant blue-hued mountains. We'd be cycling over those mountains before long.

* * *

After a claustrophobic night in our airless room, we were glad to get out of the hotel, to take breakfast on that same veranda – dried out baguettes from yesterday, toasted and with butter and marmalade. But there was Francisco hovering around the square again, waiting for us. We hadn't given him any money for showing us around yesterday. Was he still hoping to get something out of us today? He wasn't a bad chap, but he was altogether too persistent. Anyway we wanted to do our own thing today. We'd read in our Lonely Planet book about some interesting caves at Benaojan, a small village not far from Ronda. Now we looked for it on our map. It wasn't many miles from here.

Francisco came over when he saw that we'd finished breakfast, although we could have pretended to drink coffee forever, just to get rid of him nicely. "Let's tell him then," muttered Frank. So we conveyed, in our language differences, that we didn't want to look round Ronda any more, we were going to explore the area on our bikes. With tail between legs, Francisco walked away.

We fetched the bikes and prepared for our excursion before heading up a wide main road, out of town. Then, unbelievably, Francisco came racing up alongside us on a bike. Oh no, we thought, he's not coming with us, surely? But at the traffic lights at the top, he turned right and bade us 'Adios', while we turned left for Benaojan. Ah, thank goodness. He must be going back to his nine cheeldren.

When we reached the village of Benaojan, Frank was not feeling at all well. The intense heat was getting to him. I went into a bar for a bottle of something to drink and found the atmosphere distinctly hostile. A woman in Lycra shorts walking into their bar! How dare she? However, I stood my ground until I got served. We shared the drink and carried on, for we still had a couple of miles to go. But Frank now had a pounding headache, so we sat under the meagre shade of a tree for half an hour, until he felt he could continue. When we finally arrived at the cave and climbed all the way up the stone steps to the entrance (a small hole up the mountainside with an iron grill gate across it) it was locked. Closed for lunch! Frank was cross with himself for holding us up. There was nothing for it now but to carry on down the swooping road we were on to find some shelter.

At the very bottom, round a bend, was a clump of low evergreens in the valley. We crawled under them, resigned to our fate, and sat scrunched up, grumbling. Then I thought what a good opportunity this would be to write the postcards I had bought in Ronda. Frank didn't have any similar occupation, so his long, cramped wait for afternoon opening was much more tedious than mine, but his headache subsided.

At last, it was time to come out of hiding. We were quite a bit cooler now, although by the time we'd ridden back up to the 'cave' mountain, we were hot and sweaty once more. We locked the bikes and climbed the stone steps to the now open iron grill gate, where we stooped to climb through the hole.

Inside, several people were gathered in the dark. We hung on in awkward silence, wondering what would happen next, but I think the young man behind the wooden counter was waiting to see if anyone else would turn up. While we waited, he lifted three paraffin lamps onto the counter and lit them, then chose three people to carry them, Frank being one of them. Meanwhile four more people climbed through the hole to join us, bringing the number to about ten. The guide lit another lamp and now had to decide in which language to give his tour. By a show of hands, it was decided that the English predominated – very lucky for us. Most of the others were German and most Germans can speak English anyway.

These caves belonged to a local family, we learnt, discovered by the grandfather of the present owners, who had climbed through a fissure in the rocks, following bats. He wanted to collect their droppings to fertilize his fields. Inside he had found bones on the floor and drawings on the walls but thought they'd been left by Moorish occupation. A few years later, a local historian, hearing about this discovery, investigated the caves and made the wonderful revelation that the remains and paintings dated from 25,000 BC at least – on a par with many famous caves across Europe. Then in 1925, the farmer's son discovered a new opening, which is the one used today to take guided visitors. The young man who was about to take us on the tour was probably a grandson, and because the caves are family owned they haven't been exploited.

The guide locked the gate, locking us all in, then we set off cautiously following the glow of the lamps, trying to see where we were treading, as the surface was quite uneven. All around us, when we looked away from the lamplight, was pitch black and, with the chill in the caves we were shivering, perhaps from excitement as well. The young man stopped at every point of interest, first showing us cross-hatching of charcoal lines on a rock-face, indicative of man's earliest known attempts of calendar keeping, with the crossing-off of passing days. On another rock wall was a huge painting of a fish, with what looked like a seal inside its stomach. Then the loveliest one of all, I thought, depicted a pregnant mare, outlined in black but covered in brown spots. There were numerous other animals, some just outlined in black charcoal, and all these, incredibly, had been painted on the walls thousands and thousands of years ago.

To reach some of the chambers we climbed steps and to get to others there were downward slopes to negotiate. When we came to a pool of water the guide looked quite upset. Coins had been thrown into the pool and these, he said, would contaminate the water, which would poison the bats. Then he asked us to be silent while he tapped on a wall of stalactites, resembling the pipes of a gigantic church organ. We could hear musical notes echoing below us and he explained that there were even more caverns underneath, which were equally extensive. We felt very honoured to have seen these caves, doubly so because they hadn't been spoilt by modern interventions.

Although it felt much warmer when we emerged from the cave, it was considerably cooler than when we'd arrived. That was fortunate, because it was a struggle to cycle up the long hill to the main road, although after that it was an easy ride back to Ronda. In the evening, after our meal, we wandered a little aimlessly round the streets, not seeing anything of great interest. In retrospect we could have looked in on the bullring, the oldest in Spain. Or walked down to the bottom of the gorge. It's regrettable that we didn't.

* * *

The weather felt nice and fresh as we headed out of Ronda next morning, going westwards on the main road. When a long line of Harley Davidson bikers roared past us, we realised it must be a Sunday morning. They were probably heading for a mass gathering in Seville. We turned off to the left soon after, in the direction of the village of Grazalema. We had no plans to visit big cities on cycles.

We cycled through varied countryside, with woodlands of cork oaks and fields of crops. But gradually the terrain became more mountainous, although it didn't feel as arduous as our journeys to Yunquera or Ronda had been, and the valleys here seemed more lush and the mountains less barren. We reached Grazalema by early afternoon. It was a neat-looking town of pristine white houses, all with matching pinkish-brown tiles and with pretty flowers poking through the black railings of their balconies – very pleasant indeed.

In a square in the village, several families were enjoying a Sunday afternoon relax. We sat on a bench, to rest a while. It was a lovely half-hour, being entertained by a little girl on a toddler trike. She would pedal right up to our knees, to tell us something in her Spanish prattle, then throw back her head and laugh, as if she'd just told us a great joke, before pedalling off again. We never understood what the joke was but she was so endearing. Her parents grinned at us. We almost felt part of the community.

After that interlude we waved 'adios' to the little girl and set off to explore the village. At one crossroads, we had to do a double take, for the huge crest of a mountain dominated the end of the street, like some big dinosaur rearing its head above the rooftops. This was in fact called the Peñon Grande, part of the Sierra del Pinar, the mountains against which Grazalema is built.

We snacked outside a café, under the shade of an orange canopy, which gave the table and our faces a pleasant glow. This was a lovely village but we hoped to travel a little further that afternoon before finding somewhere to stay. We weren't sure how far west we would cycle on this holiday – perhaps as far as Arcos. But Jerez, further west near the Atlantic coast, would be pushing it too far, because we might not get back to Finca la Mota in time for our flight home.

I'd been complaining about the jockey wheel on my derailleur gears for the last few hours. When in my lowest gear, this little wheel was rubbing against the chain, thwarting my efforts to climb mountains. We pulled into the forecourt of a hotel so that Frank could try to mend it for me. He emptied his tools out onto a duster and set about the task in hand. Just after that a policeman walked by and came in to see if he could assist. But Frank had already sussed out the problem and competently made adjustments. He didn't want a Spanish policeman compromising his competency.

This policeman was such a nice guy though. He could speak some English and took a real interest in where we had been so far and where we planned to go from here. Then he told us that a "really splendid" route to take would be to turn north, just beyond the town and cross the mountain range to Zahara de la Sierra. Could we possibly do it before nightfall, we asked? He assured us that we could, and told us to look out for the rare fir trees growing higher up the mountainside, facing Grazalema. They are called Pinsapo pines. He described them as very tall and cone-shaped and said that in the spring they were a bluish grey in colour. He said that they had been around since before the last Ice Age.

Thanking the kind policeman, we set off to find this mountain road to Zahara, quite apprehensive about the lateness of the hour. But we tried to be calm and pedal steadily, just slowly knocking off the miles as we gained height. And as we climbed higher, the vistas beyond Grazalema and the surrounding area, known as the Sierra de Grazalema National Park, became "really splendid," just as the policeman had promised. Sometimes the road was a straight gentle incline and at others we were looping backwards and forwards up the steeper climbs. On one of the straighter sections, at a higher altitude, we could look down to see the fir trees that the policeman had told us about, ranged down a very steep mountainside. At least we thought these must *surely* be the rare trees we were looking out for, but because the sun was behind them, we couldn't tell if they were blue-grey in colour or not. All the same, we assumed that we had seen these iconic trees, which are Andalucia's chosen national tree.

This whole area on our right-hand side, as far as the eye could see, consisted of mountain ranges of limestone, with all their crags and irregular shapes, synonymous with this type of stone. The range we were cycling over was, we thought, the one we had seen from the terrace, on that beautiful sunset evening in Ronda. Although we were still in sunshine now, we stopped to put our jackets on. Down in the valleys, dark shadows were creeping slowly across the rugged terrain. Would we make it to Zahara? we wondered anxiously. When were we going to reach the top? How much further could we keep climbing? What if we had a puncture or a mishap? All these thoughts were going through our minds. It surely couldn't be far to the pass now. Then, after a series of twists and turns, we came through a gap where, suddenly, a vast new vista opened up to us, and the view over Grazalema was gone – it was like a magic trick.

The change in landscape was dramatic. Instead of craggy mountains, this side was more rounded and there were few trees growing down the slopes. The road ahead looked very exciting; a contorted mass of loops to whiz us down the mountainside. In the distance we could see a long turquoise lake, still in sunshine, with what we supposed must be Zahara at the far end. From the top it looked like a pinprick, but it was fascinating to see it grow every time we emerged from a loop in our descent. There seemed to be a tower sticking up at the far end, on top of a high rock. It was in fact a castle, built on a prominence – a dominant feature of the town.

Halfway down, we stopped to take a photo because it was quite amazing the way long shadows were cast horizontally, across from one undulating green slope to the next. These looked like overlapping folds, as the sun sank low in the sky. Soon we were coasting straight into Zahara and still in daylight. The streets of this village, built on a mountainside, slanted gradually upwards, towards the castle. It seemed like a fairy-tale setting, with its Moorish castle looking down over the turquoise lake.

We wasted no time in finding a hotel room for the night, which was on the main street and totally different from the one in Ronda – a very modern room on the ground floor, where everything was squeaky-clean and in working order. We dined in the hotel and didn't go outside for the rest of that evening, being fairly tired from our recent exploits.

* * *

Another sunny morning greeted us. No doubt it would be scorching hot again later. But before the day had time to heat up we were out on the streets, exploring the lovely village from one end to the other and down by the lakeside, taking loads of photos in the process. We were aware that we'd be moving on during the hottest part of the day, but that didn't deter us from enjoying the moment.

On seeing an old-fashioned grocery shop in the lower part of the village, I made an impulsive decision to buy some bread and cheese to sustain us on the next leg of our journey. There was a big step down into the shop and it was very dark inside. I managed to ask for cheese and as there seemed to be only one type, there was no problem in specifying which one. It was in a big round block. The shopkeeper shoved aside a lump of meat he'd been cutting up on the counter and plonked the cheese down on the blood it had left behind! I was too shocked to say anything in time and before I knew it, he had cut me a large chunk and wrapped it in greaseproof paper. I didn't dare refuse it. I'd just have to cut all the sides off before we ate it.

We'd had to make some decisions the previous night, realising it would be folly to continue cycling westwards. We needed to allow ourselves plenty of time to get back to Finca la Mota in comfort, so we revised our vague plans and decided to head north to the town of Olvera. It was quite a wrench to leave

Zahara, although there was nothing more we could do there except sit outside cafés admiring the view and spending money unnecessarily. We could have walked up to the castle, but as the temperature had soared again, we hadn't bothered.

We left the village at its northern end, crossing over the dam of that beautiful man-made lake to reach the main road. This road was wide, with a lovely smooth surface. And even though the traffic was almost non-existent, they were not the kind of roads we wanted to be cycling on, because they cut out most places of interest. So after bypassing the village of Algodanales, we turned left at a big T junction and headed south. This was going back in the wrong direction, of course, but we were looking for a small road we'd seen on our map, which would take us all the way to Olvera.

After a few miles we stopped to sit on a stone wall, to replenish our sunscreen lotion. We'd been getting through this like nobody's business during the last week. A couple of hours of cycling in the heat and it would all have sweated off again, leaving a greasy mess at the ends of our sleeves and the edges of our shorts and socks. We were getting through kitchen-roll equally quickly.

Quite soon after that, we found the little road we were looking for, going off to the left, which would lead us in a northerly direction once more. Today, our road was not heading into mountains but across a fertile undulating plain, planted out in a patchwork of various crops and olive groves. It made for an extremely pleasant and relaxing afternoon of cycling. Somewhere along the way we stopped for a snack – we ate the bread we'd bought but left the cheese where it was, in my pannier. Mañana, I thought!

We reached Olvera at the bottom end of the town and were disappointed. After the beauty of Zahara de la Sierra, as seen for the first time from the mountains above, and the neatness of Grazalema, this seemed a real comedown. We pushed our bikes uphill, up a main street which looked tired and dusty, as if we were arriving at the end of a long hot summer, not early March. Also there was litter on the pavement; something we hadn't seen much of so far. But we needed a bed for the night and our Lonely Planet book said there was accommodation somewhere up this street.

We looked and looked for this hostel but couldn't find it. We checked the book again and it gave a house number. Then we saw the number on a scruffy door, squeezed between two buildings. There was a bell with 'Hostal' written above. We pressed it. After several minutes a grumpy-looking, swarthy, middle-aged man opened the door. He didn't smile or engage with us in any nice way; just motioned us to follow him. We tapped him on the back as he turned – we weren't going to leave our bikes out on the street. He looked annoyed but let us wheel them in and down the long corridor with shabby paintwork on the walls. We assumed it would be OK to leave them at the far end, one behind the other – he didn't indicate that we couldn't. The corridor was so long that this hostel must surely be behind the buildings on the main street.

It was a really odd place, with a sense that it might once have been a public building – maybe a school or a hospital or even an asylum. He led us up a wide concrete staircase where clumps of wiring stretched across the ceiling of the landing, leading to various rooms. It looked horrible – all bodged and improvised, and everything was painted a tired, flaking cream colour. The rooms seemed to have been built from modules, as the walls were like partitions rather than solid walls. Our room was the first one along the landing. At least the double bed looked reasonable with a decent duvet on it and there was a locker (hospital type) by the side. That was it, apart from the looping wires across the ceiling, which could have been Christmas decorations, had they been any colour but black. He showed us the bathroom across the landing – another module with a smaller module inside which was the shower. He did at last manage some grunting conversation with us, for after all, we had to know how much our overnight stay would cost and also how we would be able to get in, if we went out for a meal. We went back downstairs to pay and he gave us a key, but still no smile.

* * *

We'd felt quite uneasy sleeping at this hostel. It just seemed insecure, especially as the walls didn't reach the ceiling. The cables came in at one end and out through the gap at the top, to the bathroom and other rooms. We even worried that we might get an electric shock off the metal light switch. So it was with great relief that we departed as soon as we could the following morning.

Having had a bad night, we couldn't be bothered to look round the town of Olvera, which may have had some good places or buildings of interest to see, but we didn't want to know. All we did, therefore, was cycle to the bottom of the hill, stop at a shop to buy a snack, then head off on the next leg of our journey. A few miles out of town, we found a sandy bank where we could sit for breakfast. It was high time I did something with the cheese I had in my pannier and indeed it was high by now; honking, in fact. I unwrapped it and stood it on the paper to cut off the sides with a sharp knife, but after hacking off three sides, I could stand it no longer. Frank didn't fancy any, anyway, so I tossed it behind a tree, hoping some wild animals might be glad of it.

The countryside was undulating, with mountains on the horizon. There were long slopes of olive groves, where the trees looked like dots on the hillside, set well apart – not in close proximity as they might be in an English orchard.

Around midday we arrived in an amazing village called Setenil de las Bodegas, where whole streets were built into the rock face. Some had great overhangs of rock jutting out above, creating wonderful shade. We stopped at a café beneath one of these for a lunch break. It was wonderful to sit outside in the deep shade while everywhere else was shimmering in the heat. Above us, through a gap, the sky looked a very deep blue.

This was one of the many new experiences we'd had in Andalucia, we contemplated, and as we relaxed on our cushioned wrought-iron seats, yet another one came into view. It was a man pushing a heavy-looking bike up to the corner of the street, where it opened into a small square. After setting his bike on a stand, he blew some shrill notes on a tin whistle, while turning to direct the sound all around him. We were fascinated. On closer inspection, we discovered he was a travelling knife-sharpener! But during the whole time we were finishing our coffee, no customers brought their knives to be sharpened. Maybe they were having their siestas. Then, just as we were leaving, an old lady came out to him with a handful of knives. That was good. It must be a hard toil, to ride that heavy bike from village to village, and soul-destroying if nobody wants their knives sharpening. We walked slowly past, as he began turning the pedals faster and faster to set the grinding wheel spinning.

We were in no hurry to leave Setenil. It was such an interesting place. One street we walked through was completely covered by overhanging rock, creating a tunnel. What must it be like to live permanently in a tunnel?

The road out of the village took us eastwards now, with the countryside becoming gentler. Along a long flat road we crossed a level crossing, where there was a small station, up the track on our left. This was our very first encounter with railways on this holiday. With the landscape being flatter, our cycling that afternoon was not particularly scenic or memorable, but it was nice not having to push hard on the pedals. We could create a bit of a draught by getting up speed. And in this unrelenting heat, with no shade at all, that was a bonus. Soon we were cycling into the town of Cuevas del Becerro. We were now in the province of Malaga once more, having been in Cadiz province since leaving Ronda.

We pedalled over a crossroads into the town and found a small grocery shop further up the street. We desperately needed a drink as our water bottles had long since run out. The lady behind the counter greeted us with a broad smile, then called for assistance through a curtain at the back of the shop, whereupon two pretty teenage girls appeared at her side, greeting us with "Ellow, pleeezd tew meeet yew," in joint competition. Soon we were having a lovely conversation, the girls eager to practise their English and trying to outdo each other in the process. They asked us what we had liked most about the places we had visited and if it had been hard work, especially as they were having this very hot weather in springtime. In turn, we learnt that there was a B&B just back down at the crossroads, which wasn't in our Lonely Planet bible. We were all rather reluctant to end this unexpected 'family' get-together but we really needed to get freshened up and resuscitated before nightfall.

The B&B was just around the corner from the crossroads. It was a modern house with a garage underneath, and the owners were most keen to see that our bikes were locked safely inside. The man and wife seemed very 'with it' both in dress and outlook – maybe they were from a big city, trying their hand at B&B for a career change.

Our room was light and airy. After we had showered, it was suggested that we try to get a meal at the inn across the road. This inn looked almost like an English pub. There was a forecourt for parking and the brick building was wide and symmetrical, with a large front door in the centre. The room inside was wide and fairly modern with a curved bar at the back, facing us. Two male customers, who were standing by the bar, didn't blink an eyelid that a woman had just entered their domain, unlike the attitude of men in the mountain villages we'd encountered. That was a relief.

As it happened, we didn't need to order a meal, for there were plates of tapas along the bar, something that we hadn't yet tried. (Maybe they have 'tapas' nights in Spain like we have 'steak nights' in our pubs, except that this was free.) The friendly publican encouraged us to try everything. There were fishy ones, meaty ones and some that we couldn't tell what they were, although they were most delicious. We just kept sampling them until we could eat no more. That night we slept like logs.

* * *

The morning dawned bright and sunny, just like every other on this holiday. How fortunate we had been. It was a Wednesday and in four more days we would be flying home, so we had to make the most of our last few days. Since Setenil, although our cycling had become easier, the countryside had been less exciting.

Scanning the map that Frank had spread across the bed, we could see a group of three large lakes further east, towards some mountains. They looked like long wiggly shapes with spikes, almost akin to mythical dragons with spines. We were intrigued.

"That's where I'd like to go," stated Frank.

"Me too. Let's check it out in the Lonely Planet book," I suggested.

In the book we found a place called El Chorro, just the other side of these lakes, where there were two hostels. "That's where we'll go then," Frank decided. "If one hostel's full or fallen down, we can go to the other." Now there was hope that instead of the rest of our holiday gradually grinding down to mediocrity, there might still be places of interest to see. So bidding our friendly hosts farewell, we set off with enthusiasm towards El Chorro.

We were still in undulating countryside, with olive groves spanning the slopes to the left, the right and beyond and the roads smooth and reliable to cycle on – or were they? Along one long stretch, as we were bowling nicely along, the tarmac suddenly ended and our wheels jerked down onto rough stones. This was obviously resurfacing in progress, except there was no sign of any progress being made. The project seemed to have been abandoned. But our progress was brought to near snail's pace as we bumped uncomfortably along for a mile or two. Some distance further, we rounded a bend to find the other half of the road had slipped down the slope. Luckily, these roads were almost traffic-free.

Now we were on a long straight road heading towards distant mountains. I wondered if the Romans had built it. We passed a vast, gently sloping hillside which was covered with lumps of white rock, interspersed with the odd olive tree. It seemed most odd.

Before long, we were back in hilly countryside, where we encountered yet another landslip. This time, the side of the road had disappeared dramatically down a steep bank. Again it was not on our side but this time, there was a flimsy cordon around it, with a warning sign at each end, so close to the landslip that a driver would barely have time to react.

Now we had reached the lakes – well actually, only the edge of one of them. Each one was so long and twisty that the only way to see their full extent would be from the air. But as there was a clump of dense trees at the waterside, we thankfully stopped to escape from the sun for a while, deciding that we'd rather find El Chorro first then make a proper tour of the lakes the next day.

We were amongst mountains now, which were extremely varied – on one side of us were three cone-shaped mounts covered in dark green trees, while on the other side were high craggy cliffs. It was intriguing. The best thing was that the road carved through them rather than going over them, so there were no exhaustive climbs to make.

After cycling between high cliffs for a while, we rounded a bend into sudden dazzling brightness that blinded us for a moment. The cliffs had parted and the road was now alongside a wide, fast-flowing river. We stopped to survey this impressive sight. Downstream we could see structures built partway out across the river, like hydroelectric installations. There was probably a dam somewhere beyond that. Back upstream, the river was rushing through a deep and narrow gorge. As we gazed at the scene, a train shot out of a tunnel on the opposite cliff and disappeared again, in a flash. It made us jump. We wondered if the passengers had even had time to see the gorge.

Now we had to find a hostel. We chose one on the other side of the river, which entailed cycling down the riverside for a while to a road across the dam. Eventually we found the hostel at the top of a long stony track, where we passed several houses tucked away in the trees. It was a 'climbers hostel' which seemed to be in the process of improvements, although the owners' house looked newly built; a very modern bungalow. These owners were an attractive young couple who had quite recently taken on the running of this enterprise. She was fair-skinned, fair-haired and blue-eyed, while he had black hair and brown eyes. They were not Spanish. I believe they were Swiss but they spoke good English. I marvelled at their enthusiasm and energy, especially as they had twin baby sons to cope with as well.

By contrast, my sleeping accommodation was fairly basic – the two-tiered bunk beds being in what were akin to breezeblock outhouses with shed doors, built up against the rocks. There were a couple of washbasins near the door end. I was sharing with three Irish women, who were on a climbing holiday. There were several other 'sheds' down one side of the square and also a kiosk shop, run by the husband, which was opened at specific times of the day, notably morning and evening. On the other side of the square (or patio) were views of the mountains, where most of the hostellers did their climbing.

We bought food from the kiosk, cooked it under a canopied cooking area and ate it at the large table in the centre of the patio, alongside other hostellers, who were relating their latest exploits. We were just humble cyclists with no exciting tales to tell, but were full of admiration for these intrepid climbers.

* * *

I slept well in my bottom-bunk bed. The other three ladies had been very quiet during the night – probably exhausted from climbing. I hoped Frank had faired equally well in his shed.

After breakfast we set off to do our circular bike tour, which would encompass much of the three squiggly lakes that we'd seen on the map. With luggage that consisted only of our packed picnic lunches, the map and tools, we headed back in the direction we had come the previous day. Soon we'd reached the edge of the first lake with the shady trees. We didn't stop this time but continued for several miles on our former route until we peeled off to the right, in the direction of the second lake. The main road took us across a long, flat and impressive bridge, spanning one of the many projections of this contorted lake. These lakes seemed so deep – they were most probably flooded mountain valleys.

At every opportunity we left the main road and took the more twisty minor routes, which followed the valley contours more closely. After turning off onto our very first minor road, we became aware of paragliders flying over our heads. They were taking off from a high hill to our right. It was a colourful sight and rather a strange one, as wherever we'd cycled so far on this holiday, there had been neither sight nor sound of other people's sporting activities, anywhere. We had only seen farmers leading their loaded mules or driving old tractors, or people serving us in shops and cafés. It had given us a conceited feeling that we were the only ones enjoying the Andalusian countryside. Of course, we now knew that there were climbers clambering all around El Chorro, but they were out of our sight.

It was a lovely day again – hot and sunny but with a nice breeze to cool us down somewhat. We had reached the third lake when we deemed it time for our picnic lunch. We found a beautiful, shaded, sandy bank overlooking the lake, with the mountain ranges beyond. Here we could savour our sandwiches and the splendid view at the same time – perfect.

After a relaxing lunch break, we continued our circular tour. We liked this third lake the best of the three; partly, I think, because the little road followed the ins and outs of the lake for miles. It was most beautiful. Probably because of its great beauty, we began passing cafés, people and parked cars. Tourists! How dare they intrude on our solitude, we thought. But when the road veered away from the lakes for a while, we left them behind.

Now we were passing through a small hamlet, where orange trees were growing behind a high wire fence. Juicy fruit was hanging from the branches, looking as tempting as Adam's apple must have done. We would love to have plucked and eaten one, straight from the tree. I'm sure it would have tasted much nicer than the ones shipped to England and kept in cold storage.

We felt thirsty after seeing all that luscious fruit and stopped to drink the bottled juice we'd bought at a touristy café back up the road, resting a while by the roadside. On a grassy knoll, not far from us, sat three elderly men in drab-looking jackets, chatting quietly together. One was fiddling about with bits of greenery as they whiled away their time. Then, when we stood up to leave, he called out to us and brought over a long, decorative taper of woven reeds and handed it to me with a little bow. I felt honoured that he had made this for me. I treasure it still.

The road brought us back to the lakeside once more, where we were amazed at the colour of the water – a purer turquoise than we'd ever seen before. We stopped to take photos before leaving the lakes behind us to head back to El Chorro.

Back at the hostel, our hosts were lighting a fire out on the patio, under a huge cooking vat. Thursday nights were paella nights, when they cooked a meal for all their guests. What a lovely gesture. As it was quite a long process, we had plenty of time to wash and change beforehand, salivating like Pavlov's dogs in anticipation.

When it was ready, we each took our bowls to be filled with this delicious paella, the likes of which, I can truthfully say, I have never known surpassed. We had a lovely convivial evening, chatting to other hostellers and finding out about where they were from. And when our bowls were empty, we could have refills until we were full to busting.

It was during this evening of togetherness that we learnt about the Camino del Rey (the King's Walk). This was a walkway built in the early 1900s, high up on both sides of the El Chorro gorge, to give access for the workers building the hydroelectric constructions. Although it was falling into disrepair, people still took the challenge of walking round it for a thrill. The more we heard about it, the more interested Frank became. While we were here, he insisted, we must take this wonderful opportunity. We talked it over with the three Irish couples. They somewhat surprised us by saying that they wouldn't entertain it but would gladly lend us a couple of climbing harnesses. Why, we wondered, wouldn't they want to do it? Frank was undeterred but I was unsure. We turned in for the night and slept on the idea.

* * *

It was our last day at El Chorro and the penultimate day of our holiday. Were we going to take the El Chorro challenge? After breakfast we went down to the bungalow to discuss the King's Walk with our blonde hostess, admiring her twin babies at the same time. If we'd had doubts beforehand, she quelled them by telling us that she and her husband had pushed their bikes around the whole walkway. Had they really? Was it possible, or was she just bragging? She came across as a level-headed and truthful person. Well what excuse had we now not to do it?

She explained how to get there – down to the bottom of the stony track, then up a steep hill through the woods, where we would come to the first railway tunnel that we had to walk through. At the end of a second tunnel, we would arrive at the beginning of the walkway. So with the harnesses slung over our shoulders we set off.

Just as we were turning into the first tunnel, a goods train shot out, making us jump back. Frank had just been telling me how we would hear a buzz on the tracks if a train was approaching but this one had caught us out. There was room to walk down the side of the track without coming to grief, but walking through the tunnel was excitement enough for me. I felt very brave. We emerged from the darkness into sizzling sunlight, where we followed the track to the next tunnel. If I could do this, I thought, I would have the nerve to do the walk.

We stepped out of the second tunnel onto a concrete path, several feet wide. It was the very beginning of the King's Walk. I looked down to see the river rushing out of the gorge 200 feet below. Hell! It looked terrifying, but we had come this far. Surely I could do this after walking through two train tunnels? We worked out how to put on the climbing harnesses, having hardly a clue about their worth. But it gave us confidence and made us feel prepared. Then I noticed how the path narrowed a few feet ahead of me, and froze. There was no way on earth that I could do this walk.

Frank was being macho. If those two hostel owners had pushed their bikes along here, he would surely be OK. I couldn't be persuaded to take the challenge, so Frank bravely (or foolishly) set off. With a heavy heart and a head full of woeful thoughts, I followed his slow and faltering progress. We knew that for the most part the handrail had fallen away and also that there was a long gaping hole in the path, replaced by a length of concrete and a thick plank of wood. That was the worst we knew. What condition were the supports in; the ones holding up the whole of the walkway? They must surely be rotting out as well.

After a while he disappeared around the corner into the gorge and was lost from my sight. My stomach was gnawing with anxiety as I waited and waited, not having a clue what his situation was. Then, after an eternity, I saw his bright yellow shirt appear at the corner. Hurray! "Just take your time Frank and get back to me," I whispered. Then he turned and disappeared again. Was he mucking about, trying to scare me perhaps? That's the only reason I could come up with for his about-turn. This was all too much for me. I went and sat inside the train tunnel and cried my eyes out. Would he ever make it back again?

I'd defused my emotions somewhat before I had the nerve to go out for another look. This time I could see Frank coming slowly towards me. Although I felt really cross with him for playing with my emotions, I was unbelievably happy to see him. When he finally reached the tunnel he was a dithering, shivering lump, covered in perspiration, wondering why he'd been so stupid to attempt such a thing. "Why did you try to frighten me then, by going back round the corner?" I asked. But I'd got it all wrong. It was because he'd left his camera case on the bridge that crosses the gorge and he'd gone back to fetch it, even though that was the very worst part of the experience. Apparently, the rock face protrudes outwards on the corner, so that he'd had to lean out towards the gorge. Horrifying! For a while, he told me, he'd been frozen to the spot, terrified and trembling. Then he'd felt round the corner and found a hook to clip on the harness before inching round, pressed against the rock. And he'd done that bit, there and back twice, rather than leave his camera case behind!

As we made our way back through the tunnels, our minds were full of "what ifs." If he'd fallen off the ledge, that would be curtains for sure. But what if he'd fallen off while clipped to the rock by his harness? Would he have hung in the gorge, unseen, until the vultures found him? What would I have done if he hadn't returned? How long would I have waited before going back through the tunnels to find help? We hadn't had any contingency plans whatsoever. We had blanked all bad consequences out of our minds. We'd been utter fools. Whatever! We were walking back together through the tunnels. At least Frank had walked the walk, even though it had left him a nervous wreck.

Back at the hostel we returned the harnesses and told the Irish couples of our experiences, telling them how wise they were not to have taken on such a challenge. After all, it didn't rely on climbing ability, it was just a matter of luck, really – or bad luck, whichever the case may be.

* * *

Now it's the last day of our holiday. We've left El Chorro behind us, and are here talking to Dory and Stan outside their plot of land, where they are building themselves this little house in the country. Frank still has the heeby-jeebies after that foolish expedition yesterday. I had nightmares last night and I wouldn't be surprised if he hadn't had some as well. But talking to these two down-to-earth English pensioners helps bring us down to earth – to stop our minds harping back to yesterday.

Eventually we tear ourselves away, bidding them farewell and good luck with their project. It's not many miles now to Finca la Mota for our final night before flying home in the morning. We are cycling down a very gradual slope where, running alongside the road at about waist height, is a continuous stone trough, which must have been an aqueduct, to bring water from the mountains, I reckon. Its construction is quite hefty but with a lovely smooth, basin-like hollow down the centre. I wonder how ancient it must be and when it last carried water.

Finally, we arrive back at Finca la Mota. Arun is pleased to see us back. We will enjoy one more of his evening meals with the free wine that's on offer before settling our bill for the four nights we'll have spent here. After breakfast tomorrow, we'll be transported back to Malaga airport, as arranged.

We shower and change into decent attire, looking forward to seeing Juan, the waiter, who was always so pleased to serve us when we were last here. As soon as we are seated in the dining room, Juan is by our side, with all the help he can give us in describing the meals, plus the wine list to browse through. Tonight we'll choose the very best one, as a celebration – for the wonderful holiday, the brilliant weather and the safe return of the intrepid ledge-walker.

After dinner we are told that Richard is waiting for us in the bar. He is the Englishman who met us at Malaga airport and brought us to the Finca two weeks ago. This is the first we have seen of him, since then. We buy him a drink, while he asks us about our holiday. Then we get down to the nitty gritty of paying the bill. He draws out a sheet of paper from his pocket and spreads it on the bar – it's the bill. We glance down and gasp. No, that can't be right! This is just for four nights? How can it be? We scrutinise it more closely.

"What's all this charge for wine?" we ask. "We were told the wine was free."

"Ah, that's the house wine," Richard explains.

"Then why didn't Juan tell us?" That was a bit sneaky of him, we're thinking. He could easily have explained. But then, were we so stupid as to think all that lovely wine and those extra snacks were on the house? Were we so trusting to think everyone was being so nice to us – for nothing?

Ah well, what can we say or do? At least the transport between here and Malaga was in with the charges. That's why we'd chosen to come here in the first place. So we scrape together all the money we have left and manage to pay the bill. These four days have cost us more than all the rest of the holiday put together. But hey! What a brilliant experience it has been. I doubt we'll ever match it.